The Sociology of Aging:
Selected Readings

The Sociology of Aging: Selected Readings

Robert C. Atchley and **Mildred M. Seltzer**

Scripps Foundation Gerontology Center
Miami University

Wadsworth Publishing Company, Inc.
Belmont, California

Sociology Editor: Stephen D. Rutter

Designer: Ann Wilkinson

ISBN 0-534-00451-2
L.C. Cat. Card No. 75-38172
Printed in the United States of America
1 2 3 4 5 6 7 8 9 10—80 79 78 77 76

Preface

Aging can be viewed both as a biological process and as a social process. We are interested here in biological aging only as it becomes translated into social structure and process. Because people have always grown old, all human cultures have developed ways of socially defining *old* and different ways of dealing with group members who survive long enough to be so defined. Societies deal with the aging of their members in organized ways, yet much of this organization is not readily apparent. The sociologist's job is to reveal this organization so that it can be examined, evaluated, and perhaps changed.

The literature in the sociology of aging is widely scattered and not readily available to many students. Accordingly, it seemed worthwhile to bring together a set of readings that could provide convenient access to some important sociological ideas about aging. We do not pretend to represent the full range and depth of the sociological literature on aging in this book. Specifically, it is intended to complement and to supplement *The Social Forces in Later Life* (Wadsworth, 1972). We have chosen to concentrate on a few areas that seem to us both theoretically and practically relevant.

We begin with a section on age grading and the life course, the master concepts for those who approach sociology from a structural perspective. We then include some methodological ideas that are useful to those who are interested in age changes within the individual, and some demographic ideas for those interested in an evolutionary, societal view of aging. The section on socialization illustrates a social psychological process approach to the sociology of aging. We next turn to three basic social institutions—the family, the economy, and the polity—and how they deal with older members of society. The final section of the book is devoted to ethnicity, race, social class, and sex as they influence the aging process and the social contexts in which aging takes place.

We hope that our sampler will whet the reader's appetite and encourage further inquiry into a rapidly developing field of sociology.

We would like to thank the following reviewers for their helpful comments: Leonard Cain, Portland State University; Walter

Cartwright, Texas Technical University; Steve Cutler, Oberlin College; Richard Kalish; Louis Lowy, Boston University; Hal Pope, University of Iowa; Steve Price, University of Wyoming; Richard Steinman, University of Maine; and Vivian Wood, University of Wisconsin.

Contents

Age Grading and the Life Course

Two premises are fundamental to the social structural approach to the sociology of aging:

Age is used as a prime criterion in the assignment of people to opportunities in society.

Age-related positions in society are organized into socially defined ideal sequences that, at least theoretically, require individuals to make only a few choices in order to select, or be relegated to, socially approved paths through life.

In *age grading* age is used as a criterion governing the individual's access to groups, roles, aspects of culture (including norms, attitudes, values, beliefs, and skills), and social situations. Age grading defines what individuals are allowed to do and to be and what they are required to do and to be. The system of age grading is loosely based on a set of beliefs about the significance of age for social functioning. Both children and old people are barred from various opportunities because it is *believed* that they are not fully capable. It can be easily demonstrated that such beliefs often mask large individual differences and produce individual injustices. Yet the system persists because it is useful.

The *life course* can be viewed as a crude social road map that contains quite a few alternate routes for progressing through life's stages. Other terms used synonymously are *life span, life cycle,* and *life path.* The life course is punctuated by choice points—points at which a particular path must be selected from several alternatives. For example, high school students often reach a point where they must choose a vocational, commercial, or college preparatory curriculum. With each succeeding choice point, the diversity in the population increases, and it becomes more difficult to predict precisely the positions an individual will occupy purely from the individual's age. Yet consensual standards still broadly define the age at which it is appropriate to marry, to raise children, or to retire, and it is these major life events that provide existential reality to the much subtler alternative life courses. It is important to remember that there are many life courses, not just one.

Concepts of time are central to any discussion of life course, age grading, or aging. In "Sociological Perspectives on the Life Cycle," Bernice L. Neugarten and Nancy Datan distinguish among life time, historical time, and social time. Life time is chronological age. Of itself, chronological age is a poor predictor of physical or social capacities and is socially significant only because it is closely tied to social time. The context of historical time is the evolution of society. The importance of historical time for the sociology of aging rests in the interplay between various historical epochs and the life course. For example, childhood during the Depression was different from childhood during World War II.

Social time, which refers to the system of age grading, receives the most attention. Neugarten and Datan see the age-grading system as consisting of two types of ideas about age-appropriate behavior. *Ascriptive* age norms tie certain positions in society to chronological age directly. A commonplace example is forced entry into school at six years of age. *Consensual* age norms specify an age range within which people are *expected* to take up certain positions, even though they may not do so. For example, people are expected to retire sometime in their sixties, even when they are not forced to. Consensual age norms can be powerful simply because of the bandwagon effect.

Age grading also serves as a social control. People who are chronologically out of phase with the age norms usually feel pulled to try to move back to the age norm in the next life stage. Thus, people who marry late try to have children quickly. Middle-aged and older people tell many stories about the negative consequences of being out of phase.

Finally, Neugarten and Datan discuss changes in the rhythm of the life course. They show how the family life cycle has speeded up: Marriage, parenthood, and the empty nest occurred earlier in 1966 than in 1890. Men no longer need to be breadwinners before they can marry. Entry into the labor force has been delayed. All these changes indicate that the life course and age grading are social forces that are influenced by social evolution. We therefore cannot take social time as given; it remains a variable to be constantly reassessed.

In "Social Gerontology and the Age Stratification of Society," Matilda W. Riley presents the case for a new field in sociology based on the concept of age stratification. According to Riley, the existence of the life course creates *age strata* corresponding to the various stages of life. But the age strata are not static; they are molded by periods of history. To Riley, a *cohort* in society is an aggregate of people who, because they were born at the same time, are *cohort-centric*—they view the various stages of life from the vantage point of a particular

Age Grading and the Life Course

era in historical time. Cohort-centrism solidifies age strata by encouraging the selection of friends from among age mates. A sociology of age stratification is concerned with relationships among *all* the age strata, not just the elder ones. In this view, social aging begins early in life.

There is also social mobility through the age strata—in fact, the individual cannot escape it. And it is Riley's belief that movement from one age stratum to another is subject to the same sort of personal strains that often accompany class mobility. In addition, there is a *succession of cohorts* through the various age strata, and the successive cohorts may not age in the same ways. For example, the cohort retiring in the early 1970s is oriented much more positively toward retirement than was the cohort who retired in the early 1950s.

As it now stands, Riley's theory of age stratification has several troublesome aspects. Although Riley refers to age primarily in terms of chronological age or life stage, age is also assessed in terms of physical appearance, tenure (how long the person has been in a given position), and level of physical, mental, and social functioning. As more separate ways of assessing age are brought into the discussion, it becomes harder to defend the notion that birth cohorts remain cohesive and develop a subculture. If anything, the cohort's cohesion based on similarities among its elements probably steadily decreases as it grows older. Another troublesome point is the number of years spanned by a cohort. Demographers use one-year and five-year cohorts, but unfortunately life stages range in length from nine months (infants) to several years. This would seem to pose serious problems for anyone wishing to make the theory more concrete. Finally, it seems plausible that family, sex, race, and social class may all exercise prior bids on the individual's allegiance and in effect make age stratification an insignificant aspect in the lives of many people. Yet despite its problems, Riley's approach will surely attract much effort and attention in years to come.

John Clausen's article, "The Life Course of Individuals," portrays the life course as a sequence of roles an individual plays. For Clausen, in the early part of life these roles are tied to the biological and social maturation of the organism. After maturity, age is related to roles only to the extent that specific age norms exist. The path an individual takes through the life course is shaped by personal resources, such as intelligence and temperament; individual initiative; sources of support and guidance; opportunities as influenced by ethnicity, social class, sex, and age; plus historical factors such as wars and economic depressions.

Finally, Clausen presents various efforts at making the illusive concept of the life course explicit. Role graphs, life reviews, and longitudinal studies of the life course are reviewed. Clausen's

ntribution is calling our attention to concrete problems
ie study of the life course.

ogether, the selections in Chapter 1 fairly represent the
have been developed about the social structural aspects of
ogy of aging. Age strata, age grading, and the life course are
ract concepts that attempt to help us understand the
isms through which society uses age to fit people into
s. iral niches in the social world. But this chapter also shows that
the structural approach need not be static. The concepts of historical
time and cohort succession illustrate concern with how structure
changes.

Sociological Perspectives
on the Life Cycle

Bernice L. Neugarten and Nancy Datan

Introduction

Students of the life cycle have given much attention to the biological
timetable of human development, using such concepts as maturation,
age, and stage as major dimensions in mapping significant changes.
Much less attention has been given to the socio-historical context and
to the development of concepts for mapping changes in the social
environment as they affect the way in which an individual's life is
lived. Although there have been scattered but significant attempts by
psychologists to understand the lives of noted individuals in relation
to historical change (such as Freud's [1939] study of Moses and
monotheism, and Erikson's [1958, 1969] studies of Luther and
Gandhi), for the most part, psychologists have left it to biographers,
novelists, and historians to study the personalities of the eminent and
to elucidate both the forces that shape the individual and the effect of
the individual upon his time.

Developmentally oriented studies have appeared which deal with
the impact of single historical events upon the life course of groups of
individuals. For example, the effects of World War II have been
studied in a variety of ways, as in studies of the long-term effects on
British children evacuated from London during the Blitz (Maas,
1963), or the effects of the Depression upon the subsequent social

From *Life-Span Developmental Psychology: Personality and Socialization,* Edited by
Paul B. Baltes and K. Warner Schaie, Academic Press, 1973. Reprinted by permission of
the publisher and authors.

Age Grading and the Life Course

development of children (Elder, 1973), or in a study of middle-aged women 25 years after they had experienced concentration camps (Antonovsky, Maoz, Datan, & Wijsenbeek, 1971).

While there are many such studies of the significance of given historical events, the socio-historical perspective on the life cycle has not as yet received widespread, systematic treatment. On the contrary, studies of development are more often characterized by a search for a universal sequence of personality change comparable to, if not paced by, the maturational timetable, rather than a search for the sequences of personality changes that can be shown to reflect sequences of historical and social events. A major problem lies in the fact that we lack a set of conceptual tools by which to integrate maturational, psychological, sociological, and historical perspectives on the life cycle.

The purpose of this paper is to remind the reader of a few sociological concepts that have been of significance in understanding human personality, and then to turn to the life cycle seen in three dimensions of time: life time, or the individual's chronological age; social time, or the system of age grading and age expectations that shapes the life cycle; and historical time, or the succession of political, economic, and social events that shape the setting into which the individual is born and make up the dynamic, constantly changing background against which his life is lived.

Sociological Concepts

From the sociological perspective, personality is generally seen as an emergent of the interaction between the biological organism and the social context, and the task of the sociologist has been to explore this interaction from the standpoint of social organization. Thus, speaking very generally, sociologists often move from a study of the social organization to the consideration of its consequences for personality, viewing personality as the outcome of social learning.

In relating the individual to his social surroundings, the concepts of social system, social role, and socialization have repeatedly been set forth in the sociological and social–psychological literature. (Recent expositions are given, for example, in Brim & Wheeler, 1966; Clausen, 1968; Goslin, 1969; and Riley, Johnson, & Foner, 1972.) Although not each of these concepts was originally intended for this purpose, each can be related to a time dimension in looking at the life course.

The Social System and Social Role Parsons and Shils (1951b) have expressed the distinction between the psychological and sociological levels of analysis in their description of the social system as made up of the actions of individuals. The actions constituting the *social system* are the same actions that make up the personality systems of the individual actors, but these two systems are analytically discrete entities despite the identity of their basic components. The difference lies in the different focuses of organization and each system involves different functional problems in operation. The individual actor is not the unit of study in the social system; rather, for most purposes, it is the *role* that is being examined. A role is a sector of an individual actor's range of action, but it is also a specific set of behaviors having a particular function for a social institution—e.g., fatherhood is a role with specific functions for the family (and thus for the larger society) and at the same time, it is a role with specific functions for the individual. Any role or role constellation has different significance according to whether it is viewed from the individual or the societal perspective; but from both perspectives, the individual learns to think and to behave in ways that are consonant with the roles he plays, so that performance in a succession of roles leads to predictable personality configurations. Indeed, for some sociologists, personality itself is perceived as the sum of the individual's social roles. For purposes of the present discussion, the life cycle can be seen as a succession of roles and changing role constellations, and a certain order and predictability of behavior occurs over time as individuals move through a given succession of roles.

Socialization and Social Learning   The process by which the human infant is transformed into a member of a particular society and learns the roles appropriate to his or her sex, social class, and ethnic group, is called socialization. (Social classes have been shown by sociologists to be subcultures with differentiated norms and institutions.) LeVine (1969) has distinguished three different views of the process of socialization which correspond approximately to the disciplinary orientations of cultural anthropology, personality psychology, and sociology. For the anthropologist, socialization involves the transmission of cultural values and traditions from generation to generation. To some psychologists, the major task in socialization is the channeling of instinctual drives into socially useful forms. For the sociologist, socialization is a process of training the child for participation in society, with the emphasis upon positive social prescriptions growing out of the needs of the social structure.

In all three views, however, socialization can be seen as a process of social learning or of training through which individuals acquire the knowledge, skills, attitudes and values, the needs and motivations, and the cognitive, affective and conative patterns that relate them to their socio-cultural setting. The success of the socialization process is measured by the ability of the individual to perform well in the roles he takes on (Inkeles, 1969).

While socialization was once conceived as a process by which the infant was transformed into an adult of his culture, and thus the process was essentially complete at adulthood, more recently, sociologists have come to describe socialization as a lifelong process (Brim & Wheeler, 1966), one that involves new learning in adulthood in response to rapid social change and in response to the succession of life tasks. Although anthropologists such as Benedict (1938) have long pointed to discontinuities in cultural conditioning at various points in the life cycle, the recognition of the need for resocialization in adulthood is relatively new.

In summary then, from the sociological perspective, the life cycle can be described as a succession of social roles, and personality can be described as the product of changing patterns of socialization.

Three Dimensions of Time

Life Time   From the ancient poets through Shakespeare to Erikson (1950, 1959), people have viewed the life cycle as a series of orderly changes, from infancy through childhood, adolescence, maturity, and old age with the biological timetable governing the sequence of changes in the process of growing up and growing old. Although for the developmental psychologist there are a host of conceptual and methodological issues involved in the use of chronological age or *life time* as an index of change (see, e.g., Baer, 1970; Baltes & Goulet, 1971; Wohlwill, 1970a), chronological age is nevertheless the most frequently used index. It is a truism that chronological age is at best only a rough indicator of an individual's position on any one of numerous physical or psychological dimensions, for from earliest infancy on, individual differences emerge in development. Nor is age a meaningful predictor of many forms of social and psychological behavior, unless there is accompanying knowledge of the particular society as a frame of reference. An obvious example is the fact that in the United States the typical 14-year-old girl is a schoolgirl, while in a rural village in the Near East she may be the mother of two children. The significance of a given chronological age, or a given marker of life time, when viewed from a sociological or anthropological perspective, is a direct function of the social definition of age, or of *social time*.

Social Time   *Social time* refers to the dimension that underlies the age-grade system of a society. Anthropologists were the first to introduce the concept of age grading (see, e.g., Eisenstadt, 1956; Warner, 1958). It is characteristic in a preliterate society to have *rites-de-passage* marking the transition from one age status to the next, such as the passage from youth to maturity and to marriageability (Van Gennep, 1960). Only a rough parallel exists between social time and life time, for although in simple societies a girl may be considered marriageable when she reaches puberty, in a modern society, she is not considered marriageable until long thereafter. In short, social timing is not synchronous with biological timing. There are also different sets of age expectations and age statuses in different societies, further demonstrating that neither chronological age (nor maturational stage) is itself the determinant of age status, but that it merely signifies the biological potentiality upon which a system of age norms and age grading can operate to shape the life cycle.

Historical Time   *Historical time* shapes the social system, and the social system, in turn, creates a changing set of age norms and a changing age-grade system which shapes the individual life cycle. Aries (1962) has traced the social history of family life in Western society, suggesting that not until the seventeenth and eighteenth centuries, with the growth of industrialization, the formation of a middle class, and the appearance of formal educational institutions, did the concept emerge that childhood is a distinct phase of life, a period that has its specific characteristics and needs. The concept of adolescence as a distinctive period in the life cycle appeared in the twentieth century (Demos & Demos, 1969). Keniston (1970) has suggested that in the past few decades, when the speed of social change has been so great, a stage called youth, in which a new form of reconciliation of the self with the changing social order follows upon the earlier task of identity formation, can now be noted. Similarly, the period of middle age is a recently delineated stage in the life cycle resulting from this enormous increase in longevity that has occurred since the beginning of this century, together with the changing rhythm of the work cycle and the family cycle.

Historical time refers not only to long-term processes, such as industrialization and urbanization which create the social-cultural context and changing definitions of the phases of the life cycle. History is also a series of economic, political, and social events that directly influence the life course of the individuals who experience those events. The life cycle of an individual is shaped, then, by the long-term historical processes of change that gradually alter social institutions; but the life cycle is also affected by discrete historical events. Some sense of the interplay between historical time and life time emerges if, for example, one considers World War II as it impinged on a young man, a child, or a young mother.

In the first case, a young man who becomes a soldier may achieve some resolution of masculine identity by taking on a highly stereotyped male role. In the second case, the child may go fatherless for the first few years of his life, with the attendant consequences for parental identification and oedipal resolution. In the third case, a mother whose husband has gone to war faces child rearing with reduced economic, physical, and psychological resources as she takes on both father's and mother's roles. This example merely illustrates the obvious point that the same historical event takes on very different psychological meanings depending on the point in the life cycle at which the event occurs.

Behavioral scientists have recognized the importance of the timing of major historical events in the life line of the individual, and *cohort analysis* (cf. Cain, 1967; Schaie, 1968) is a tool originally developed by demographers in an attempt to relate life time to historical time. A *cohort* is a group defined by calendar year of birth (a given year or some prescribed number of years). The characteristics of cohorts are analyzed in an attempt to explore *cohort effects*, that is, the effect of membership in a particular cohort with its unique background and demographic composition (cf. Riley, 1971; Riley *et al.*, 1972). For instance, Cain (1967) has presented sets of data to show that a historical "hinge" or "watershed" developed in America at the end of World War I with regard to levels of education, fertility patterns, sexual mores, reduction of hours in the work week, labor force participation patterns, and so on. This watershed produced a sharp contrast in life styles between the cohort of persons born before the turn of the century (persons who are presently over 70) and the cohort born after 1900 (persons who are now entering old age), with the results indicating that the needs of the new cohort of the aged will be very different from the needs of cohorts that preceded it. Another watershed probably occurred with the Great Depression of the 1930s.

It might be pointed out that cohort, like the dimension age, is in itself without psychological meaning, and that psychologists must eventually be able to specify the events that give meaning to cohort differences. For the present it is not known, except in the most general way, which historical events are more significant than other events in influencing the course of personality development over the life cycle—a problem which must somehow be resolved if cohort analysis is to become a powerful tool in analyzing life histories.

Social Time and the Age Status Structure

The concepts of historical time and life time are well understood, even though they have not often been used in juxtaposition in studies undertaken by developmental psychologists. The concept of social time, on the other hand, probably needs fuller exposition.

Age grade systems are expressions of the fact that all societies rationalize the passage of life time, divide life time into socially relevant units, and thus can be said to transform calendar time (or biological time) into social time. As already noted, the concept of age grading comes from anthropological studies of simple societies where the life cycle may consist of a succession of formally age-graded, ascriptive roles: A male, for example, may pass from infancy to childhood to warrior-apprentice to warrior (and simultaneously to husband and father), and finally to elder, a status terminated by death. Age-strata and age-status systems emerge in all societies; and duties, rights, and rewards are differentially distributed to age groups which themselves have been socially defined. In societies where the division of labor is simple and the rate of social change is slow, a single age-grade system becomes formalized; and family, work, religious, and political roles are allocated and regulated accordingly. A modern complex society, by contrast, is characterized by plural systems of age status that become differentiated in relation to particular social institutions.

American society is characterized by a comparatively fluid and differentiated age-status system; yet despite its fluidity, and despite overlapping systems of age grading, there are some ascriptive age statuses that are systematically tied to chronological age, such as entry into school, age at eligibility to vote, age of legal responsibility, and so on.

The age-grade system institutionalizes cultural values and constitutes a social system that shapes the life-cycle. Every society has a system of social expectations regarding age-appropriate behavior, and these expectations are internalized as the individual grows up and grows old, and as he moves from one age stratum to the next. There is a time when he is expected to go to work, to marry, a time to raise children, a time to retire, even a time to grow sick and to die.

As an example of the way in which age expectations are institutionalized, most children in American society must attend school between the ages of 6 and 16; at 18, they acquire the right to vote. This is to say that American society views a lengthy education as a prerequisite for adult responsibility; there are social institutions to provide this education; there is an age-grade and age-norm system that prevents the assumption of adult responsibilities—work, marriage, voting, legal liability—until compulsory education is ended. The total network of age-associated institutions is far more complex than this example can indicate, and the system of age grading is primarily consensual rather than formal, but the example serves to illustrate the close correspondence between age norms and age expectations on the one hand, and social and cultural values on the other.

That these concepts of social time, age grading, age status, and age norms refer to present-day social realities is demonstrated in a series of empirical studies by the first-named author begun over 15 years ago. Many of these studies remain unpublished and some are still in progress, but it will be useful to draw upon them here in elaborating upon the concept of social time.

One of the first in this series of studies explored regularities in age expectations among adults. It was found that middle-aged people perceive adulthood as composed of four different life periods, each with its characteristic pattern of personal and social behavior: young adulthood, maturity, middle age, and old age (Neugarten & Paterson, 1957). Progression from one period to the next was described along one or more of five underlying dimensions of life: career line (e.g., major promotion, retirement), health and physical vigor, the family cycle (e.g., children entering school, children departing the family home), psychological attributes (e.g., "Middle age is when you become mellow."), or social responsibilities ("Old age is when you can take things easy and let others do the worrying.").

From these data it was possible to delineate the first gross outline of an age structure and a system of age expectations that cross-cut various areas of adult life. There appears to be a set of social age definitions that provide a frame of reference by which the experiences of adult life are perceived as orderly and rhythmical. Although perceptions vary somewhat by age and sex, and especially by social class (for example, middle age and old age are seen as beginning earlier by working-class men and women than by middle-class), it was the high degree of consensus that was striking in these data.

Expectations regarding the timing of major life events can also be charted. Interviewees respond easily to questions such as: "What is the best age for a man to marry?"; or "the best age to become a grandmother?" and they readily give chronological ages for phrases such as: "a mature woman"; or "when a man should hold his top job." Moreover, there is widespread consensus on items such as these that deal with the timing of work and family events, attitudes, and psychological characteristics. There also appears to be a prescriptive timetable by which major events are ordered along the individual's life line, and consensual definition of the chronological ages that correspond to phases in the life span. For example, most middle-class men and women agreed that a man is young between 18 and 22, middle-aged between 40 and 50, and old between 65 and 75; and that men have the most responsibilities between 35 and 50. Youth, middle age, and old age were similarly defined for women, but women are seen as moving through major phases of the life line earlier than men (Neugarten, Moore, & Lowe, 1965). There is greater consensus regarding age-appropriate behavior for women than for men; and greater consensus regarding age expectations for the period of young adulthood, as if the normative system bears more heavily on individuals as they enter adulthood than when they move on to successive phases of maturity and old age.

Age Norms as a System of Social Control

If the system of age expectations is a normative one, as hypothesized, then it should be more or less compelling for everybody; that is, individuals should feel some degree of social pressure to conform to expectations. One of the ways this issue was pursued was to ask to what extent an individual is consistent in meeting various age norms. The data were examined to identify persons who fell at the extremes of the age distribution on an early life event—for instance, men who had married comparatively early or late—and to see to what extent these persons maintained an early or late position relative to their own social class group on successive life events. Although these data are spotty thus far, and the size of the sample precludes statistical testing, in examining individual cases it was observed that early or late individuals move toward the norm on the next major event in the life line. The implication is, then, that there is a "pull" in the age system, just as there is in other normative systems, so that individuals who are age-deviant on one event tend to move back toward the norm on the next event.

Individuals themselves are aware of age norms and age expectations in relation to their own patterns of timing. In adults of varying ages, it has been found that every person can report immediately whether he was "late," "early," or "on time," on one life event after another (e.g., "I married early," or "I was late getting started, because of the Depression"). This high degree of awareness of timing has been interpreted as further evidence that age expectations form a normative system, that social definitions of age are commonly accepted and meaningful, and that patterns of timing play an important role with respect to self-concept and self-esteem.

Another question relates to the process of socialization by which age norms are learned. Respondents have been asked how their ideas about age norms originated, but people seem to take age-norms so much for granted that they are unable to describe their learning experiences. One conclusion has been that the norms are probably learned in such a wide range of contexts and are so imbedded in experience that it is not feasible to attempt to disentangle the socialization experiences by direct questioning.

It may be reasoned, however, that if a normative system is operating, people are probably aware of the sanctions in the system and are sensitive to social approval and disapproval. Attempts to explore this question through a study of individuals who were "off-time" in major life events convinced the investigators that age deviancy is always of psychological significance to the individual, even though a systematic elucidation has not yet been achieved of the mechanisms involved in the social sanctioning of age deviancy.

Another research approach has permitted some inferences about age norms as a system of social constraints. Such questions as these were asked:

> Would you approve of a woman who decides to have another child at 40? at 35? at 30?
> What about a couple who moved across the country to live near their married children when they are 40? 55? 75?

In analyzing responses to such items, a significant increase with age has been found in the extent to which respondents attach importance to age norms and view age appropriateness as a constraint upon behavior. It can be inferred then, that the middle-aged and the old, who see greater constraints in the age-norm system than do the young, have learned that to be off-time with regard to major life events entails negative consequences, and that, therefore, age and age appropriateness are reasonable criteria by which to evaluate behavior. The young, by contrast, tend to deny that age is a valid criterion by which to judge behavior (Neugarten *et al.*, 1965).

These studies illustrate the point that the age-status structure of a society, age-group identifications, the internalization of age norms, and age norms as a network of social controls are important dimensions of the social and cultural context in which the life course must be viewed. Many of the major punctuation marks of the life cycle are not only orderly and sequential, but many are social rather than biological in nature, and their timing is socially regulated. These concepts point to one way of structuring the passage of time in the life span of the individual; and in delineating a social time clock that can be superimposed upon the biological clock, these concepts are helpful in comprehending the life cycle.

Age Stratification

A complementary perspective on the dimension of age emerges from the literature on age stratification in society. Mannheim (1952b) and more recently, Riley and her associates (Riley, 1971; Riley *et al.*, 1972) have viewed the study of the age structure of society along two dimensions: the life course dimension; and the historical dimension, seen as coordinates for locating the individual in the age structure of society.

Sociological Perspectives on the Life Cycle

The life course dimension is roughly indexed by chronological age which serves as an indicator of the individual's experience, including age-related organic changes affecting physical and mental functioning, and including the probability of certain psychological and social experiences. The historical dimension includes the political, social, and cultural changes in society. In Riley's view, integration of these two dimensions provides a perspective on the life course, and the concept of cohort is a link between the two dimensions.

In Mannheim's concept of a generation, he bridges historical time and life time. Mannheim suggested that the sociological significance of generations is predicated upon, but not defined by, the rhythm of the biological succession of generations. Individuals sharing the same year of birth are endowed with a potentially common location in "the historical dimension of the social process." A common year of birth does not in itself constitute a similarity of location: rather, a generation by its date of birth is limited to a particular range of possible experiences. Similarity of location results from the fact that a particular generation, or what we now call age cohort, experiences the same events at the same points in the life cycle, and thus "these experiences impinge upon a similarly stratified consciousness. [Mannheim, 1952b, p. 310]." The sense of belonging to a generation is only a *potentiality* based upon the biological succession of generations. Furthermore, "whether a new *generation style* emerges every year, every thirty, every hundred years, or whether it emerges rhythmically at all, depends entirely on the trigger action of the social and cultural process [Mannheim, 1952b, p. 310]." Mannheim thus moves from the historical context to the level of individual consciousness by the intervening concepts of "generations" and "generational consciousness."

Riley (1971), using Mannheim's dimensions of historical time and life time, deals with the effect of the process of aging on the social structure of society. After describing a society as a structure composed of age strata, her concern is the sociology of age stratification as the expression of the rhythm of generations. Following Mannheim's conceptualization, each cohort by the fact of its year of birth is limited to a certain range of experience; and the consequence is that when, at a given point in time, individuals of varying age levels are studied, they differ in ways that cannot be accounted for solely on the basis of aging. Instead, each age stratum has its distinctive subculture which is the product of the historical events the individuals experience at a particular period in their lives.

At any point in time, then, society consists of a set of age strata each of which is characterized by its own pattern of labor force participation, consumer behavior, leisure-time activities, marital status, religious behavior, education, nativity, fertility, and child-bearing practices. Differences (or similarities) between age strata are to be understood on the two dimensions of life course and historical change.

Both Mannheim and Riley, then, are concerned with only two of the three time dimensions under discussion here, and both of them link historical time to life time by the use of such intermediary concepts as generation and age cohort. The relations between historical time and life time can be better understood, however, if social time is added as a third interrelated dimension and if age statuses and age norms can be seen as forming a social–psychological system that stands parallel to the age-stratification structure.

The conceptual framework put forward here, then, might be restated as follows: The age-stratification structure described by Riley and the age-status structure as described in the present paper can be seen as descriptions of two types of sociological reality. Age norms as a system of social control can be seen as a description of social–psychological reality. All three are based upon age as a dimension of social organization; and all three imply that an individual can be located within an age structure and that his behavior is controlled by the age system of which he is part. Similarly, in turning from concepts of social structure to dimensions of time, historical time and life time need to be complemented by the dimension of social time. In moving from the socio-historical context to the form and content of the life cycle, and in considering the psychological significance of historical events, social time and social age become particularly useful as intermediary concepts. The effects of historical events upon the individual can be said to be "filtered" through the age-status system. For example, the effect of World War II upon an 18-year-old man is different from its effect upon a 25-year-old man not only because the second, having lived longer, is different biologically from the first, but because he is different sociologically from the first. The two individuals have been socially "placed" in different age strata; they have different age statuses, and the age-related expectations of behavior that are binding upon them are different.

Some of these points will emerge again in the following illustration of how historical time, social time, and life time are intertwined in the currently changing rhythm of the life cycle.

The Changing Rhythm of the Life Cycle

As American society has changed from agrarian to industrialized, from small town to metropolis, there have been corresponding changes in the social definitions of age groups, in age norms, and in relations between age groups. Only a few aspects of the changing rhythm of the life cycle will be described here to show how major life events are now differently timed and to indicate that the difference in timing is an accompaniment of underlying biological, social, and economic changes in the society. (Much of this section is taken from Neugarten & Moore, 1968.)

Medical advances are among the many factors that have led to growth and redistribution of the population, with presently high proportions of the young and the old, due in turn to reductions in infant mortality and to a striking increase in longevity. Technological change and urbanization have created alterations in the economic system and the family system which are superimposed upon this changing biological base. One result is a new rhythm of life timing and aging.

Concepts of social age and age status are readily illustrated within the institution of the family. The points along the life line at which the individual moves from "child" to "adolescent" to "adult" are socially defined, although they are timed in relation to biological development. After physical maturity is reached, social age continues to be marked off by relatively clear-cut biological or social events in the family cycle. Thus, marriage marks the beginning of one social age period, as does the appearance of the first child, the departure of children from the home, and the birth of the first grandchild. At each stage, the individual takes on new roles and his prestige is altered in relation to other family members.

As shown by the data for women in Table 1, changes in timing in the family cycle have been dramatic over the past several decades as age at marriage has dropped, as children are born earlier in the marriage and are spaced closer together, and as longevity of both sexes, and consequently the duration of marriage has increased. (The data for men show parallel trends. In 1890, the median age at

Table 1   Changes in the Timing of Life Events

Median age at:	1890	1966
Leaving school	14	18
Marriage	22	20
Birth of first child	24–25	21
Birth of last child	32	26
Death of husband	53	64
Marriage of last child	55	48
Death	68	78

*Data are taken from Glick, Heer, and Beresford, 1963. The entries in the table do not, of course, represent the same women, but various groups of women at each of the two calendar years. The timing of future events for, say, women who in 1966 were marrying at average age 20 cannot be directly extrapolated from the table. At the same time, the interpretation of these data may be seen as a quickening family cycle over calendar time. This is but another instance in which developmental psychologists draw longitudinal inferences from cross-sectional data.

marriage for men was 26; at birth of first child, 36; at marriage of last child, 59; at widowhood, 57. In 1959, the respective median ages were 22, 28, 49, and 66.)

Changes in work patterns have been even more dramatic (see Fig. 1). In 1890 less than 30% of all women at age 20 were in the labor force, and this was the highest percentage for any age group. The proportions dropped by age, so that at age 50 only about 12% were workers. But by 1966, women's participation in the labor force had increased so dramatically that over 50% of all 20-year-old women were working. The percentage dropped off only a little among 30-year-olds, and then rose again so that over 50% of all 50-year-old women were in the labor force.

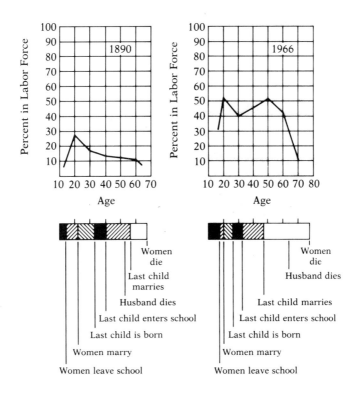

Figure 1 Work in Relation to Significant Stages in the Lives of Women. [From Neugarten (Ed.), *Middle age and aging: A reader in social psychology.* Chicago: The University of Chicago Press, 1968. © 1968 by the University of Chicago Press. *Sources:* National Manpower Council, *Womanpower* (New York: Columbia University Press, 1957), p. 307. Right-hand portion of figure has been revised based on labor-force data taken from *1967 Manpower Report,* U.S. Department of Labor, Table A-2, p. 202, and on family cycle data taken from Glick, Heer, and Beresford, 1963, p. 12.]

Historically, then, the family cycle has quickened as marriage, parenthood, empty nest (and grandparenthood) all occur earlier. The trend is toward a more rapid rhythm of events through most of the family cycle, then an extended interval (now some 16 years) when husband and wife are the remaining members of the household. Widowhood occurs much later, and the life span for women has lengthened enormously.

These general trends are not expected to be reversed, even though today a slight upturn in age of marriage (in 1972, it was 20.8 rather than 20.2 for women), more unmarried families, more communal and other experimental forms of family life may be noted. While the family cycle runs its course a few years later for women at higher-than-average levels of education, the general pattern of historical change just described is the same for both highly-educated and poorly-educated women.

Over the past 80 years, an interesting and important difference has been developing between men and women with respect to the timing of family and work cycles. Marriage no longer signifies that the man is ready to be the breadwinner. With the needs of the American economy for technical and professional workers, the length of time devoted to education has increased for more and more young persons, but there has not been an accompanying delay of marriage. In 1966 of all men attending college or graduate school, nearly one in four was married (for those men aged 25–29, it was nearly three out of four) as was one of every seven women.

The accompanying phenomenon is the young wife who works to support her husband through school. The changing sex-role patterns are reflected in the rising proportion of young married women in the labor force: In 1890, it was only 6% of those aged 14–24; in 1960, it was 31%. While these percentages reflect marriages in which husbands are working as well as those in which husbands are still in school, they show in both instances not only that young wives are increasingly sharing the economic burdens of new households, but also that women are doing so at younger and younger ages. Thus, the age of economic maturity has been deferred for men, but not for women. It has become socially acceptable for men to reverse the traditional sequence of events, and for family maturity to precede rather than to follow economic maturity.

Furthermore, men's work life has been shortened over the past decades as young men are increasingly delayed from entering the labor force (at technical and professional levels, because of the diminishing need for unskilled workers) and as older men are increasingly retiring at younger ages (for men over 65, only one of four is now in the labor force). In short, the trend for men is to be older when they start to work, and younger when they retire. Women still spend much less time in the labor force than men, on the average, but the historical trend for women is the opposite—women are younger when they start to work; they work much longer than before, whether or not they are married and whether or not they have children; and they are older when they retire.

The new rhythms of social maturity impinge also upon other aspects of family life. Parent-child relationships are influenced in many subtle ways by the fact that half of all new fathers in the 1960s were under 23 and half of all new mothers under 21. Changes in parental behavior, with fathers reportedly becoming less authoritarian and with both parents sharing more equally in tasks of homemaking and child-rearing, may reflect, in part, this increased youthfulness. It is the relative youth of both parents and grandparents, furthermore, that may be contributing to the complex patterns of help between generations in the family that are now becoming evident, including the widespread financial help that flows from parents downward to their adult children. Similarly, with more grandparents surviving per child, and with an extended family system that encompasses several generations, new patterns of child-rearing are emerging in which child–grandparent relations may be taking on changing significance.

Toward a Social Psychology of the Life Cycle

Changes in the life cycle, such as those just described, have their effects upon personality, and it is likely that the personalities of successive age cohorts will, therefore, be different in measurable ways, especially if the sociologist's view of personality is adopted. (This is not the occasion to discuss varying conceptions of personality, except to acknowledge their great diversity, and to suggest that from most points of view, including those of psychoanalysis and ego psychology, social change can be expected to have at least some systematic effects upon personality development.) It nevertheless remains for future personality psychologists to turn attention to the interplay between history and personality, as indicated at the outset of this chapter, and to undertake empirical studies that will elucidate, for example, the changes in self-concepts, the sense of efficacy, and even the balance between the rational and the impulsive components of personality as these are affected by the changing social context.

Developmental theorists are lacking, as yet, an overarching theory of development over the life cycle. In part, this is so because we have not fully recognized the complex interplay between maturational sequences and social-cultural forces, and have often tended to view the latter as complications that "obscure" the invariant sequence of developmental change. What is needed is to view maturational change as only one of the major components of development, and to forego the constraining analogy that compels us to search only for corresponding invariant timetables of psychological change. The present authors are not, of course, the first to argue that the specific historical context is as valid a frame of reference for the study of the development of personality as is the maturational timetable, and that both are required. The point can be stated more accurately: namely, the task is to study sequences of change for the purpose of determining *which ones* are primarily developmental (in the sense of being tied to maturational change), and *which ones* are primarily situational—if, indeed, this distinction can be made at all.

For example, how will life-cycle change and social change be related in the life course of present-day youth, a problem that is as current as this morning's headlines and as relevant as any to which the developmental psychologist can address himself? As this chapter is being written, the morning newspaper carries a story about high school radicals and the fact that by the time they reach college they seem to have exhausted their political energies—that is, the "little brother" about whom the campus radical used to warn us only a year or two ago seems already to have burned out and to be leading a more conventional life as a college student than his big brother. What is the relation of *timing* and commitment to social causes, and the relation of both to personality development? What does it mean to become an activist at 15, as compared to 20, or 45?

Shall we re-examine our earlier views that extremism and idealism among the young are an accompaniment of underlying biological change? Why was it the 20-year-old who was the activist in 1968, the 15-year-old in 1970, but neither in 1972? And what difference will it make to the particular individuals by the time they reach middle age?

To take another example, what are the changes in the personalities of women that may be anticipated as the accompaniment of the women's liberation movement? Specifically, what are the effects if the woman is young and is choosing to postpone marriage and child-bearing, perhaps to forego them altogether, as compared to the effects if the woman is 40 and engaged in that period of self-evaluation whose outcome will determine the course of her old age?

Obviously the relations of life time, social time, and historical time pose enormously complicated questions, but it is precisely this complexity to which students of the life cycle should be willing to address themselves.

References

Antonovsky, A., Maoz, B., Datan, N., and Wijsenbeek, H. Twenty-five years later: A limited study of sequelae of the concentration camp experience. *Social Psychiatry*, 1971, *6*, 186–193.

Aries, P. *Centuries of childhood.* New York: Random House, 1962.

Baer, D. M. An age-irrelevant concept of development. *Merrill-Palmer Quarterly*, 1970, *16*, 230–245.

Baltes, P. B., and Goulet, L. R. Exploration of developmental variables by manipulation and simulation of age differences in behavior. *Human Development*, 1971, *14*, 149–170.

Brim, O. G., & Wheeler, S. *Socialization after childhood: Two essays.* New York: Wiley, 1966.

Cain, L. D., Jr. Age status and generational phenomena: The new old people in contemporary America. *Gerontologist*, 1967, *7*, 83–92.

Clausen, J. A. (Ed.) *Socialization and society.* Boston: Little, Brown & Company, 1968.

Eisenstadt, S. N. *From generation to generation: Age groups and social structure.* Glencoe, Illinois: Free Press, 1956.

Elder, G. H., Jr. *Children of the great depression.* New York: Markham Press, 1973.

Erikson, E. H. *Childhood and society.* New York: Norton, 1950, 1963.

Erikson, E. H. *The young man Luther.* New York: Norton, 1958.

Erikson, E. H. Identity and the life cycle. *Psychological Issues*, 1959, *1*, Whole No. 1.

Erikson, E. H. *Gandhi's truth on the origins of militant nonviolence.* New York: Norton, 1969.

Freud, S. *Moses and monotheism.* Translated by K. Jones, New York, Knopf, 1939.

Goslin, D. A. (Ed.) *Handbook of socialization theory and research.* Chicago: Rand McNally, 1969.

Inkeles, A. Social structure and socialization. In D. A. Goslin (Ed.), *Handbook of socialization theory and research.* Chicago: Rand McNally, 1969.

Keniston, K. Youth as a stage of life. *The American Scholar*, 1970, *39*, 631–654.

LeVine, R. A. Culture, personality, and socialization: An Evolutionary view. In D. A. Goslin (Ed.), *Handbook of socialization theory and research.* Chicago: Rand McNally, 1969.

Looft, W. R. Socialization and personality throughout the life span: An examination of contemporary psychological approaches. In P. B. Baltes and K. W. Schaie (Eds.), *Life span developmental psychology: Personality and socialization.* New York: Academic Press, 1973.

Maas, H. Long term effects of early childhood separation and group care. *Vita Humana*, 1963, *6*, 34–56.

Mannheim, K. The problem of generations. In K. Mannheim (Ed.), *Essays on the sociology of knowledge.* New York: Oxford University Press, 1972. (b)

Neugarten, B. L., and Moore, J. W. The changing age-status system. In B. L. Neugarten (Ed.), *Middle age and aging: A reader in social psychology.* Chicago: University of Chicago Press, 1968.

Neugarten, B. L., Moore, J. W., and Lowe, J. C. Age norms, age constraints, and adult socialization. *American Journal of Sociology*, 1965, *70*, 710–717.

Neugarten, B. L., and Paterson, W. A. A study of the American age-grade system. In *Proceedings of the Fourth Congress of the International Association of Gerontology*, Vol. 3, 1957.

Parsons, T., and Shils, E. A. The social system. In T. Parsons and E. A. Shils (Eds.), *Toward a general theory of action*. Cambridge: Harvard University Press, 1951. (b)

Riley, M. W. Social gerontology and the age stratification of society. *Gerontologist*, 1971, *11*, 79–87.

Riley, M. W., Johnson, M. E., and Foner, A. (Eds.), *Aging and society: A sociology of age stratification*. Vol. 3. New York: Russell Sage, 1972.

Schaie, K. W. Age changes and age differences. In B. L. Neugarten (Ed.), *Middle age and aging: A reader in social psychology*. Chicago: University of Chicago Press, 1968.

Van Gennep, A. *The rites of passage*. Chicago: University of Chicago Press, 1960.

Warner, W. L. *A black civilization*. New York: Harper & Row, 1958.

Wohlwill, J. F. The age variable in psychological research. *Psychological Review*, 1970, *77*, 49–64. (a)

Social Gerontology and the Age Stratification of Society

Matilda White Riley

One decade after "the" White House Conference, and on the eve of another, the Gerontological Society and all of us involved in research in the field can survey with satisfaction the amount of information accumulated in these 10 years and the impact of this information upon professional practice, public policy, and popular attitudes. That much remains to be done is patent to all gerontologists, but that the title of this symposium is "Research Goals and Priorities in Gerontology" suggests that we have reached a point where we can pick and choose among alternative strategies.

What we propose as a high priority for the future is a sociology of age stratification. Gerontologists working in the social science fields have amassed a remarkable body of facts on two main topics: being old and growing old. Our immediate aim is not so much to add to these facts and ideas as to look at them from a fresh perspective. This perspective emphasizes not just old age, but all the age strata in the society as a whole; it emphasizes not just aging, but also the societal processes and changes that affect aging and the state of being old.

From *The Gerontologist*, Vol. 11, No. 1, Part I, Spring 1971. Reprinted by permission of the Gerontological Society and the author.

What do we mean by age *stratification*, which is only now emerging as a new field of sociology? A comparison with the well-established sociology of class stratification is provocative. In that field, two concepts, heuristically stimulating as analogues to our concepts of age strata and aging, have demonstrated their power in explaining diverse social phenomena. These concepts are *social class* (variously defined in terms of inequality of income, prestige, or power) and *social mobility* (consisting of upward or downward movement between lower and higher classes). These concepts of social class and social mobility, which any one of us can grasp intuitively from first-hand experience, have proved scientifically useful in defining and suggesting answers to many important questions. We shall list four sets of these questions briefly, as they may stimulate us to find answers to similar questions in relation to age and aging.

First, how does an individual's location in the class structure channel his attitudes and the way he behaves? Here there is much evidence that, for example, a person's health, his desire to achieve, his sense of mastery over his own fate, or the way he relates to his family and to his job depend to a considerable extent upon his social class.

Second, how do individuals relate to one another within, and between, classes? Within class lines, many friendships are formed, marriages often take place, and feelings of solidarity tend to be widespread. Between classes, relationships, even if not solidary, are often symbiotic, as people of unlike status live harmoniously in the same society. However, there seems to be greater opportunity between, than within, classes, for cleavage or conflict, as in struggles over economic advantages or clashes in political loyalties.

Third, what difficulties beset the upwardly (or downwardly) mobile individual, and what strains does his mobility impose upon the group (such as his parents of one class) whom he leaves behind and upon the new group (such as his wife's parents of a different class) who must now absorb him?

Fourth, to the extent that answers can be found to these three sets of questions, what is the impact of the observed findings upon the society as a whole? If there are inequalities between classes, for example, what do these portend for the prosperity, the morality, or the stability of the over-all structure of classes? What pressures for societal change are generated by differences, conflicts, or mobility between classes?

The literature on these four aspects of class stratification is impressive, pregnant with insights that might be extended to analyses of kindred phenomena. Our concern is to test the utility of the questions it evokes for understanding old age as just one stratum in a society stratified or differentiated, not by class, but by age. Thus we shall start by thinking of society as divided into strata according to the age of its members. *People* at varying ages differ in their capacity and willingness to perform social roles (of student, spouse, worker, or retiree, for example). Moreover, the age strata differ in the social *roles* members are expected to play and in the rights and privileges accorded to them by society. At any given period of time, old people must live as members of such a society, finding their place in relation to the other members who are younger than they, and making choices among whatever opportunities are available to them. Over time, not only old people but people of different ages are all growing older, moving concurrently through a society which itself is undergoing change.

Age Stratification and the Individual

To ask our first question, then: how does an individual's location within the changing age structure of a given society influence his behavior and attitudes? (Mannheim, 1952). In the sociological literature generally it has been well established that individuals are conditioned by society. As Robert Merton puts it, "Structure constrains individuals variously situated within it to develop cultural emphases, social behavior patterns and psychological bents" (Merton, 1957). Similarly, it has been well established in the literature of social gerontology that the state of old age reflects the structural context, showing wide variations (as well as some similarities) when primitive and modern societies are contrasted (Simmons, 1960), or even when modern Western nations are compared with one another (Burgess, 1960, Havighurst, Munnichs, Neugarten, & Thomae, 1969; Shanas & associates 1968). But how does it come about that, *within a given society at any given time*, individuals located in *different age strata* differ from one another? How are older individuals set off from the middle-aged and from the young?

The answer to such a question as this involves two distinct dimensions of time: a life course dimension and an historical dimension. These two dimensions can be thought of as coordinates for locating the individual in the age structure of society. On the first dimension, individuals at the *same* stage of the *life* course have much in common. They tend to be alike in biological development, in the kinds of roles they have experienced (such as worker, spouse, parent of dependent child), and in the sheer number of years behind and potential years ahead. People at *different* life course stages tend to differ in these very respects. The rough index of this life course dimension is years of chronological age—we say that a person is aged 20, or in the age category of 45 to 60. But chronological age is of interest to us, not intrinsically, but only because it can serve as an approximate indicant of personal (that is biological, psychological, and social) experience—and this experience carries with it varying probabilities of behavior and attitudes. This life course dimension is the familiar one that includes the age-related organic changes

Age Grading and the Life Course

affecting physical and mental functioning and that links the biological and the social sciences.

But there is a second time dimension for locating an individual in the age strata that also affects his probability of behaving or thinking in particular ways. This dimension refers to the *period of history* in which he lives. People who were born at the *same* time (referred to as a cohort) share a common historical and environmental past, present, and future. For example, when Americans born in 1910 had reached the age of 30, they had all (in one way or another) experienced World War I and the Great Depression, they were all currently exposed to World War II, and they all confronted the future of the 1940s through the 1970s. People who were born at *different* times (that is, different cohorts) have lived through different intervals of history; and even when they encounter the same historical situation, they may, because they differ in age, experience it differently. Thus any one of us—just as we might be ethnocentric—is almost certainly (to add a needed term to our vocabulary) *"cohort-centric."* That is, we view old age, or any other stage of life, from the unique point of historical time at which we ourselves are standing. The rough index of this historical (or environmental) dimension is the date, or the calendar year. Here again our concern is not with dates themselves, but with the particular socio-cultural and environmental events, conditions, and changes to which the individual is exposed at particular periods.

It comes as no surprise, then, that each of the age strata has its own *distinctive sub-culture.* By age differences in sub-culture we mean that a cross-section view of society shows, for myriad characteristics, patterns that are closely related to age. In our own society today, familiar instances of the differing sub-cultures among young, middle-aged, and old include such varied aspects of life as labor force participation, consumer behavior, leisure-time activities, marital status, religious behavior, education, nativity, fertility and child-rearing practices, or political attitudes—to name only a few. Such age-related patterns differ from time to time and from place to place, as all the age strata in a society—not the old alone—display differ-ences (or similarities) in behavior and attitudes on the two dimen-sions of life course and history.

If we want to go beyond a mere description of these age-related sub-cultures, however, we must examine them further, which leads to our next topic.

Age Stratification and Social Relationships

The second set of questions suggested by the analogy between class stratification and age stratification points to the utility of exploring *relationships* both *between* and *within* age strata. For not only the behavior and attitudes of discrete individuals, but also social relationships—people's positive or negative feelings and actions toward each other—are channeled through the age structure of the particular society. Thus a sociology of age stratification, by investigating these relationships, should help to illuminate the nature of old age.

Many aspects of the cleavages or the bonds *between* old and young, dramatized by philosophers and poets of the ancient past, are still widely discussed today. Is there an inevitable gap between generations? Do the elderly constitute a disadvantaged minority group, regarded with prejudice by the majority? Or do they control important centers of power, refusing to yield to the young? Are old people likely to form political blocs, seeking to solve their own problems with little regard for the rest of society? And, if many conditions foster intergenerational conflict or exploitation, what other conditions foster relationships of harmony or reciprocity?

As a preliminary to addressing such momentous issues, one small illustration of the *sequential relations* among generations within the family will point out the interconnectedness of the age strata. If we start with the elderly generation of parents and their adult offspring, a well-known finding from the gerontological literature reports widespread exchanges of material support. This support varies in amount and kind, ranging from financial contributions and care in illness to baby-sitting and help with housework and home repairs. Contrary to previous notions of an upward flow of contributions *to* older people, the flow of support between aged parents and their adult offspring appears to be two-directional, either from parent to child or from child to parent as need and opportunity dictate (Riley et al., 1968). Indeed (in the United States, at least), the proportions of older people who *give* help to their offspring appear to exceed the proportions who *receive* help from their offspring (Shanas, 1966; Streib, 1965; Streib & Thompson, 1960).

Let us now, however, include in the example still a third generation of the family, for it is our contention that many a commonplace observation about old people can take on new significance through extension to other age strata. Let us move from the flow of material assistance between aged parents and their middle-aged children to the flow between this middle generation and *their* young children. The principle can be illustrated by one small study (Foner, 1969) in which parents of high school students were asked what they would do with money unexpectedly received. Only 2% said they would use it to help their aged parents. But this was not because they would spend it on themselves or save it for their retirement; it was rather because, in the main, they would reserve it to help their children get started in life. Furthermore, the aged generation concurs; they do not expect repayment. The middle generation, then, does not neglect the old because of pre-occupation with their own needs (in fact, they are far readier to offer help than are their aged parents to want or to accept it), but because of their pre-occupation with the needs of their young children. In short, the flow of material support tends to be, not reciprocal, but sequential—with each generation (regardless of its means) attempting to aid the next younger generation.

As such a finding intimates, many middle-aged parents, by investing their resources in the future of their young children, are not only restricting any potential help they might give to the older generation; they are also restricting the accumulation of assets for their own later life. In this example, then, extension of the analysis from the oldest to the youngest generation in the family helps to clarify one aspect of the meaning of old age. Any lack of family support for aged parents now appears, not as willful indifference or neglect, but as an expression of normative agreement among all the generations about the direction in which aid should flow.

Many other conditions of the aged might similarly be better understood against the backdrop of the other strata with whom old people live and relate. Consider the work force data on older men as this might be compared with the differing circumstances of employment of younger people at various periods of history. In the early days of the Industrial Revolution in England, the father (or grandfather), as a skilled workman in his own right, could take his children with him into the factory, himself training the adult sons and supervising the little children throughout the long workday (Smelser, 1968). Thus his authority within the family could penetrate into the workplace, preserving traditional ties among the generations. If such an arrangement encouraged between-strata solidarity, then the subsequent changes in conditions of work may have undermined this basis. More recently, in the United States, quite another set of changes have marked the relative positions of older men and boys in the work force. Between 1900 and 1930, while the majority of older men remained economically active, the proportion of boys aged 10 to 15 who were fully employed declined from 25% to only 6%. Since World War II, as older men have been winnowed from the labor force, boys too are being extruded; the Census no longer counts children under 14 in compiling labor force statistics, and the participation rates of boys from 16 through 19 show slight but consistent declines. Thus older men today live in a society where the situation of both the old and the young must be interpreted in relation to the productivity and economic prestige of men in their middle years (Kalish, 1969).

Such examples suggest a general principle: important increments to gerontological knowledge are obtainable by studying the entire age-differentiated society, not merely the old. The same principle holds when the research focus is on relationships *within* rather than *between* age strata. Here we shall simply allude to the concern of gerontologists with questions of age-similarity as a basis for friendship, or age-homogeneity as a feature of residential settings for older people (Madge, 1969; Riley et al., 1968). It has been shown that, outside of family groups, older people tend (although by no means exclusively) to have friends who are similar to themselves in status characteristics—notably age—that signal mutuality of experiences, tastes, or values. However, as the sociological literature shows (Hess, 1971), such choice of age-mates is only a special case of the widespread phenomenon of homophily (or similarity among friends in status or in values) (Lazersfeld & Merton, 1954).

Age homophily, not only among the old but also at younger age levels, may be especially pronounced in the United States today as a number of factors converge to produce solidarity within age lines. Simply the rapidity of social change, for example, can sharpen the differences among strata and can thereby contribute to a sense of uniqueness among members of each single stratum. The expansion of education has extended the social (and often the physical) segregation of age-similars from children in the lower schools to older adolescents and even to young adults in colleges and universities (Parsons & Platt, 1971). Today's middle-aged people, too, many of whom have left the city to rear their children in the suburbs, have experienced long years of age-homogeneous neighborhood settings (Starr, 1971). And old people because of increasing longevity retain larger numbers of their age peers as associates (Spengler, 1969). In many respects, then, we live in an *age-graded* society, with a high potential for strong ties to develop within each age stratum.

However, the possible long-term consequences of such heightened conditions of within-stratum solidarity may be double-edged. On the one hand, homophily may be beneficial to the individuals involved. Age peers have long been recognized as easing the transition from childhood to adulthood (Eisenstadt, 1956); and they may perhaps aid adjustment in old age and at other points of transition in the life course as well. On the other hand, if age peers increasingly turn to each other for aid and comfort, detriments to relationships between strata may ensue as ties between generations may become attenuated or the potential for cleavage or conflict may be increased.

Aging and Cohort Flow

It is the third set of questions—those relating to the processes of *mobility* of individuals from one stratum to another—that brings into bold relief certain similarities, but also the essential differences, between class stratification and age stratification.

At points of similarity between the two processes, much can be learned about aging from the rich literature on class mobility. We tend to take aging for granted (much as before the development of physiology as a science, laymen took their bodily functioning for granted). Yet, when aging (social, psychological, and biological) is viewed as mobility through the age strata, it is revealed as a process that entails many of the same tensions and strains as class mobility. Aging individuals must pass through key transition points in the society—from infancy to childhood, for example, from one school grade to the next, from adolescence to adulthood, or from work-life to retirement (Clausen, 1971). And the degree of strain engendered by such transitions depends upon diverse social conditions—upon the continuity or discontinuity in the role sequences (Benedict, 1938); upon how fully institutionalized a particular role may be (Donahue, Orbach, & Pollak, 1960); upon the internal consistency of role expectations, facilities, and sanctions;[1] or upon how effectively people are trained or socialized at every stage of life (Brim, 1968; Brim & Wheeler, 1966). For example, consider the stress entailed in our society because we crowd formal education almost exclusively into the younger stages of life rather than spreading it over the life course as individuals require it. Since we do not regard students as full-fledged adults, what tensions must be endured by the young person who stays in the role of student beyond adolescence well into adulthood (tensions that are all too evident in universities today)? What difficulties beset the older person if, in order to obtain the further education he needs or desires, he must sacrifice his job? Like social mobility, too, aging places strains not only upon individuals but also upon the groups through which the aging individual passes. Thus a family must regroup itself after the marriage of its youngest child, or a community after the death of an elder statesman. Similarly, group adjustments are necessitated by the advent of new members like the birth of a child into a family, the entry of a new class of children into a school grade, or the move of a widowed old person into the household of her married daughter.

Despite such similarities, however, aging differs from class mobility in certain fundamental respects. Exactly because the analogy breaks down in these respects is age stratification revealed in its full uniqueness and in its intrinsicality to social change. In the first place, mobility across social classes affects only selected individuals, who can move either upward or downward, and who can reverse direction at different stages of life. But mobility through the age strata is, of course, universal, unidirectional, and irreversible. Everybody ages. Everybody changes over his life course as personality develops, experience accumulates, and adjustments are made to new roles. Nobody can ever go back, although individuals may age in different ways and at different rates.

In the second place, knowledgeable as we are about the

inevitability of aging, we take much less cognizance of the inexorability of birth and death, and of the endless succession of cohorts (or generations of individuals born at the same time)—for which there is no precise parallel in class mobility. Yet the sociology of age stratification requires examination of the fact that, within a given society, different cohorts can age in different ways. Each cohort is tied through its date of birth to societal history. Thus the aging of each new cohort is affected by the special situation of that cohort's particular era in history—by the changing cultural, social, and material conditions in the society and by events in the external environment. While all the members of one particular cohort move together over their life course through the same period of time, the various cohorts in the society can differ because they start at distinct times. Cohorts can also differ markedly in size and in composition (in the proportions of males and females, for example, or of blacks and whites, or of natives and foreign-born).

Consider a few examples of inter-cohort differences in the way people have aged in our own society in the *past*. Epidemiologists tell us that, in comparison with women born a century ago, today's women have experienced menarche at earlier ages and menopause at later ages. (National Center for Health Statistics, 1966; Susser, 1969; Tanner, 1962). That is, the period of potential fertility has appreciably lengthened. In practice, however, *recent* cohorts spend fewer years of their lives in child-bearing. Women have telescoped the phase of actual reproduction, having fewer and more closely spaced offspring nowadays than did their mothers or grandmothers (Glick & Parke, 1965). Moreover, the trauma of reproduction have been drastically reduced, as fewer women die in childbirth and fewer of their infants die.

Most striking of all the cohort differences, perhaps, are those in longevity—in the proportions of cohort members who outlive the ills of infancy, who escape maternal deaths and the other mortality risks of young adulthood, and who thus survive into the higher ages of the life-span. The average lifetime (estimated at only two to three decades among cohorts born in ancient Rome or in medieval Europe) has risen in the United States from four decades among cohorts born in the mid-nineteenth century to an estimated seven decades among those born in the mid-twentieth—a situation apparently unparalleled in human history.[2] The profound implications of such cohort differences in longevity can be intimated by just one of the many associated changes, the one called the "revolution in family structure" (Glick & Parke, 1965; Shanas, 1969).[3] The single nuclear household of a century ago (parents and their children, sometimes including a grandparent) has been replaced, because of increased joint survival, by several generations of related nuclear households: the young couple with their dependent children, the middle-aged parents, the aged generation of grandparents, and the great-grandparent who also often survives.

What do such differences between earlier and later cohorts presage for the people who will become old in the *future?* Speculation about many of these differences can prove fruitful of hypotheses. We might speculate, for example, about the extended period of husband-wife relationships in the middle years: the more recent couples have had more time to accumulate assets, or to learn independence from their offspring, or to prepare themselves for retirement. But not all predictions about future implications of cohort differences are entirely speculative, since everybody who will reach 65 during this century or during the early decades of the 21st century is already alive. Much information is already in hand about the size of existing cohorts, for example, or about their place of birth or their educational level. Thus, apart from unforeseeable changes (as through wars, depressions, or major shifts in migration or in values), fair estimates can be made about numerous characteristics of old people at particular dates in the future. The *size* of the aged stratum at the turn of the century will reflect the small numbers of babies in the Depression cohorts; but the size of the aged stratum will predictably increase again in the early decades of the coming century with the influx of the "baby boom" cohorts born after World War II (Spengler, 1969). In respect to *nativity*, the much-studied cohort who had passed age 65 or more by 1960 had contained a sizeable proportion of early immigrants who were largely illiterate and unskilled, whereas the more recent cohorts who will reach old age in subsequent decades contain fewer and better educated immigrants. Or in respect to formal *education*, we know that over 70% of the cohort aged 75 or more in 1960 had had less than 9 years of school, contrasted with only 17% of the cohort aged 25 to 29, who will not reach age 75 before the year 2,005 (Riley et al., 1968). We are aware, also, of many changing societal or environmental conditions, not all of them salutary, that may influence in special ways the future life course of existing cohorts—as, for example, the spread of pollution might have the greatest effect on young cohorts subject to a full lifetime of exposure, or as the increase of smoking among women might bring female death rates more nearly into line with the currently higher male rates. We cannot overestimate the importance of charting such cohort differences for an understanding of old age.

Age and Social Change

We have been discussing the dual processes affecting individuals (or cohorts of individuals) in a society: aging as a social, psychological, and biological process; and the succession of cohorts which do not all age in exactly the same ways. We shall now ask how these processes relate to the macrocosm of the changing society (Ryder, 1965) of which the old people who concern us are one integral part.

Mannheim (1952) once proposed a tantalizing mental experiment. Imagine, he said, a society in which one generation lived on forever, and none followed to replace it. Let us, as social scientists, policy-makers, and professional groups, make such an experiment! If everybody grows old together, what distinctions might remain between old and young? A few moments' thought are enough to suggest the ineluctable connections among the succession of cohorts, aging, and age stratification. For, in contrast to Mannheim's imaginary society, our own consists of successive cohorts, each with its own unique life-course pattern. It is clear that these cohorts fit together at any given time to form the age structure of young, middle-aged, and aged strata. And over time, as the particular individuals composing the particular strata are continually moving on and being replaced, the society itself is changing.

Certain connections now become apparent between the flow of cohorts and the age-related societal patterns and changes in individual behaviors, attitudes, and relationships (noted in the first sections of the paper). In the simplest case, because successive cohorts often age in different ways, some of these societal patterns and changes can be viewed as direct reflections of the differing cohorts that comprise the age strata at particular periods. Education is a noteworthy example of the significance of cohort flow for cross-sectional differences among age strata (Riley et al., 1968). The rapid pace of educational advance over the century, leaving its mark on successive cohorts of young people, now sets the age strata clearly apart from one another. And these strata differences in education have incalculable importance for many aspects of behavior and attitude—for prejudice, feelings of powerlessness, narrow ranges of interests and friendships, and the like. Of course, such strata differences do not remain fixed. Not only do new cohorts come along, but society itself can change in its related institutions and practices. The age pattern of education today is a reversal of that in earlier societies where the old were honored for their greater knowledge. If one looks ahead from today's knowledge explosion, the information gap between the very young and even the not-so-young is deepening, creating pressures to change the entire structure of education if people beyond the earliest years are to maintain competitive equality.[4]

In another example, the cross-section age patterns for drinking or smoking have shown a general decline from younger to older strata; and these differences among strata are in part reflections of the past tendency for each new cohort to espouse these practices to an

Age Grading and the Life Course

increasing degree (Riley et al., 1968). Today's younger cohorts, however, may be introducing new habits that could, over the next decades, drastically change the cross-section age pattern. A recent campus interview elicited the student comment, for example, that

. . . upperclassmen still prefer beer, but a large majority of underclassmen prefer pot. Pot is big in the high schools, and it is very popular with freshmen who just came out of that environment. The trend is definitely away from beer (Cicetti, 1970).

Are these newcomers to the college likely to set the pace for the cohorts that follow?

In such instances, changes in societal age strata can be interpreted as the shifting composite of cohorts who, themselves affected by differing historical backgrounds, have aged in differing ways. In other instances, life course differences among cohorts in one social sphere appear to stimulate further changes in other spheres. For example, far-reaching shifts in the relations between men and women at various ages—the decreasing differentiation between the sexes or the greater freedom of sexual behavior—might be traced in part to a reversal in cohort patterns of female participation in the labor force (Riley et al., 1968, 1971). Many cohorts of women born during the late 19th century showed steadily declining rates of participation over the life course. Following World War II, a new pattern began to emerge, as many married women entered the labor force during their middle years, although work force participation of young women in the child rearing ages remained low. The conjunction of these cohort trends meant that, for a considerable period, it was only the young mothers with little children whose labor force participation was low. This situation may have prompted a classic observation (foreshadowing the full force of the Women's Liberation Movement) that "for the first time in the history of any known society, motherhood has become a full-time occupation for adult women" (Rossi, 1964). Women at other times and places shared motherhood with demanding labor in the fields, the factory, or the household.

Can we expect that full-time motherhood is now institutionalized and will persist into the future? If so, we may be victims of our own "cohort-centrism"—one more proof that our understandings of society are influenced by our particular historical background. For this full-time preoccupation of American mothers with their young children seems already to be eroding as recent cohorts have developed a rather different pattern. Not only have the proportions of married women in the labor force during their middle years more than doubled, but there have been pronounced increases also among young married women, even those with little children (Manpower Report of the President, 1970). Thus it may appear to historians of the future that full-time motherhood was a peculiar phenomenon, existing in American society only for a few decades of the twentieth century. Whatever the future may actually hold, the example begins to suggest how the confluence of cohorts with differing life course patterns in one respect (economic activity of women) can change society in other respects as well. Think, for example, of the mature women who no longer "retire" from major social roles many years before their husbands retire from work. Or think of the young husbands and wives who now share the work of homemaking and infant care. May such changing work habits result in entirely new modes of relationship in the family and—if only because of the widespread unavailability of working wives for daytime activities at home or in the community—in other social institutions?

In addition to the impress of cohort succession upon the history of society, it can sometimes happen that innovations emanating from a single cohort ramify rather quickly through the other age strata, without awaiting the lag over a long series of cohorts. Thus the excessive size of the "baby boom" cohort born after World War II has required drastic adjustments throughout a society unprepared to absorb it—from the initial requirements for obstetrical facilities through the successive pressures on housing, schools, the job market, the marriage market, and so on into the future. Among the many other widely discussed instances are the increased financial burden borne (through transfer payments) by the remainder of society because so many retired old people have inadequate incomes (Bernstein, 1969; McConnell, 1960); or the potential changes in the ethos surrounding work and leisure as large numbers of old and young no longer participate in the work force (Donahue et al., 1960; Riley, Foner, Hess, & Toby, 1969). It has even been suggested that a completely revolutionary "consciousness," now informing the values and behaviors of many young people, may affect the entire society (Reich, 1970).

To return to the immediate topic of this essay, we offer a special challenge to the oncoming cohorts of social gerontologists—not merely to continue looking for new materials, but also to re-examine and fit together the existing materials in a new way. We suggest a review of old age as one ingredient in the societal macrocosm, inseparable from, and interdependent with, the other age strata. We suggest a review of aging and of the succession of births and deaths as integral parts of societal process and change that follow their own rhythm and that in themselves constitute immanent strains and pressures toward innovation. Such a sociological review can, we submit, help to explain old age and aging and can at the same time suggest potential solutions to some of the problems of great immediate concern.

In sum, the forces of social change, whether through deliberate intervention[5] or as an indirect consequence of existing trends, are not only constantly affecting the aging process, but are also bringing new influences to bear on the situation, on the characteristics of persons who are old, and on the younger age strata with whom old people are interdependent. Discovery and evaluation of the implications for old age of these forces for change constitutes a whole new field of opportunity for social scientists, professional groups, and policy makers in gerontology.

References

Back, K. W. The ambiguity of retirement. In E. W. Busse and E. Pfeiffer (Eds.) *Behavior and adaptation in late life.* Boston: Little, Brown & Co., 1969.

Benedict, R. Continuities and discontinuities in cultural conditioning. *Psychiatry*, 1938, *I*, 161–167. (Reprinted in Kluckhohn, C., Murray, H. A., & Schneider, D. (Eds.), *Personality in nature, society and culture.* New York: Alfred A. Knopf, 1953.

Bernstein, M. C. Aging and the law. In M. W. Riley, J. W. Riley, Jr., & M. E. Johnson (Eds.), *Aging and society*, Vol. 2, *Aging and the professions.* New York: Russell Sage Foundation, 1969.

Brim, O. G., Jr. Adult socialization. In J. A. Clausen (Ed.), *Socialization and society.* Boston: Little, Brown, & Co., 1968.

Brim, O. G., Jr., & Wheeler, S. *Socialization after childhood: Two essays.* New York: John Wiley & Sons, 1966.

Burgess, E. W. (Ed.) *Aging in Western societies.* Chicago: University of Chicago Press, 1960.

Cicetti, F. Campuses revisited: New trend at Seton Hall. *Newark Evening News*, Sept. 30, 1970.

Clausen, J. A. The life course of individuals. In M. W. Riley, M. E. Johnson, & A. Foner, *Aging and society.* Vol. 3, *A sociology of age stratification.* New York: Russell Sage Foundation, 1971.

Donahue, W., Orbach, H. L., & Pollak, O. Retirement: The emerging social pattern. In C. Tibbitts (Ed.) *Handbook of social gerontology.* Chicago: University of Chicago Press, 1960.

Eisenstadt, S. N. *From generation to generation; age groups and social structure.* Free Press: Glencoe, Ill., 1956.

Foner, A. The middle years: Prelude to retirement? PhD dissertation, New York University, 1969.

Glick, P. C., & Parke, R., Jr. New approaches in studying the life cycle of the family. *Demography*, 1965, *2*, 187–202.

Havighurst, R. J., Munnichs, J. M. A., Neugarten, B. L., & Thomae, H. (Eds.) *Adjustment to retirement; a cross-national study.* Assen. The Netherlands: Koninklijke van Gorcum, 1969.

Hess, B. Friendship. In M. W. Riley, M. E. Johnson, & A. Foner. *Aging and society*. Vol. 3, *A sociology of age stratification*. New York: Russell Sage Foundation, 1971.

Kalish, R. A. The old and the new as generation gap allies. *Gerontologist*, 1969, *9*, 83–89.

Lazarsfeld, P. F., & Merton, R. K. Friendship as social process: A substantive and methodological analysis. In M. Berger, T. Abel, & C. H. Page. *Freedom and control in modern society*. New York: D. Van Nostrand Co., 1954.

McConnell, J. W. Aging and the economy. In C. Tibbitts (Ed.), *Handbook of social gerontology*. Chicago: University of Chicago Press, 1960.

Madge, J. Aging and the fields of architecture and planning. In M. W. Riley, J. W. Riley, Jr., & M. E. Johnson (Eds.), *Aging and society*. Vol. 2, *Aging and the professions*. New York: Russell Sage Foundation, 1969.

Mannheim, K. The problem of generations. In P. Kecskemeti (Ed. & Trans.), *Essays on the sociology of knowledge*. London: Routledge & Kegan Paul (1928), 1952.

Manpower Report of the President, Mar., 1970. Washington: Government Printing Office.

Merton, R. K. *Social theory and social structure*. (Rev. Ed.) Glencoe, Ill.: Free Press, 1957.

National Center for Health Statistics. Age and menopause, United States 1960–1962. *Vital and health statistics, 1966*, PHS Pub. No. 1000-Series II, No. 19, Washington: Government Printing Office.

Parsons, T., & Platt, G. M. Higher education and changing socialization. In M. W. Riley, M. E. Johnson, & A. Foner. *Aging and society*, Vol. 3, *A sociology of age stratification*. New York: Russell Sage Foundation, 1971.

Reich, C. Reflections: The greening of America. *New Yorker*, Sept. 26, 1970, 42 ff.

Riley, M. W., Foner, A., & Associates. *Aging and society*. Vol. 1, *An inventory of research findings*. New York: Russell Sage Foundation, 1968.

Riley, M. W., Riley, J. W., Jr. & Johnson, M. E. *Aging and society*, Vol. 2, *Aging and the professions*. New York: Russell Sage Foundation, 1969.

Riley, M. W., Johnson, M. E., & Foner, A. *Aging and society*. Vol. 3, *A sociology of age stratification*. New York: Russell Sage Foundation, 1971.

Riley, M. W., Foner, A., Hess, B., & Toby, M. L. Socialization for the middle and later years. In D. A. Goslin (Ed.), *Handbook of socialization theory and research*. Chicago: Rand McNally, 1969.

Rossi, A. S. Equality between the sexes: An immodest proposal. *Daedalus*, Spring, 1964, 607–652.

Ryder, N. B. The cohort as a concept in the study of social change. *American Sociological Review*, 1965, *30*, 843–861.

Shanas, E., & Associates. Family help patterns and social class in three countries. Paper presented at the meetings of the American Sociological Assn., Miami, 1966.

Shanas, E. *Old people in three industrial societies*. New York: Atherton Press, 1968.

Shanas, E. Living arrangements and housing of old people. In E. W. Busse & E. Pfeiffer (Eds.), *Behavior and adaptation in late life*. Boston: Little, Brown & Co., 1969.

Simmons, L. W. Aging in preindustrial societies. In C. Tibbitts (Ed.), *Handbook of social gerontology*. Chicago: University of Chicago Press, 1960.

Smelser, N. J. Sociological history: The industrial revolution and the British working-class family. In N. J. Smelser (Ed.), *Essays in sociological explanation*. Englewood Cliffs, NJ: Prentice-Hall, 1968.

Spengler, J. J. The aged and public policy. In E. W. Busse & E. Pfeiffer (Eds.), *Behavior and adaptation in late life*. Boston: Little, Brown & Co., 1969.

Starr, B. C. The community. In M. W. Riley, M. E. Johnson, & A. Foner. *Aging and society*. Vol. 3, *A sociology of age stratification*. New York: Russell Sage Foundation, 1971.

Streib, G. F. Intergenerational relations: Perspectives of the two generations on the older parent. *Journal of Marriage & the Family*, 1965, *27*, 469–476.

Streib, G. F., & Thompson, W. E. The older person in a family context. In C. Tibbitts (Ed.), *Handbook of social gerontology*. Chicago: University of Chicago Press, 1960.

Susser, M. Aging and the field of public health. In M. W. Riley, J. W. Riley, Jr., & M. E. Johnson (Eds.), *Aging and the professions*. New York: Russell Sage Foundation, 1969.

Tanner, J. M. *Growth at adolescence*. (2nd ed.) Oxford: Blackwell, Davis Co., 1962.

[1]Back (1969) claims ambiguity of retirement which, although socially defined as a right of the individual, offers low rewards and is socially under-valued.

[2]To be sure, infant deaths weigh heavily in these averages. Moreover, the data are based on hypothetical, rather than true, cohorts. See Riley et al. (1968).

[3]Among couples born a century ago, the last child in the family was married, on the average, at about the same time as the death of one of the parents. But among recent cohorts, husbands and wives typically survive together as two-person families for a good many years after the last child has married and left home. Changes in family structure are associated with changes, not only in longevity, but also in child-bearing and in household living arrangements; see Riley et al., 1968.

[4]If such a change is not effected, we may expect increasing convergence of age and class stratification as education achieves preeminence among the distinguishing criteria of social class.

[5]Many possibilities for intervention in the several professional fields are discussed in the series of essays in Riley, Riley, & Johnson, 1969, in which experts discuss the implications of social science knowledge for public policy and professional practice affecting older people.

The Life Course of Individuals

John Clausen

Whatever the age structure of a society and however sharp the boundaries between age levels, individuals move more or less smoothly from each stratum to the next highest, somehow integrating their experiences into a coherent whole, which may be viewed from a variety of perspectives. From the perspective of the Bible's "dust to dust, ashes to ashes," the process is but one cycle in an infinite series. The early growth and late decline of strength and power over the course of a life also evokes the image of the "life cycle." Another related image is that of successive generations coming into being and then dying out.

Yet few individuals seem to experience their lives as cyclical in nature. The decline of physical strength and sexual power that accompanies aging is by no means comparable to the tremendous thrust of early development. In many respects, in fact, an individual may show continued development until extreme old age. There is not only continuity but also a continual unfolding of new possibilities almost to the very end. For most of the life history, then, the term "life cycle" seems to be somewhat inappropriate.

However, the course of a human life does entail many events that from a generational perspective may be viewed as cyclical. The sequence of events that has been called the "family cycle," in which one moves from dependent family member to independent individual, spouse, and parent and then (potentially) back to "empty nest," to widowhood and possibly dependency is certainly the prime subsidiary cycle. But other social roles and role sequences may entail similar ebbs and flows of involvement and vital investment. Thus, how one labels the whole of the life history depends upon particular images, though in the pages that follow, we shall use the terms "life course" and "life cycle" interchangeably.

The life course is, most simply put, the course of aging, but . . . the passage of years has several facets and many implications. Biological aging involves a number of interrelated processes of growth and maturation, of differentials in the attainment of maturity and in the decline of optimum performance. The individual must adapt recurrently to the facts of his own development and aging. Inevitably, aging also brings a continual accretion of experiences, which the

From *Aging and Society:* Volume three (chapter 11): A Sociology of Age Stratification, by Matilda White Riley, Marilyn Johnson, and Anne Foner, et al., © 1972 by Russell Sage Foundation. Reprinted by permission of Basic Books, Inc. and the author.

individual draws upon in formulating who he is and where he is going. Beyond this, almost from the very start, aging brings the development of interests and goals that will influence an individual's choice among alternative paths or even lead him to cut out a path through heavy underbrush that deters most of his peers from leaving the beaten paths.

Parallel to biological aging, and largely setting the frame of reference within which the individual defines and redefines his goals and self-image, is the structure of expectations and relationships through which he sequentially passes. Certain possibilities exist for him as positions to be occupied, roles to be played. One role may link to another: college graduation makes possible admission to law school, and law school graduation makes possible a legal career. Conversely, failure in a given role may preclude the assumption of others. A life is made up of several subcycles of interlinked roles: student roles, family roles, career roles, community roles. Within a subcycle, role sequences may be closely linked; between cycles— family and career, for example—the linkages are likely to be lesser. Nevertheless, a marked change in one sequence is likely to mean some change in the others and in their relative saliences.

The general aim of the present chapter, then, is to examine the life course for the light it throws on the nature and meaning of age for the individual member of a given cohort. Attention will be focused on the role sequences experienced by individuals in contemporary society and the selection and socialization processes that influence the life course. We shall also examine a number of issues concerning personality development, identity, and the psychological dynamics entailed in role transitions and the process of aging.

The Analysis of the Life Course

Consideration of the life course almost immediately leads to an effort to break down that course into constituent phases or stages. Shakespeare's seven ages of man (*As You Like It*, II, vii) and Erikson's eight stages of psychosocial development (1950, 1968) are the best known such formulations. Of Shakespeare's seven ages, the first two and the last two are specifically age-linked: "At first the infant, muling and puking in the nurse's arms; then the whining schoolboy" and, at the other end, "the sixth age shifts into the lean and slippered pantaloon, with spectacles on nose and pouch on side . . ." and finally, "last scene of all, . . . is second childishness and mere oblivion." The other three "ages" are really social roles—lover, soldier, justice—that have a strong age reference, especially if one considers each as a kind of ideal type. Romeo, the lover, is strictly an adolescent; the soldier, "full of strange oaths," is *par excellence* the young adult male; and the lawyer does not often become a justice until he has acquired the wisdom and the round belly of middle age. Shakespeare's seven ages are a dramatic statement of the fact that persons change markedly from one age level to the next in the images they evoke and in the selves they present to the world. One is a different person by virtue of changing physique, changing major social roles, and changing participation in society.

If Shakespeare's seven ages are most widely known by the general population, Erikson's eight stages are certainly the most widely quoted in social science and psychiatric literature. Erikson's formulation of the life cycle is psychoanalytically based and seeks "to make explicit those psycho-social insights that often remain implicit in clinical practice and theory" (1968, p. 286). Erikson's concern is with the development of personality, especially of identity. He postulates a series of crises or critical problems that must be resolved in the course of development, each defining a stage and (potentially) resulting in the attainment of a more mature level of functioning for the individual. Each such attainment is said to depend on the proper sequence of prior attainments, though precursors of each level of maturity exist prior to the critical time for its emergence. In infancy, the critical task is attainment of trust; in early childhood (age 2 or 3) the child must achieve autonomy or be faced with shame and doubt; at the "play age" (3 to 4) the child achieves initiative and conscience by resolving his Oedipal guilt; at the school age he develops a sense of industry and competence or comes to see himself as inadequate. Adolescence is the time for achieving an integrated sense of identity. Young adulthood brings true intimacy in relationships, according to Erikson, while maturity brings concern with establishing and guiding the next generation. Old age is seen as the period for achieving and maintaining full integrity and wisdom or falling into despair.

Erikson has addressed his attention to aspects of personality development and life experience that are almost universally salient in social functioning. They are problematic in that they must be achieved through socialization and adaptation. It is this fact, I believe, and not the sequence of stages in which Erikson has embedded his clinical insights, that has made his formulation so popular. Individual and group departures from Erikson's postulated sequence are frequent, and there is little evidence to support the thesis that autonomy, initiative, and intimacy—or even identity—tend to be definitively achieved *at* any given stage or *by* any given time. Each of these attributes has different meanings at different age levels, as Erikson himself notes, and some degree of each may be demanded at more or less clearly specified times in any given social milieu, but phase movements differ sharply. Erikson's stages, then, are valuable principally as a medium for his insightful analysis of developmental aspects of identity. Neither the stages nor the concepts they illuminate are precisely enough defined to permit systematic research, though they give rise to many hypotheses worth formulating with sufficient precision to make testing possible.

Problems of Delineating Life-Course Stages When stages can be linked to the maturational level of the organism, as in childhood and early adolescence, it is not difficult to delineate specific tasks and developmental phases that are particularly salient in a given period. One can evaluate the individual's performance of these tasks or, perhaps more important, note how persons in his social set evaluate his performance. It then becomes a problem for empirical research to ascertain the consequences for the individual's later development of success or failure in resolution of the tasks of any particular stage.

In addition to accomplishment of specific developmental tasks, the effects of possession of certain characteristics can also be examined within the framework of life stages. Physical attributes, for example, may have greater importance at certain ages than at others. How does possession of valued attributes at the critical phases influence the life course? Do athletic ability in a young man or early glamour and beauty in a young woman—attributes that lead (in the United States, at least) to popularity in the adolescent peer group— give lasting advantages to their possessors? Or, to take another example, how does the age-structure of one's closest friends and associates influence or vary with the life course?

The decision to analyze the life course as a sequence of stages forces evaluation of the constancy of the points dividing the stages. The life course consists of many sequences, and some developmental accomplishments and status transitions are more closely linked with age than others. During the early years of life, maturational stages tend to occur within fairly narrow ranges. Still, even these narrow ranges may shift historically. We know, for example, that sexual maturity comes earlier now than in Shakespeare's time, though perhaps not much earlier than for the precocious Romeo and Juliet. And individual differences do exist. Almost all children start the first grade at 5 or 6 in the United States, but some move ahead more rapidly than others. As the spread increases, cumulative achievement in relation to grade level becomes a criterion for evaluation. Indeed, distinctions are noted much earlier, as a child is termed a "late talker," or an "early walker." Thus, as Bernice Neugarten and her associates (1965) have noted, we have personal timetables that reflect social norms as to when various events and role changes should take place. An important question to examine, then, is the extent to which being early or late in some sequences affects one's timing in others. For example, do girls and boys who mature early—who are "old for their years"—have an advantage over late maturers? How much difference does such acceleration make for the life course?

Once full physical maturity has been achieved, age as such becomes a basis for stage definitions primarily to the degree that there are clear age norms for status transitions. In simpler societies, where there is less role differentiation, nearly all persons of the same sex may be expected to make a given transition at a particular time, and such transitions may be highly ritualized. We emphasize, they *may* be expected to make the transition together, but only to the degree that age-grading is an important basis for social organization. For example, among the Nyakyusa, a West African society in which the villages themselves are organized on the basis of age level (beginning as new settlements of boys aged 10 to 13 or 14), power and influence are passed along from one age cohort to another in rituals that constitute a rededication of the social structure (Wilson, 1951). One's life course is to a large extent dependent on the composition of his age-village and the family status of the highest ranking male in that village.

In the contemporary United States, role transitions within the adult years are differently patterned within the social structure, especially according to one's social class, ethnic background, and occupation. This is most obvious for such transitions as college attendance, entry into first job, military service, and age of marriage. Age-linked expectations impinge differently on later careers as well. Because of these variations, stage analyses of the adult years are likely to be fruitful primarily as we deal with sequences within particular roles. Even here, the postulation of definable stages may be less fruitful than the analysis of how roles come to be ordered for a particular individual. This will be a major concern of the present essay.

Determinants of the Life Course The trajectory of a human life is the product of many forces—genetic, physiological, ecological, social, and cultural. Physical and social-psychological development interact in a social matrix made up of group memberships and of shared or conflicting expectations that bind men to each other or divide them and that contribute crucially to the individual's own identity. What an individual is at any given time—what goals he pursues, what meanings events have for him, how he relates to others, and how others view him—depends upon the complex sequence of interactions among the influences upon him and the patterns that he himself has evolved for coping with his world.

There appear to be four major components underlying the

development of the life course and the individual's performance of the major social roles that make up so large a part of that course: (1) the personal resources that the individual can command—his intelligence, appearance, strength, health, temperament; (2) the sources of support and guidance that help to orient him to his world and assist him to cope with it; (3) the opportunities available to him or the obstacles he encounters as these are influenced by his social class, ethnic membership, age, sex, and personal contacts, as well as the effects of war, depression, and major social changes that impinge differentially upon particular birth cohorts; and (4) investments of effort that the individual makes in his own behalf (his commitments) and his mobilization of effort toward these ends. There is, then, an enormous range of influences to be considered. Only the most gross sequences and interactions have been studied . . . .

The Representation of the Life Course

As noted earlier, the life course is not easily encapsulated in a set of stages or in any single body of theory. At every period beyond early childhood, the individual has the potential to direct or modify large segments of his activities and relationships. He does this within a framework of roles and expectations that are often strongly age-linked, but they are not inexorable constraints. Individuals can and do differ in the extent to which they set themselves goals and invest themselves. The school dropout *may* become a highly creative, industrious, and successful rock musician, though obviously this is not the most likely result.

What we want to know perhaps more than anything else about a given life history is how that individual came to carve out the goals he pursues or how he came to abandon his incipient goals. Every life has turning points, though they may seem imperceptible either because the person never moved far enough to see where he was going or because a whole series of subtle influences escaped notice. Anselm Strauss (1959) writes of "status forcing" or transforming experiences by which an individual comes to redefine himself and the possibilities open to him. The art student whose efforts are singled out for favorable comment and encouragement by an eminent artist, or the unassuming underling who emerges as the only competent leader in the face of a disaster, may have new views of themselves and where they are going. Events that bring discontinuity into one life may actually bring meaning into another.

If we cannot encapsulate the life history, it is at least possible to focus on aspects that can be examined more systematically. One can examine how role priorities were established and how role conflicts have tended to be resolved. As noted in the discussion of occupational careers, many men acknowledge that their job comes first except for dire crises in the family. Many others would say that their families come first, an assertion that some wives and children might dispute. It would be helpful to have a schematic representation of a life in terms of the relative salience of various roles throughout the entire life course. Charlotte Buhler (see Volume I, p. 410; also Buhler and Massarik, 1968) has provided one form of schematic representation showing the duration of each major role commitment or salient activity by lines on a time grid. It is apparent at a glance how many major roles or activities the individual was engaged in at a given time and at what points in time roles were taken up or relinquished. What is lacking, however, is some feeling for the shifting importance of particular roles as one's identity becomes more fully involved or as one turns away from heavy commitment to a particular role. Such shifts are often the focal points of novels and of autobiographies.

Several investigators have experimented with the graphing of a life review as part of an interview. Subjects of whatever age are asked to "draw their lives" as they view the whole course or to evaluate for each year from early childhood to their current age the relative quality of their experiences. Back and Bourque (1970) have used the technique as part of a public opinion survey, thereby getting a large sample of persons at varied ages. Moreover, respondents were asked to evaluate their lives not merely up to the present but to project into the future what they think the quality of life will be like up to age 80. In general, the future looks more promising than the past, though a peak is reached between 50 and 70, after which decline is predicted.

In longitudinal studies at Berkeley, subjects have been asked periodically to discuss the most and least satisfying periods of their lives. In their late 30's, subjects in two of the studies were also asked to check "high-low charts," rating each year in terms of their recalled morale at the time, using a grid marked from 0 ("rock bottom") to 9 ("absolute tops"). Such graphs show great individual variation. Some cover the full range of ratings, with frequent shifts, while others show only minor variation from year to year. When the average ratings accorded each year of age are plotted, they reveal trends that reflect both aging and cohort patternings. Ratings by women indicate a relative positive evaluation of the first five years, then a drop during the early school years, reaching a low point early in adolescence, from which there was a steady climb until the early 20's. Most frequently mentioned as reasons for the low point of adolescence were feelings of not belonging or of lacking social skills. Men show less of a dip in adolescence but otherwise rather similar tendencies. (See Figure 1.)

The high points of early adulthood for both men and women tend to be marriage and the birth of the first child, though for men indications of occupational success were almost as frequently cited as the reason for life approaching "absolute tops." Most women who had several children in rather close proximity show a marked dip in morale for this period. The late 20's and early 30's show a slight drop, but for each of the cohorts with which we have used this technique, the average rating given the most recent year tends to be close to previous peaks.

Subjects currently being interviewed at age 48–50 who had completed "high-low charts" a decade ago are not asked to reconstruct the entire graph but to report on the most and least satisfying periods. A substantial proportion rate their 40's as most satisfying. Very, very few of our study members seem to feel that they are "over the hill" at 50. In general, retrospective reconstruction of high and low points in personal morale or life satisfaction over the life course seems reasonably consonant with the person's reported feelings at the time or relatively soon thereafter. That is, years marked by personal triumphs or tragedies, or years that were exceptionally pleasant (or on the contrary full of strife or other stress) were to a considerable degree subsequently reported as highs or lows. On the other hand, the general level at which various periods were subsequently rated seems to have relatively little relationship to feelings that the individual had reported at the time or to assessments of him by others at that time. For example, the professional whose life plot at age 37 is given in Figure 2 reports a rather favorable picture of his later high school years. They were undoubtedly less dismal for him than were the grade school and junior high school years, but at the time he could hardly have been characterized as sitting on top of the world. By contrast with what had been before and what came later, this period now appears in a most favorable light. This man, it may be noted, uses the full range of the scale. Others seems to be unwilling to rate any period "absolute tops" or "rock bottom." It is as if they were saying that they have yet to experience either extreme. Some laboriously plot year by year, keying to events that mark highs or lows or turning points. A few "draw pictures" of their lives, sketching the major trends rather than giving a set of points that might be connected as in Figures 1 and 2.

The reconstruction of one's past can be usefully combined with longitudinal data to indicate how features of past experience influence current perspectives. Figure 3 illustrates one such use. It is based on "high-low charts" at age 36–38 by subjects of the Berkeley Growth Study, a group studied from birth. Mother's behaviors toward these subjects during the first three years had been recorded and were subsequently rated along a number of dimensions. One such dimension was the mother's positive evaluation of the child (which correlated highly with expression of affection, attentiveness to the

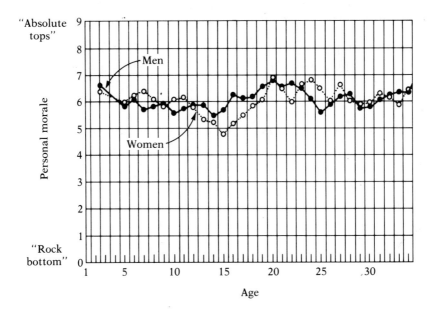

Figure 1 Average Morale Scores Assigned Each Earlier Year of Life, by Men and Women of Berkeley Growth Study, Aged 36–38

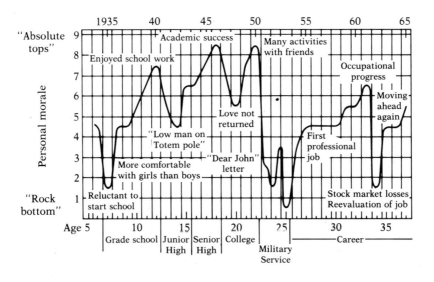

Figure 2 "High-Low Chart" of Male Professional, Aged 37

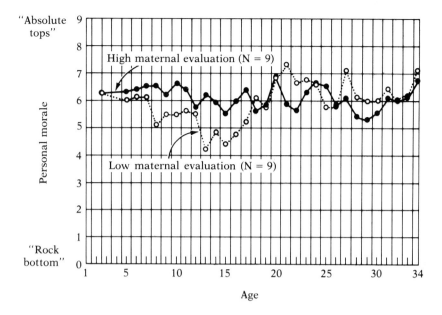

Figure 3 Average Morale Scores Assigned Each Earlier Year of Life, by Women Aged 36–38 Whose Mothers Had Been Rated High or Low in Maternal Evaluation of Child in Infancy

child, and nonpunitiveness).[1] The mother's positive evaluation of the child was in general correlated with positive behaviors on the part of the child (friendliness, cooperativeness, facility) throughout childhood. It is not entirely surprising, then, to find that more than thirty years later those women whose mothers had been critical and unaccepting of them in infancy recall their childhood years more negatively than do women whose mothers had been positively rated. Even for the small sample of subjects for whom all of the necessary data are available so that fixed samples can be compared over the entire period, the differences in reported morale are highly significant (reaching $p < .01$ at age 13, for example). It is interesting to note, however, that the differences largely disappear in the adult years, after the women are no longer in close contact with their mothers.

Assessment of the high and low points of one's life course not only permits one to single out crucial events and turning points, as perceived by the individual himself, but also gives clues as to the goals and values that have exerted a governing effect. Failure to achieve satisfying goals may sometimes be noted by the rating of the high school years as the peak of life satisfaction. This seems to occur especially often among those who were highly popular as young people. For example, in one sample the most popular girl in her high school class never again reached the peak achieved at age 17. Everything thereafter was anticlimactic, for she had little purpose except to be the center of a social whirl. As noted above, early adolescence is far more often viewed subsequently as a low point in life and subsequent movement up the scale of life satisfaction is closely keyed to developing purpose and commitments to particular goals and particular relationships.

There are, of course, many dimensions of individual performance and involvement that might be graphed, at least theoretically, if data were available. The dependency-power axis is one that is highly relevant, though not easily assessed by the individual himself except at times of marked shifts or desired shifts. In infancy the individual's only power is that which he exercises by virtue of the love his parents have for him; his dependency is absolute. Through the childhood years his dependency lessens and changes in nature, and his power to influence others increases. In adulthood, power is closely linked to occupational role, except as power over one's children is concerned; one is supposed to be self-dependent. For the infirm adult, or one who loses his source of livelihood, dependency again becomes a major problem. Now dependence tends to shift onto the succeeding generation.

Autonomy increases as dependency wanes, up to a point, but then come the commitments of adulthood—to occupational career and to family—and now autonomy is again sharply curtailed. Even though occupational and family roles often do not entail any substantial number of highly specific norms that are general to the whole population, normative expectations among members of a given role set tend to become consensual. When they do, it is the individual's commitment to the role and his conception of himself as performing that role adequately that holds him to the pressure of demands. Autonomy is not so much lost as constrained.

More interesting than the simple graphing of dimensions of change is the analysis of the meaning of change and the consequences of various modes of coping. Many role transitions are anticipated events toward which the individual is favorably (or unfavorably) oriented and more or less prepared. Others are a consequence of unforeseen events that lead to the opening up or closing off of opportunities, as occurs when a person receives high recognition or is publicly labeled as a deviant.

Transitions may be incremental, leading to expanded obligations and spheres of participation, or decremental, representing the loss of powers, opportunities, relationships. Marjorie Lowenthal and her associates are now in process of formulating a theoretical framework for the study of adaptation in adulthood by examining alternative responses to incremental and decremental transitions in the light of the individual's preexisting goals, especially as the latter are constricted or expansive in nature. By examining a number of transitions as different periods of the life course, data will be brought to bear on the theory. Only as this is done will we move toward more adequate conceptualizations of stability and change in the course of a life.

In this essay we have been concerned with the ways in which age gives patterning to the life space and to the sequences of roles, relationships, and activities that make up the life course. Within all segments of society the years provide a structure of expectations, opportunities and challenges. If these are to a considerable degree integrated by the individuals who experience them, they remain largely unintegrated insofar as a general theory of the life course is concerned. Perhaps it is unrealistic to think of a theory of the life course. Perhaps we can only look forward to more limited theories relevant to aspects of the life course—for example, more adequate theories bearing on types of role transition in different kinds of social settings. It is hoped that the present essay has at least indicated some of the elements that will be incorporated in more adequate formulations in the future.

Works Cited

Back, Kurt, and Linda B. Bourque, 1970, "Life graphs: aging and cohort effects," *Journal of Gerontology* 25:249–255.

Buhler, Charlotte, and Fred Massarik (eds.), 1968, *The Course of Human Life*, New York: Springer.

Erikson, Erik, 1950, "Eight stages of man," pp. 219–234 in Erik Erikson, *Childhood and Society*, New York: Norton.

———, 1968, "Life cycle," Vol. 9, pp. 286–292 in David L. Sills (ed.), *International Encyclopedia of the Social Sciences*, 17 volumes, New York: Macmillan and Free Press.

Lowenthal, Marjorie Fiske, and David Chiriboga, 1969, "The midlife crisis," paper presented at the Symposium, "The Context of Marriage," San Francisco Medical Center, University of California, November 8.

Neugarten, B. L., Joan W. Moore, and J. C. Lowe, 1965, "Age norms, age constraints and adult socialization," *American Journal of Sociology*, 70:710–717.

Shaefer, Earl S., and Nancy Bayley, 1963, "Maternal Behavior, Child Behavior and Their Intercorrelations from Infancy through Adolescence," monographs of the Society for Research in Child Development 28, No. 3 (Serial No. 87).

Strauss, Anselm, 1959, *Mirrors and Masks: The Search for Identity*, New York: Free Press.

Wilson, Monica, 1951, *Good Company: A Study of Nyakyusa Age-Villages*, London: Oxford University Press.

[1]For details of the use of these ratings and their relationships to child behavior, see Shaefer and Bayley (1963).

.

Individual Aging and Social Evolution: Methodological Issues

For sociologists who study individuals, it is important to be able to distinguish between cohort effects, effects of aging, and effects of contemporary social events. K. Warner Schaie presents a lucid summary of how research can be designed in order to make these crucial distinctions. The concepts of birth cohort and historical time series (time of measurement) are used to distinguish between "Age Changes and Age Differences." Although Schaie uses examples from the literature on intelligence, the principles he presents are applicable to the study of any sort of change. They provide much help in evaluating the adequacy of social research on the aging individual.

In "Age Status and Generational Phenomena: The New Old People in Contemporary America," Leonard D. Cain, Jr., illustrates how the concepts of birth cohort and historical time can be used to study change in *society*. Cain begins with an insightful discussion of the problems of defining *generation* and *cohort*. As we pointed out when we discussed Riley's paper (Chapter 1), a standard length of time to be spanned by a generation on a cohort has yet to be established. But Cain's real purpose is to use cohort analysis to test the proposition that people born just before the turn of the century are quite different from those born just after. Using mainly data from the United States Census, Cain systematically illustrates that compared to the cohort born from 1890 to 1899, the members of the cohort born from 1900 to 1909 were better educated, had fewer children, married and had their children earlier, entered the "empty nest" earlier, entered the labor force at substantially higher wage rates, were less likely to occupy physically taxing manual jobs, and were less likely to be immigrants. In 1975 those in the favored cohort were between the ages of sixty-six and seventy-five. They have "come of age" as the new old people in America, and there are definite signs that they are indeed more articulate and more action oriented than the preceding cohort. Ten years ago Cain forecast that the new old people would have styles, needs, and aspirations that would contrast markedly with those of their predecessors.

Cain's work is imaginative in several areas. It shows how historical statistics can be used in the study of aging, how cohort analysis works, and how the general framework can be used to study not only the past and present but the future as well. However, the problems of operationally defining *cohort* persist even in Cain's painstaking work.

Age Changes and Age Differences

K. Warner Schaie

Almost as soon as objective measures were defined which could be used to index intellectual abilities and other cognitive functions, researchers began to express interest in individual differences on such measures. One of the most persistent of such interests has been the investigation of developmental changes in cognitive behavior. Most treatments covering age changes in cognitive behavior have closely followed the prevalent approaches in the description of developmental theories. Although great attention has always been paid to early development, and maturation during childhood and adolescence is fully described, very little is said about the further development of intelligence and other cognitive variables during adulthood or senescence. In fact, the concern with age changes in cognitive behavior during adulthood did not come to be of serious interest to psychologists until it became clear that the I.Q. concept used in age scales was inapplicable for the measurement of intelligence in adults. As a consequence of the work of Wechsler (1944) in developing special measures for the description of the intelligence of adults but also due to the earlier descriptive works of Jones and Conrad (1933) with the Army Alpha and that of the Stanford group working with Miles (1933), it soon became clear that somewhat different conceptual models would be required for the proper understanding of adult cognitive development.

It will be noted that emphasis has been placed upon the term "age changes." The literature on the psychological studies of aging has long been haunted by a grand confusion between the terms "age change" and "age difference." This confusion has beclouded the results of studies involving age as a principal variable and has loaded the textbook literature with contradictory findings and what will be shown to be spurious age gradients. This presentation intends to clarify in detail the relationship between age changes and age differences and to show why past methodologies for the study of age-related changes have been inadequate.

From *The Gerontologist*, Vol. 7, No. 2, Part I, June 1967. Reprinted by permission of the Gerontological Society and the author.

Much of the literature on aging and cognitive behavior has been concerned with describing how older individuals differ from their younger peers at a given point in time. Such a descriptive attempt is quite worth while and is necessary in the standardization of measurements. This approach, however, is restricted to a description of the very real differences between organisms of various lengths of life experience at a given point in time. Unless some very strong assumptions are made, these attempts beg the issue and fail to produce relevant experiments on the question of how the behavior of the organism changes over age. This is a strong statement, and it is not made rashly since it clearly questions much of the work in the current literature. But it is required since we find ourselves increasingly puzzled about the results of our own and others' studies of age differences. Let us be explicit in clarifying the basis of our concerns and in tracing the resulting implications for the interpretation of much of the data in the developmental literature.

A general model has been developed which shows how the previously used methods of developmental analysis are simply special cases which require frequently untenable assumptions. This model has been described elsewhere in more detail (Schaie, 1965). At this time, however, it would be useful to state the most important characteristics of a general model required for the explanation of aging phenomena as they pertain to the relationship between age changes and age differences.

Let us begin then by clearly distinguishing between the concepts of age change and age difference. Before we can do so effectively, we must also introduce some new concepts and redefine various familiar concepts. The concept of *age* is, of course, central to our discussion. It needs to be carefully delineated, however, and whenever used will be taken to denote the age of the organism at the time of occurrence of whatever response is to be measured. Even more precisely, age will refer to the number of time-units elapsed between the entrance into the environment (birth) of the organism and the point in time at which the response is recorded.

In addition, it is necessary to introduce two concepts which are relatively unfamiliar in their relevance to developmental study. The first of these concepts is the term *cohort*. This term has frequently been used in population and genetic researches and is useful for our purpose. The term implies the total population of organisms born at the same point or interval in time. Restrictions as to the nature of the population and the latitude in defining the interval in time designated as being common to a given cohort or generation must be determined by the special assumptions appropriate to any given investigation.

The second concept to be introduced is that of *time of measurement*. It will take on special significance for us as it denotes that state of the environment within which a given set of data were obtained. In any study of aging it is incumbent upon the investigator to take pains to index precisely the temporal point at which his measurements occur. Such concern is most pertinent since changes in the state of the environment may contribute to the effects noted in an aging study.

With these definitions in mind let us now examine Figure 1 which will help us in understanding the distinction between age changes and age differences. Figure 1 contains a set of six independent random samples, three of which have a common age, three of which have been given some measure of cognitive behavior at the same point in time, and three of which have been drawn from the same cohort; i.e., whose date of birth is identical. If we compare the performance of samples 1, 2, and 3 we are concerned with *age differences*. Discrepancies in the mean scores obtained by the samples may be due to the difference in age for samples measured at the same point in time. But note that an equally parsimonious interpretation would attribute such discrepancies to the differences in previous life experiences of the three different cohorts (generations) represented by these samples.

		Sample 3	Sample 5	Sample 6
	1910	Age 45	Age 50	Age 55
		$A_1C_3T_1$	$A_2C_2T_2$	$A_3C_3T_3$
Time of Birth (Cohort)		Sample 2	Sample 4	
	1905	Age 50	Age 55	
		$A_2C_2T_1$	$A_3C_2T_2$	
		Sample 1		
	1900	Age 55		
		$A_3C_1T_1$		
Time of Testing		1955	1960	1965

A–Age level at time of testing.
C–Cohort level being examined.
T–Number of test in series.

Figure 1 Example of a Set of Samples Permitting All Comparisons Deducible from the General Developmental Model

If, on the other hand, comparisons were made between scores for samples 3, 5, and 6, we are concerned with *age changes*. Here the performance of the same cohort or generation is measured at three different points in time. Discrepancies between the mean scores for the three samples may represent age changes, or they may represent environmental treatment effects which are quite independent of the age of the organism under investigation. The two comparisons made represent, of course, examples of the traditional cross-sectional and longitudinal methods and illustrate the compounds resulting therefrom.

Lest it be thought that there is no way to separate the effects of cohort and time differences from that of aging, we shall now consider a further set of differences which may be called *time lag*. If we compare samples 1, 5, and 6, it may be noted that the resulting differences will be independent of the organism's age, but can be attributed either to differences among generations or to differences in environmental treatment effects or both.

Any definitive study of age changes or age differences must recognize the three components of maturational change, cohort differences, and environmental effects as components of developmental change; otherwise, as in the past, we shall continue to confuse age changes with age differences and both with time lag. Hence, it may be argued that studies of age differences can bear upon the topic of age changes only in the special case where there are no differences in genetically or environmentally determined ability levels among generations and where there are no effects due to differential environmental impact. It follows, therefore, that findings of significant age differences will bear no necessary relationship to maturational deficit, nor does the absence of age differences guarantee that no maturational changes have indeed occurred.

As a further complication, it is now necessary to add the notion that differences in the direction of change for the confounded developmental components may lead to a suppression or an exaggeration of actual age differences or changes. As an example, let us suppose that perceptual speed declines at the rate of one-half sigma over a five-year interval. Let us suppose further that the average level of perceptual speed for successive five-year cohorts declines by one-half sigma also. Such decrement may be due to systematic changes in experience or to some unexplained genetic drift. Whatever their cause, if these suppositions were true, then a cross-sectional study would find no age differences whatsoever because the maturational decrement would be completely concealed by the loss of ability due to some unfavorable changes in successive generations.

As another example, let us suppose that there is no maturational age decrement but that there is systematic improvement in the species. In such a case successive cohorts would do better than earlier ones, and cross-sectional studies would show spurious decrement curves, very much like those reported in the literature for many intelligence tests.

One of the most confusing facets of aging studies therefore is the fact that experimental data may reveal or fail to reveal a number of different combinations of underlying phenomena. Yet the understanding of the proper conceptual model which applies to a given set of data is essential before generalizations can be drawn. Let us illustrate the problem by considering some of the alternative models that might explain the behavior most typically represented in the literature on developmental change. Reference here is made to cross-sectional gradients such as those reported by Wechsler (1944) or by Jones and Conrad (1933). These gradients typically record a steep increment in childhood with an adult plateau and steep decrement thereafter.

When we address ourselves to the question of what developmental changes are represented by such data, we face relatively little difficulty in determining whether maturational changes are contained in the age differences noted during childhood and adolescence. Our own children provide us with at least anecdotal evidence of the longitudinal nature of such change. Whether this portion of the developmental curve, however, is a straight line or a positive asymptotic curve is still in doubt. Also, it should be remembered that even if we agree upon the validity of evidence for maturational changes, we must still consider that such changes will be overestimated by cross-sectional data if there are positive cohort differences and/or negative environmental experience effects. Similarly, maturational growth will be underestimated in the event of cohort decrement or the effect of positive environmental influences.

For the adult and old-age portions of the developmental span, matters are much more complicated. While we can readily accept the fact of psychological maturational growth during childhood, similar evidence of maturational decline on psychological variables by means of longitudinal study remains to be demonstrated. As a consequence, we also must at least entertain models which would account for age differences in the absence of maturational age changes.

The detailed analysis of the general developmental model (Schaie & Strother, 1964a) shows that it is possible to differentiate as many as 729 models to account for developmental change if one considers the direction and slope as well as the three components involved in developmental change gradients. Of the many possible models, three will be considered now which seem to be high probability alternatives for the classical textbook age-gradients. Our three examples are models which not only would fit these textbook gradients but would furthermore predict that the cross-sectional data depicted by the gradients could not possibly be replicated by longitudinal studies.

The first of these models might be called an "improvement of the species" model. It holds that the form of the maturational gradient underlying the typical representatives of the textbook gradients is positive asymptotic; i.e., that there is systematic increment in performance during childhood, slowing down during early adulthood, and that there is no further maturational change after maturity. The model further holds that the cohort gradient, or the differences between generations, should also be positive asymptotic.

Successive generations are deemed to show improved performance for some unspecified genetic or prior experience reason, but it is also assumed that improvement has reached a plateau for recent generations. The effect of the environment is furthermore assumed to be constant or positive asymptotic also. When these components are combined they are seen to provide a cross-sectional age gradient which shows steady increment during childhood, a plateau in midlife, and accelerating decrement in old age.

The same model, however, when applied to longitudinal data will predict steady increment during childhood, but slight improvement in midlife, and no decrement thereafter. The only reason the cross-sectional gradient will show decrement is that the younger generations start out at a higher level of ability and thus in the cross-sectional study the older samples will show lower performance. Of course, this means no more than that the older samples started out at a lower level of ability even though they showed no decrement over their life-span.

A second no less plausible alternative to account for the textbook age gradients might be called the "environmental compensation" model. This model also specifies a concave maturational gradient with increment in youth and decrement in old age, much as the cross-sectional gradient. In addition, however, this alternative calls for a positive environmental experience gradient. Here the effect of an environmental experience increases systematically due to a progressively more favorable environment. The effects of cohort differences in this model are assumed to be neutral or positive asymptotic.

If the second model were correct, then our prediction of longitudinal age changes would result in a gradient with steep increment in childhood but no decrement thereafter, since maturational changes would be systematically compensated for by a favorable environment. Since the environmental component of change over time is not measured in the cross-sectional study, assessment would be made only of the maturational decrement yielding information on the state of a population sample of different ages at a given point of time. But it would provide misleading information as to what is going to happen to the behavior of this population sample as time passes.

Third, let us propose a more extreme alternative which we might label the "great society" model. This model specifies a positive asymptotic maturational gradient; i.e., increment during childhood and a plateau thereafter. The model further specifies a positive asymptotic cohort gradient; i.e., successively smaller increments in performance for successive generations. Finally the model specifies increasingly favorable environmental impact. The reason for calling this alternative the "great society" model should be readily apparent. The model implies (a) that maturity is an irreversible condition of the organism, (b) that the rapid development of our people is reaching the plateau of a mature society, and (c) that any further advance would now be a function of continually enriching the environment for us all. Note that the cross-sectional study of groups of different age at this time in our history will still conform to the textbook cross-sectional gradients. Their longitudinal replication, however, would result in a gradient which would be steep during childhood, which would level off during adulthood, but which would show continued growth until the demise of the organism.

Obviously, it is still possible that the straightforward decrement model might hold equally well for the classical gradients. The information we have on longitudinal studies such as those of Owens (1953) and Bayley and Oden (1955) and the more recent sequential studies by Schaie and Strother (1964b; 1964c) let it appear that any one of the above alternatives may be a more plausible one.

It is hoped that the examples just given have alerted the reader to some of the flaws in the traditional designs used for the studies of aging phenomena. Caution is in order at this time lest the premature conclusion be reached that the increase in sophistication of our methods has indeed led to a better understanding of how and why organisms age. Thus far it seems just as likely that all which has been investigated refers to differences among generations and thus in a changing society to differences which may be as transient as any phase of that society. Only when we have been successful in differentiating between age changes and age differences can we hope therefore that the exciting advances and methods in the more appropriate studies now in progress will truly assist us in understanding the nature of the aging process.

Summary

The concepts of age change and age difference were differentiated by introducing a three-dimensional model for the study of developmental change involving the notions of differences in maturational level (age), differences among generations (cohorts), and differential environmental impact (time of measurement). It was shown that age differences as measured by cross-sectional methods confound age and cohort differences while age changes as measured by the longitudinal method confound age and time of measurement differences. Conceptual unconfounding permits specification of alternate models for the prediction of age changes from age differences and resolution of the meaning of discrepancies in the findings yielded by cross-sectional and longitudinal studies. Examples of alternative models for aging phenomena were provided.

Individual Aging and Social Evolution

References

Bayley, N., and M. H. Oden: The maintenance of intellectual ability in gifted adults. *J. Geront., 10:* 91–107, 1955.

Jones, H. E., and H. S. Conrad. The growth and decline of intelligence: a study of a homogenous group between the ages of ten and sixty. *Genet. Psychol. Monogr., 13:* 223–298, 1933.

Miles, W. R.: Age and human ability. *Psychol. Rev., 40:* 99–123, 1933.

Owens, W. A.: Age and mental abilities; a longitudinal study. *Genet. Psychol. Monogr., 48:* 3–54, 1953.

Schaie, K. W.: A general model for the study of developmental problems. *Psychol. Bull., 64:* 92–107, 1965.

Schaie, K. W., and C. R. Strother: Models for the prediction of age changes in cognitive behavior. Unpubl. mimeo. paper, West Virginia Univ. Also abstract in *Gerontologist, 4:* 14, 1964 (a)

Schaie, K. W., and C. R. Strother: *A cross-sequential study of age changes in cognitive behavior.* Paper presented at Midwestern Psychological Ass., St. Louis. Unpubl. mimeo. paper, Univ. of Nebraska, 1964. (b)

Schaie, K. W., and Strother, C. R.: The effect of time and cohort differences upon age changes in cognitive behavior. Unpubl. multilith paper, West Virginia Univ. Also abstract in *Amer. Psychol., 19:* 546, 1964. (c)

Wechsler, D.: *The measurement of adult intelligence.* Williams & Wilkins, Baltimore, 1944.

Age Status and Generational Phenomena: The New Old People in Contemporary America

Leonard D. Cain, Jr.

Sociologists are confronted repeatedly with the task of interpreting the relationship between social statics and social dynamics, between the persisting and the changing. The concept "generation," although defined and applied in a wide variety of ways, offers promise of assisting in this task. A French sociologist (Durkheim, 1925), accentuating the static, observed:

> Early generations are replaced by later ones, and meanwhile society remains with its own structure and its own peculiar character. . . .

From *The Gerontologist*, Vol. 7, No. 2, Part I, June 1967. Reprinted by permission of the Gerontological Society and the author.

There is an identity between France of the Middle Ages and contemporary France that one cannot fail to recognize. And so, while generations of individuals succeed one another, throughout this perpetual flux of particular personalities there is something that persists, society [culture] with its own mode of thought, its particular temperament. . . .

Indeed, "generation" is frequently used discursively simply to distinguish old people from young people. When used to distinguish between parents and their children, the term does not necessarily connote a dynamic quality. However, studies of occupational mobility between generations, or studies of assimilation among first-, second-, and third-generation immigrants, do reflect theoretical consideration of the dynamic.

Another frequent use of "generation," and the one having the most theoretical potential for sociology, is that associated with the formation of distinctive life styles among discrete groups. Crises (e.g., wars, depressions), intellectual or technological "breakthroughs" (e.g., new art forms, the atomic age), or modifications in social structure (e.g., urbanization, the "baby boom") seem to force those coming of age during the crisis or the breakthrough or the change in social structure to develop responses to life different from those just older. This suggests what may be called a "historical hinge," or a "generational watershed." Although the significance of chronological age *per se* is in dispute (Berger, 1960), several writers accept the interpretation that those approaching adulthood form the nucleus of newly forming generations.

On the one hand, there is "something that persists." Concepts such as "culture," "institution," "social system," and "social structure" convey this theme. Yet, on the other hand, there is "something that changes." The son does not necessarily duplicate the performance of his father. Thus, the "needs" of institutions (as manifested, for example, in age status systems) and the "needs" of generations (as manifested in innovation and protests by the young) may periodically be in conflict.

Although generational analysis of the latter type abounds, crucial definitional and methodological problems remain unsolved, hardly even identified. The issue of termini—when one generation ends and another begins; of the length of a generation, and the related question of membership; the role of chronological age in determining generational identity; the issue of whether an individual joins a generation or has it imposed upon him by the inexorable forces of history—these are among the avoided questions.

Cohort analysis, developed by the demographers, aids in resolving some of the methodological problems, but not all. A recent article on the dynamics of public opinion (Evan, 1959) recommended cohort analysis, handling the "generations" issue this way:

. . . we propose to use the cohort technique, which for present purposes will be roughly equated with a generational analysis, as a means of inquiring into the impact of types of historical events on the opinions, attitudes or ideologies of different generations.

But Evan's definition of cohort does not help to clarify the termini question:

. . . a cohort is a group of persons born at a particular time, whether in a given year, in a five-year period, or in any other interval.

Historical events and periods may not correspond to the calendar year, to the decimal system, or to a census bureau's customs. Yet, cohort analysis provides a significant advance over the pundits' presumptuous attachment of generational labels to fleeting fads. Likewise, it provides a prognostic instrument for the sociologist and the social planner. Evan advanced a very important question when he asked if the impact of historical events on those who entered the labor force during the Depression years was distinct from the impact of a different set of events on those who entered the labor force prior to, say, World War I.

A demographer (Ryder, 1965) has proposed recently that cohort analysis become a tool for studying social change:

Each new [birth] cohort makes fresh contact with the contemporary social heritage and carries the impress of the encounter through life. . . . [The new cohorts] do not cause change; they permit it. If change does occur, it differentiates cohorts from one another, and the comparison of their careers becomes a way to study change.

Ryder does not confront the question of the span of a cohort. If no change occurs over a several-year period, are not those born during this period of the same cohort? Otherwise, cohort is nothing but a demographic artifice. I propose to alter the phrase, "if change does occur," to read, "when crisis does occur," and suggest that herein lies the terminus of a generation. Still unresolved is the issue of what sort, or intensity, of change Ryder is talking about. Also unresolved is the issue of to what extent change creates a new generation, and to what extent a new generation creates social change.

The above is prelude. The purpose is to introduce a perspective on gerontology, using cohort and generational analysis. Essentially, I want to advance the hypothesis that those who are already past 65 in contemporary America represent a style of life and have needs and aspirations which are in sharp contrast to the style and needs and aspirations of those who are now beginning to enter the old-age category. To put it in cohort terms, I hypothesize that Americans born in the years before the turn of the century (let us focus on the 1890–1899 cohort, and call it Cohort A) are distinct in ways of special significance for gerontological planning from those born in the first years of this century (let us focus on the 1900–1909 cohort, and label it Cohort B). Put in generational terms, a historical "hinge" or "watershed" developed at the end of World War I which has directed Cohort A down one path of life and Cohort B down another. Implicit in this formulation is a criticism of the gerontological practice of using those already old as the population universe for research, followed by use of the results of the research to propose public policies for the aged. Insofar as those who are currently "coming of old age" in America are on the other side of a generational watershed from those already old, policies based on studies of the older generation are likely to be unsound. . . .

Many of the data to follow are from rather conspicuous sources, mainly the United States Census. Eventually more refined and comprehensive data will be necessary if the hypothesis is to be tested satisfactorily. The effort now is more to propose a perspective than to seek to prove the proposition.

It is rather obvious that educational opportunities for American children have improved over the decades. But did our younger cohort, Cohort B, have a significantly greater opportunity than those immediately older, our Cohort A? Data on median years of schooling completed, by cohorts (Table 1), reveals that the three successive cohorts (——1882, 1883–1892, 1893–1902) experienced a gradual increase in median years—7.7 years, 8.1 years, and 8.5 years—but that the cohort born in 1903–1912 (approximately Cohort B) jumped to a median of 9.9 years. That is, Cohort A (adjusted) had only one semester beyond grammar school, or the eighth grade, whereas Cohort B (adjusted) probably had typical experience with high school, lacking only one year to graduate under the 11-year system widespread at the period. Just as college is becoming the expected experience for the majority of youths today, high school apparently became typical for the first time with those who are now entering old age.

A report of the percentage of 17-year-olds who graduated from high school in successive decennial census years (Table 2) indicates a steady percentage increase. For those born between 1893 and 1903, the average increase was only eight-tenths of one per cent per year (8.8% to 16.8%). During the following ten-year period, however, the average increase in graduates was over one and two-tenths per cent per year (16.8% to 29.0%). These figures do not reveal a generational watershed, but nonetheless the continuing increase of educational opportunities suggests that the oncoming aged are better educated than those already old. However, the percentage increase between the 1893 and 1903 cohorts (90.0%) does suggest a watershed of sorts.

Table 1 Median Years of School Completed by Ten Year Cohorts, Through 1922

Age in 1965	Year of Birth	Median Years of School Completed
43–52	1913–1922	11.7
53–62	1903–1912	9.9 (Cohort B, Modified)
63–72	1893–1902	8.5 (Cohort A, Modified)
73–82	1883–1892	8.1
83+	–1882	7.7

Source: U.S. Bureau of the Census, *Statistical Abstract of the United States: 1950* (Seventy-first edition.) Washington, D.C., 1950, Table 17.

Table 2 Percentage of Seventeen Year Olds Who Had Finished High School, by Ten Year Periods, 1890–1940

Graduated by	Year of Birth	Age in 1965	%	% Increase
1890	1873	92	3.5	—
1900	1883	82	6.4	82.8
1910	1893 (Cohort A)	72	8.8	37.5
1920	1903 (Cohort B)	62	16.8	90.9
1930	1913	52	29.0	72.6
1940	1923	42	50.8	75.2

Source: U.S. Bureau of the Census, *Historical Statistics of the United States, Colonial Times to 1957*, Washington, D.C., 1960, Series H 223–233.

Table 3 provides two more relevant variables—the changes in percentage of children enrolled in school each ten-year period, and the changes in average number of days per year of school attendance. Although the trend from 1870 to 1930 was toward both larger percentage enrollment and increased attendance, the rates of growth fluctuated, and the two variables did not grow together. For example, for children born in 1903–1915, the percentage increase in enrollment (1920) was higher than either the preceding or succeeding

Table 3 The Percentage of Children Five–Seventeen Years of Age, Enrolled in School, and Their Average Days of Attendance per Year, by Ten-Year Intervals, 1870–1930

Year of Study	Years Children Born	% 5–17 Years of Age Enrolled in School	% Increase	Average Days Attended	% Increase
1870	1853–1865	57.0	—	78.4	—
1880	1863–1875	65.5	14.9	81.1	3.4
1890	1873–1885	68.6	4.7	86.3	6.5
1900	1883–1895	72.4	5.5	99.0	14.7
1910	1893–1905 (Coh. A)	73.5	1.5	113.0	14.1
1920	1903–1915 (Coh. B)	77.8	5.8	121.2	7.3
1930	1913–1925	81.3	4.5	143.0	17.9

Source: U.S. Bureau of the Census, *Statistical Abstract of the United States: 1950* (Seventy-first edition.) Washington, D.C., 1950, Table 137.

decade, but the percentage increase in days attended school was considerably lower than in 1910 or 1930.

Table 4 suggests that a watershed may have occurred in education about five years later than in our hypothesis, especially for white males. The figures also indicate that Cohort B females expanded their educational accomplishments over the males (especially the white) more than any females before or since.

Table 4 Median Years of School Completed, by Cohort, Sex, and Color, 1950

	Male		Female		
Cohort	White	Non-White	White	Non-White	Total
1875–79	8.1	3.9	8.4	4.2	8.2
1880–84	8.2	4.0	8.4	4.5	8.2
1885–89	8.3	4.7	8.5	5.3	8.4
1890–94	8.5	5.1	8.7	5.8	8.5
1895–99	8.7	5.6	8.9	6.1	8.7
1900–04	8.9	6.0	9.5	6.7	8.9
1905–09	9.9	6.5	10.5	7.2	9.8
1910–14	10.7	7.1	11.2	7.8	10.7
1915–19	11.9	7.8	12.1	8.4	11.6
1920–24	12.4	8.4	12.2	8.9	12.1

Source: U.S. Bureau of the Census, *Historical Statistics of the United States, Colonial Times to 1957*, Washington, D.C., 1960, Series H 395–406.

The above tables provide data for simple cohort analysis. To complement these data generational analysis of changes in curricula, teacher certification, consolidation of schools, etc. is needed to determine if the kind and quality of education also varied between Cohorts A and B.

Another way of testing the major hypothesis is to examine changes in the family structure of the two cohorts. Data on cohort fertility, for example, tend to confirm a watershed between Cohorts A and B. A special census report (U.S. Bureau of the Census, 1953) put it quite succinctly:

Women 45 to 49 years old in 1952 [that is, born in 1903–1907] had the lowest national average on record for completed fertility. They had borne only about 2,172 children per 1,000 women. . . . This is the first cohort known to have had a completed fertility rate below the replacement level.

Whelpton's (1954, Table A) classic venture in cohort fertility provides even more important clues to the distinctiveness of Cohort B. Table 5 shows that a sharp drop in fertility occurred for women born in 1900 and 1901, and that their younger sisters continued the trend until an upturn toward the end of the decade cohorts.

Table 5 Total Births per 1,000 White Women, at Age 40, by Age Cohort

Cohort (Year of Birth)	(Total Births per 1,000 Women: Cumulative to Age 40)	Change in Birth Rate from Previous Year
1891	2,793	—
1892	2,759	− 34
1893	2,726	− 33
1894	2,692	− 34
1895	2,660	− 32
1896	2,623	− 37
1897	2,593	− 30
1898	2,564	− 29
1899	2,538	− 26
1900	2,416	−122
1901	2,364	− 52
1902	2,358	− 6
1903	2,320	− 38
1904	2,275	− 45
1905	2,255	− 20
1906	2,232	− 23
1907	2,239	+ 7
1908	2,195	− 44
1909	2,235	+ 40

Source: P. K. Whelpton, *Cohort Fertility*, Princeton University Press, Princeton, 1954, Table A.

Table 6 gives a somewhat different perspective. Whelpton (1966), with more accurate data and more refined techniques than were available in his pioneer study (1954), computed fertility rates which reveal that the women of the 1890's (Cohort A) actually reduced fertility rates more rapidly than Cohort B, although the new data still reveal very clearly that it was Cohort B women who had the fewest number of children of any cohort before or since in America. And these are the women now entering old age in contemporary America.

Glick and Parke (1966) provide another important clue (Table 7). Women of Cohort B married earlier, completed giving birth earlier, launched their children into marriage earlier, and experienced a longer "empty nest" period with their husbands, than the women of Cohort A. Of significance for our analysis is the evidence that Cohort A experienced a post-parental period of 5.9 years with both husband and wife living, whereas Cohort B extended the post-parental period to 10.4 years. Will bereavement at the loss of a mate be deeper, at least different, from previous periods?

Again, the evidence presented is fragmentary. Trends in divorce rates, in kinship solidarity and interdependence, and in attitudes toward family life need to be added. Nonetheless, there are indications of changes in family structure which have relevance to our hypothesis. Gerontologists need to concern themselves with the consequences of these shifts. The earlier release from parental burdens appears to have freed women for work (as Table 10 will indicate), and may have contributed to a higher family income in later years, although retirement may nip this and make the reduction in income extra vexing. These trends may have increased the opportunity for new grandparents to visit their children more frequently, to lavish more gifts on grandchildren, and thus to promote a new type of interdependence.

Table 6 Actual or Projected Total Births per 1,000 American Women, by Age Cohort

Year of Birth	Year Reached Age 50	Year Reached Age 65	Actual or Projected Total Births per 1,000 Women (Cumulative to Age 50)	Change in Birth Rate from Previous 5-Year Period
1881–85	1931–35	1946–50	3,384	—
1886–90	1936–40	1951–55	3,205	−179
1891–95 (Cohort A)	1941–45	1956–60	2,962	−243
1896–1900 (Cohort A)	1946–50	1961–65	2,672	−290
1901–05 (Cohort B)	1951–55	1966–70	2,420	−252
1906–10 (Cohort B)	1956–60	1971–75	2,271	−149
1911–15	1961–65	1976–80	2,315	− 44
1916–20	1966–70	1981–85	2,565 (projected)	−250
1921–25	1971–75	1986–90	2,895 (projected)	−330

Source: P. K. Whelpton, A. A. Campbell, and J. E. Patterson, *Fertility and Family Planning in the United States*, Princeton University Press, Princeton, 1966, Table 210, p. 392.

Table 7 Median Age of Women at Selected Stages of the Family Life Cycle, for Women Born from 1880 to 1919, by Ten Year Cohorts

Median Age of Cohort

Year of Birth	First Marriage	Birth of First Child	Birth of Last Child	First Marriage of Last Child	Death of One Spouse
1880–89	21.6	22.9	32.9	56.2	57.0
1890–99 (Cohort A)	21.4	22.9	31.1	53.5	59.4
1900–09 (Cohort B)	21.1	22.6	30.4	51.9	62.3
1910–19	21.7	23.7	31.5	53.0	63.7

Source: Paul C. Glick and Robert Parke, Jr., "New Approaches in Studying the Life Cycle of the Family," *Demography*, 2: 1966, 187–202. (p. 190).

A recent newspaper report (*New York Times*, 1966) gives the women of Cohort A still another distinction:

> The real change [in sexual morality], sociologists say, came in the nineteen-twenties. In particular, it was the generation born between 1900 and 1910 that revolutionized American sexual behavior.

To illustrate what "sociologists say," the *Times* story referred to Terman's (1938) report on changing patterns of virginity. Terman reported that the 1880–1889 cohort of women in his sample reported that 86.5% were virgins at marriage, that the figure for Cohort A was 74.0% and for Cohort B, 51.2%.

A significant shift in career patterns, in types of jobs performed, in rewards and protections and hours of work per week between Cohorts A and B would also be important for our analysis. Any trend in reduction of hours in the work week would provide indicators of several changes of status and attitude, in health, in recreational opportunities, in family participation. DeGrazia (1962), for example, calculated that the non-agricultural work week in 1850 was 65.7 hours, that this was reduced less than ten hours per week in the next 50 years (1900, 55.9 hours), but that during the next 20 years the figure dropped another ten hours or more (1910, 50.3 hours, and 1920, 45.5 hours). In 1940 the work week was still over 40 hours (41.1 hours).

The U.S. Department of Labor (1929) has provided more refined data on employment trends, including wages (Table 8). The table vividly reveals that after World War I wages rose steadily over a several year period (with the exception of the Depression year of 1922) and that during the same years the hours of work per week declined steadily. Cohort A, which began entry into the labor force before 1910 and had probably almost completed its entry by 1917, experienced an increase in wages between 1910 and 1917 from index 95.2 to 112.4. Cohort B, which began entry into the labor force possibly during World War I, experienced an increase between 1918 and 1928 from index 129.6 to 240.6.

Cohort B surely launched its members into careers under auspicious and optimistic circumstances. Unfortunately, data refined enough to permit tracing the career opportunities throughout the life course of our cohorts are not available at this time. Rather, some general information on unemployment rates must suffice. Table 9 reveals two peaks of unemployment when Cohort A entered the labor force (1908, 1914–1915), and another peak when Cohort B entered (1921). Of overwhelming significance is, of course, the high rate of unemployment during the 1930's. A task for gerontologists today is

Table 8   Index Number of Union Wage Rates and Hours of Labor from 1912 to 1928 (1913 = Index of 100)

Date	Rate of Wages per Hour	Increase from Previous Year	Hours per Full Time Week	Decrease from Previous Year	Rate of Wages per Full Time Week	Increase from Previous Year
1910	94.4	—	101.1	—	95.2	—
1911	96.0	1.6	100.7	0.4	96.5	1.3
1912	97.6	1.6	100.3	0.4	97.7	1.2
1913	100.0	2.4	100.0	0.3	100.0	2.3
1914	101.9	1.9	99.6	0.4	101.6	1.6
1915	102.8	0.9	99.4	0.2	102.3	0.7
1916	107.2	4.4	98.8	0.6	106.2	3.9
1917	114.1	6.9	98.4	0.2	112.4	6.2
1918	132.7	8.6	97.0	1.4	129.6	17.2
1919	154.5	21.8	94.7	2.3	147.8	18.2
1920	199.0	44.5	93.8	0.9	188.5	40.7
1921	205.3	6.3	93.9	+0.1	193.3	4.8
1922	193.1	− 12.2	94.4	+0.5	183.0	− 10.3
1923	210.6	27.5	94.3	0.1	198.6	15.6
1924	228.1	18.5	93.9	0.4	214.3	15.7
1925	237.9	9.8	93.0	0.9	222.3	8.0
1926	250.3	12.4	92.8	0.2	233.4	11.1
1927	259.5	9.2	92.4	0.4	240.8	7.4
1928	260.6	1.1	91.9	0.5	240.6	− 0.2

Source: U.S. Department of Labor, Bureau of Labor Statistics, Bull. No. 482. 1929, p. 14.

to determine anew the differential impact on cohorts of the un-employment of the Depression. It can only be suggested that Cohort B, younger and better educated than Cohort A, may have fared better than Cohort A.

Another indicator of change is to be found in reports of labor force participation by age categories (Table 10). Participation by males over 65 has dropped steadily over the years, whereas partici-pation by women has risen. Possibly the most significant figure for our purposes in Table 10 is that which reports that in 1965 almost one half (46.6%) of the women in the 45–64 age group were employed. This surely represents a second income in many in-stances. The increase in the percentage of older women in the labor force is likely to produce changes in the status and the attitudes and expectations of older males and females. These changes need to be studied, even anticipated, by gerontologists.

Ironically, there are also indications that, during a transition from blue collar jobs which involve strenuous physical exertion to white collar jobs which require mental exertion, the physically taxing jobs have often been occupied by older men. Adequate data on type of job by age are not readily available, although Table 11, based on a 1930 study, gives some indication of the rapid increase in the median

Table 9 Unemployment: 1900 to 1957 (In Thousands, 14 and over)

Year	Unemployed	% of Civilian Labor Force	Year	Unemployed	% of Civilian Labor Force
1900	1,420	5.0	1929	1,550	3.2
1901	710	2.4	1930	4,340	8.7
1902	800	2.7	1931	8,020	15.9
1903	800	2.6	1932	12,060	23.6
1904	1,490	2.8	1933	12,830	24.9
1905	1,000	3.1	1934	11,340	21.7
1906	280	0.8	1935	10,610	20.1
1907	600	1.8	1936	9,030	16.9
1908	2,960	8.5	1937	7,700	14.3
1909	1,870	5.2	1938	10,390	19.0
1910	2,150	5.9	1939	9,480	17.2
1911	2,290	6.2	1940	8,120	14.6
1912	1,960	5.2	1941	5,560	9.9
1913	1,680	4.4	1942	2,660	4.7
1914	3,110	8.0	1943	1,070	1.9
1915	3,840	9.7	1944	670	1.2
1916	1,920	4.8	1945	1,040	1.9
1917	1,920	4.8	1946	2,270	3.9
1918	560	1.4	1947	2,142	3.6
1919	950	2.3	1948	2,064	3.4
1920	1,670	4.0	1949	3,395	5.5
1921	5,010	11.9	1950	3,142	5.0
1922	3,220	7.6	1951	1,879	3.0
1923	1,380	3.2	1952	1,673	2.7
1924	2,440	5.5	1953	1,602	2.5
1925	1,800	4.0	1954	3,230	5.0
1926	800	1.9	1955	2,654	4.0
1927	1,890	4.1	1956	2,551	3.8
1928	2,080	4.4	1957	2,936	4.3

Source: U.S. Bureau of the Census. *Historical Statistics of the United States, Colonial Times to 1957*, Washington, D.C., 1960, Series D 46–47.

age of workers such as blacksmiths, boilermakers, locomotive engineers, draymen, firemen, furnacemen, and longshoremen. The combination of urbanization (and thus less farm labor), unionization (and protection of workers), shorter work weeks, and white collar jobs suggests that Cohort B is the first age group in America from whom the burden of toil has been lifted. The implications for health status are manifold.

Immigration to the United States was at its peak during approximately those years when our cohorts were born. The hypothesis is that Cohort A is an immigrant or immigrant-competing cohort and Cohort B is a native-born cohort. Between 1845 and 1879 America had experienced only five years during which between 400,000 and 500,000 immigrants had disembarked on its shores. The usual flow was closer to 200,000. Between 1880 and 1914 this country received a larger

Table 10   Labor Force Participation Rate, by Age and Sex, 1890–1965

% of Males 14 and over

Year	% of Total Population in the Labor Force	All Ages	14–19	20–24	25–44	45–64	65+
1890	52.2	84.3	50.0	90.9	96.0	92.0	68.3
1900	53.7	85.7	62.0	90.6	94.7	90.3	63.1
1910	—	—	—	—	—	—	—
1920	54.3	84.6	51.5	89.9	95.6	90.7	55.6
1930	53.2	82.1	40.1	88.8	95.8	91.0	54.0
1940	52.7	79.7	35.4	88.4	95.6	89.4	42.2
1950	53.4	79.0	39.5	81.9	93.3	88.2	41.4
1960	—	77.4	—	—	—	89.0	30.5
1965	—	78.3	—	—	—	90.9	27.8

% of Females 14 and over

Year		All Ages	14–19	20–24	25–44	45–64	65+
1890		18.2	24.5	30.2	15.1	12.1	7.6
1900		20.0	26.8	31.7	17.5	13.6	8.3
1910		—	—	—	—	—	—
1920		22.7	28.4	37.5	21.7	16.5	7.3
1930		23.6	22.8	41.8	21.6	18.0	7.3
1940		25.7	19.0	45.6	30.6	20.0	6.0
1950		29.0	22.6	42.9	33.3	28.8	7.8
1960		34.5	—	—	—	41.6	10.3
1965		38.0	—	—	—	46.6	10.0

Source: U.S. Bureau of the Census, *Historical Statistics of the United States, Colonial Times to 1957*, Washington, D.C., 1960, Series D 13–25. *The Gerontologist*, 7: 6, 1967.

stream of immigrants than any other nation has probably ever known (Table 12). Note that during the years of the heaviest influx (about 1900 to 1914), the percentage of children was relatively low, meaning that few of the immigrants were in Cohort B. It would appear that the vast majority of the immigrants of the period were in Cohort A, or possibly the 1880–1889 cohort.

A life course of the "immigrantness" of the two cohorts is provided by Table 13. When the 1880's cohort was 40–49 years of age, it contained 22.3% immigrants; Cohort A at 40–49 years had 16.2% immigrants; Cohort B had only 9.6%; and the 1910's cohort had only 4.6%. At age 50–59, Cohort A had 16.4% immigrants, and Cohort B, 10.0%. Again, the watershed issue is evasive. Whether one can say that a population with one-sixth immigrants is an "immigrant" population and one with one-tenth is a "native" population is conjectural; but we can at least conclude that the presence of the immigrant in the aged population is now rapidly diminishing.

The stemming of the tide of immigration with the restrictive legislation of the 1920's has contributed to another factor of possibly great importance for our analysis. Before 1920, much of the inter-ethnic contact of Americans was with Caucasian immigrants. Hostilities and prejudices were centered in national and religious, possibly

Individual Aging and Social Evolution

Table 11 Median Ages of Workers 16 to 64 Years of Age in Selected Occupational Groups, 1910, 1920, and 1930*

Occupation	Male			Female		
	1910	1920	1930	1910	1920	1930
All gainful workers	33.9	35.4	36.5	27.8	28.5	30.0
Total of 53 occupations	31.3	33.6	34.6	28.5	28.7	29.8
Professional persons						
Musicians and teachers of music	32.6	34.8	33.0	29.2	31.8	35.4
Teachers (schools and colleges)	31.8	34.2	33.5	28.4	27.6	29.7
Proprietors, managers and officials						
Wholesale and retail dealers	40.3	41.2	41.6	40.9	41.6	42.6
Clerical Workers						
Bookkeepers, cashiers and accountants	30.5	31.3	32.4	25.5	23.8	27.1
Clerical workers (proper)	24.0	29.1	30.1	24.0	23.9	26.3
Office boys, telegraph and other messengers	20.9	21.3	21.2	20.9	21.4	21.5
Stenographers and typists	23.6	23.6	24.3	23.0	22.8	23.7
Telephone operators	24.7	29.4	32.6	22.1	22.4	23.8
Sales people						
Commercial travelers	37.0	38.0	38.8	36.9	38.1	39.8
Newsboys	22.6	23.7	22.5	27.3	30.4	25.9
Real estate and insurance agents	41.9	42.4	41.7	40.4	42.3	44.1
Salesmen and saleswomen (proper)	30.2	31.6	32.7	24.7	26.3	29.5
Skilled workers and foremen						
Blacksmiths, forgemen and hammermen	38.4	39.5	43.6	—	—	—
Boilermakers	34.0	35.1	39.8	—	—	—
Brick and stone masons and tile layers	38.3	41.5	39.9	—	—	—
Cabinet makers	39.4	41.0	41.3	—	—	—
Carpenters	39.4	41.5	43.4	—	—	—
Electricians	29.3	30.0	33.1	—	—	—
Locomotive engineers and firemen	34.7	35.6	41.6	—	—	—
Machinists, millwrights and tool makers	32.4	33.1	37.0	—	—	—
Molders, founders, casters (metal)	35.2	37.1	39.9	—	—	—
Painters, enamelers and varnishers (building) and paperhangers	36.0	40.6	39.7	—	—	—
Plasterers and cement finishers	37.9	40.5	38.6	—	—	—
Plumbers, gas and steam fitters	32.0	34.8	37.2	—	—	—
Sawyers	34.7	37.7	38.1	—	—	—
Structural iron workers (building)	33.8	35.2	37.0	—	—	—
Tailors and tailoresses	35.2	39.0	43.1	27.7	32.5	37.1
Tin and coppersmiths	33.8	33.9	37.5	—	—	—
Skilled workers, printing, publishing and engraving	30.8	34.5	33.9	23.9	27.3	30.9
Semi-skilled workers						
Painters, glaziers, enamelers, and varnishers in factories	33.8	35.3	34.8	22.6	24.4	23.6
Bakers	32.3	35.0	34.3	36.4	37.0	38.9
Dressmakers, seamstresses and milliners	34.9	38.2	39.1	33.3	38.8	42.8
Grinders, filers, buffers and polishers (metal)	31.2	34.9	36.5	23.4	24.8	25.8

Table 11 (continued)

Occupation	Male			Female		
	1910	1920	1930	1910	1920	1930
Operatives in cigar factories	33.0	38.1	40.0	23.9	26.1	27.2
Operatives in clothing factories	31.1	34.4	36.8	24.1	26.9	29.3
Barbers, hairdressers and manicurists	34.0	37.2	38.2	30.0	32.6	30.7
Boarding and lodging house keepers ..	44.7	47.3	49.1	43.2	46.1	46.8
Brakemen	30.9	32.7	37.3	—	—	—
Housekeepers, stewards and practical nurses	36.5	38.8	39.7	38.6	41.7	44.6
Watchmen, guards and doorkeepers ...	47.4	51.6	51.0	35.8	41.7	46.0
Unskilled workers						
Farm laborers	24.1	24.7	24.5	26.4	27.0	25.6
Charwomen, cleaners and laundresses	36.8	38.6	37.6	36.4	38.8	40.6
Elevator tenders	28.0	36.5	33.2	—	—	—
Porters	31.9	35.6	34.8	—	—	—
Servants	32.9	35.4	34.7	27.5	31.4	31.7
Waiters, waitresses and bartenders ...	32.4	33.4	32.7	24.5	26.5	25.9
Other laborers						
Draymen, teamsters and expressmen	31.9	33.5	39.8	—	—	—
Firemen (except locomotive and fire department)	34.0	37.0	40.3	—	—	—
Fishermen and oystermen	35.5	38.1	38.1	34.9	33.4	38.3
Furnacemen, smelter men, heaters and puddlers	33.7	34.6	37.9	—	—	—
Longshoremen and stevedores	35.3	36.5	39.6	—	—	—
Lumbermen, raftsmen and woodchoppers	32.8	33.9	35.8	—	—	—
Miners, oil, gas and salt well operatives	32.4	33.8	35.8	24.6	27.0	24.3

*In calculating the median age, it has been assumed that the ages of workers form a discrete series the basic unit of which is one-tenth year. Where no median age is given there were too few cases for measures of central tendency to be reliable.

Source: Smith, M.: Trends in the ages of gainful workers, by occupation, 1910–1930, *Amer. Stat. Ass. J.*, *30;* 678–687; 1935, Table 1, p. 680.

language, issues. Since 1920, America's interethnic contacts have been increasingly racial. During the last 45 years the Southern, rural Negro population has become a Northern, urban population. Mexicans, racially "visible" although infrequently classified as a "racial" minority, did not enter the United States in large numbers until the 1920's and after. Filipinos did not immigrate in large numbers before the 1920's. Since the 1920's, the Chinese and Japanese on the West Coast have been more mobile (Handlin, 1954). Although it is not possible at this time to even suggest the implication of these observations for the two cohorts, the replacement of a nationality-oriented group of aged with a racially-oriented group may have vast latent consequences for politics, housing, etc.

Table 12 Immigrants to the United States, by Age Group, 1880–1920

Year	Total Number	% Male	Children (Under 15 Years)	% Children	Youth and Young Adults (16 to 40 Years)	Older Adults (Over 40 Years)
1880	457,257	62.9	87,154		327,662	42,441
1881	669,431	61.4	153,480		454,495	61,456
1882	788,992	63.2	171,021		540,677	77,294
1883	603,322	60.3	143,865		390,406	69,051
1884	518,592	59.5	123,562		335,572	59,458
1885	395,346	57.3	92,880		257,551	44,915
1886	334,203	60.1	66,188		232,118	35,897
1887	490,109	62.6	94,278		345,575	50,256
1888	546,889	63.2	97,287		396,990	52,612
1889	444,427	59.2	92,534		303,835	48,058
1890	455,302	61.9	86,404		315,054	53,844
1891	560,319	63.2	95,879		405,843	58,597
1892	623,084	62.4	89,167		491,839	42,078
1893	502,917	63.8	57,392		419,701	25,824
1894	314,467	59.3	41,755		258,162	14,550
1895	279,948	57.6	33,289		233,543	13,116
1896	343,267	61.9	52,741		254,519	36,007
1897	230,832	58.5	38,627		165,181	27,024
1898	229,299	59.2	38,267		164,905	26,127
			(Under 14 Years)		(15 to 40 Years)	(Over 40)
1899	311,715	62.6	43,983	14.1	248,187	19,545
1900	448,572	67.8	54,624	12.2	370,382	23,566
1901	487,918	67.9	62,562	12.8	396,516	28,840
1902	648,743	71.9	74,063	11.4	539,254	35,426
1903	857,046	71.5	102,431	12.0	714,053	40,562
1904	812,870	67.6	109,150	13.4	657,155	46,565
1905	1,026,499	70.6	114,668	11.2	855,419	56,412
1906	1,100,735	69.5	136,273	12.4	913,955	50,507
1907	1,285,349	72.4	138,344	10.8	1,100,771	46,234
1908	782,870	64.8	112,148	14.3	630,671	40,051
1909	751,786	69.2	88,393	11.8	624,876	38,517
1910	1,041,570	70.7	120,509	11.6	868,310	52,751
1911	878,587	64.9	117,837	13.4	714,709	46,041
1912	838,172	63.2	113,700	13.6	678,480	45,992
1913	1,197,892	67.5	147,158	12.3	986,355	64,379
1914	1,218,480	65.6	158,621	13.0	981,692	78,167
1915	326,700	57.2	52,982	16.2	244,472	29,246
1916	298,826	61.0	47,070	15.8	220,821	30,935
1917	295,403	59.1	47,467	16.1	214,616	33,320
			(Under 16 Years)		(14 to 44 Years)	(45 and over)
1918	110,618	55.9	21,349		76,098	13,171
1919	141,132	59.0	26,373		97,341	17,418
1920	430,001	57.6	81,890		307,589	40,522

Source: U.S. Bureau of the Census, *Historical Statistics of the United States, Colonial Times to 1957*, Washington, D.C., 1960, Series C 133–138.

Age Status and Generational Phenomena

Table 13 The Ratio (in Percentages) of the Foreign-Born White Population to the Entire Population, by Age Cohorts, 1881–1890, 1891–1900, 1901–1910, and 1911–1920, for the United States

Years of Age	1890 (1880's cohort)	1900 (1890's cohort)	1910 (1900's cohort)	1920 (1910's cohort)	1930	1940	1950	1960
		"A"	"B"					
		"A"	"B"					
1–9	2.2%	1.1%	2.0%	0.9%				
			"A"	'B"				
10–19		5.6%	5.7%	4.3%	2.4%			
			"A"	"B"				
20–29			17.9%	13.0%	9.0%	2.8%		
				"A"	"B"			
30–39				21.4%	16.5%	8.9%	3.7%	
					"A"	"B"		
40–49					22.3%	16.2%	9.6%	4.6%
						"A"	"B"	
50–59						22.0%	16.4%	10.0%
							"A"	
60+							21.9%	17.9%

Source: U.S. Bureau of the Census, *Historical Statistics of the United States, Colonial Times to 1957*, Washington, D.C., 1960, Series A 71–85. U.S. Bureau of the Census, *U.S. Census of Population: 1960, Vol. 1, Characteristics of the Population, Part 1, United States Summary*, Government Printing Office, Washington, D.C.: 1964. Table 158.

This paper began with an emphasis on generational analysis. Most of the information so far has been classified as cohort analysis. Before seeking to draw conclusions and suggest the general import of this study for gerontology, let me introduce some efforts at generational analysis.

Lenski (1961) has considered trends in political party preferences among Catholics and white Protestants. A study ten years previously (Berelson, 1948) had reported that party-preference differences between the two religious groups were declining. Lenski's Detroit data suggested, however, that the trend toward diminishing the significance of the religious variable had ended, even reversed itself. The interviewees over 50 (in 1958?) had a Protestant-Catholic gap in preferences of 39 points, those 35–49 a 23-point gap, but those under 35 had a 26-point gap. Lenski resorted to cohort analysis to interpret the trend:

For persons born from the late nineteenth century to the middle 1920's, events conspired to produce a political homogenization of white Protestants and Catholics. . . . For persons born since the middle 1920's, however, the trend seems at least to have been halted, and possibly even reversed.

Individual Aging and Social Evolution

Unfortunately, Lenski did not define the "late nineteenth century," nor did he identify the "conspiring events," although it is apparent that he meant the Depression and possibly World War II.

Since Hofstadter (1955) placed the terminus of the age of Social Darwinism as World War I, his observations are pertinent.

> The social-Darwinian generation . . . had to learn to live with and accommodate to startling revelations of possibly sweeping import; . . .
>
> Hard work and hard saving seemed to be called for, while leisure and waste were doubly suspect [by social Darwinists] . . . .
>
> Today we have passed out of the economic framework in which that ethic was formed. We demand leisure; we demand that we be spared economic suffering; we build up an important business, i.e. advertising, whose function it is to encourage people to spend rather than save; we devise institutional arrangements like installment buying that permit people to spend what they have not earned; . . .

Hofstadter sought to place the emergence and persistence of social Darwinism in chronological perspective:

> Spencer, and the men of Spencer's generation in America [those who came of age between 1865 and 1890?], thought that he had written a grand preface to destiny. Their sons [who came of age between 1890 and 1915?] came to wonder at its monumental dullness . . . and thought of it . . . only as a revealing commentary on a dead age.
>
> While Darwinian individualism declined, Darwinian collectivism of the nationalist or racist variety was beginning to take hold. . . . The survival of the fittest had once been used chiefly to support business competition at home; now it was used to support expansion abroad.

Then, abruptly, Americans supposedly turned their backs on Darwinism, on both the individualistic and the nationalistic varieties. Insofar as Hofstadter has identified the period of the decline of an ideology, we have added evidence that the world that Cohort A matured in was dramatically different from that of Cohort B.

Hoffman (1965) identified a similar generational terminus, although with a different emphasis from that of Hofstadter. The literature of the 1920's was the vehicle that Hoffman used to understand the "hinge" in American history produced by World War I.

> However distorted and exaggerated, [a pattern of rejection by those who took over critical roles in the post-World War I period] followed rather closely the lines of a threefold criticism of the prewar generation and of the civilization it had made: there was, first, a failure of communication; second, a failure of social meaning and value; and third, a failure of morality. . . . Faith in the

older generation, not unmixed with criticism of its enormities, persisted through what Van Wyck Brooks has called 'the confident years' (1885–1915); but when the war had ended, this generation discovered that it had lost most of its influence. . . . Before 1915 the liberal, the dissident, the progressive member of society hoped for a moral, intellectual, and aesthetic resurgence . . . These hopes . . . were all but abandoned at the end of World War I.

Hoffman's entire study seeks to document that the 1920's were marked by the general repudiation of tradition.

There is space only to recall some of the dramatic events of the 1920's. Women's suffrage and the prohibition of the sale of alcoholic beverages were introduced into the Constitution in 1920. The ubiquitous bootlegger and speakeasy suggest that those now entering old age were aware of the frequent violation of the law. Model T's began rolling off the assembly line in large numbers at this time; America has not been the same since. Radio, and then the movies, became a part of the communications system. Harding was elected President, then Coolidge and Hoover, conservatives all. Cannot a cohort who came of age in the 1920's be expected to demand some sort of modification in the status of the aged in these next few years?

Our analysis is only partial. It must terminate without our examining the differential impact of the Depression, World War II, the McCarthy era, continuing prosperity, and the recent strains and crises on the two cohorts.

The data presented hint that Cohort B in many ways has been a "favored" generation. Its members have not had to fight a war. They may have fared better than any other age group during the Depression. This is the cohort which filled the lucrative defense jobs of World War II and which has continued to ride the crest of probably the longest period of uninterrupted prosperity in the nation's history. This cohort had fewer children to educate and more double paychecks than any other cohort to date. What all this means for the status of the aged in these next few years I cannot tell, but it is obvious that gerontologists need very much to ask new types of questions, to develop new methods and to use their imagination in new ways if the aged are to be served.

References

Berelson, B., P. F. Lazarsfeld, and W. McPhee: *Voting: A Study of Opinion Formation in a Presidential Campaign.* University of Chicago Press, Chicago, 1954.
Berger, B. M.: How long is a generation? *Brit. Jour. Sociol., 11:* 10–23, 1960.

Cain, L. D.: The AMA and the gerontologists. *In:* Gideon Sjoberg, (editor), *Politics, Ethics, and Social Research.* Schenkman Press, Cambridge, Mass., 1967.

Davis, K., and J. W. Combs: The sociology of an aging population. *In:* D. B. Armstrong (chmn.), *The Social and Biological Challenge of Our Aging Population.* Columbia University Press, New York, 1950.

DeGrazia, S.: *Of time, work, and leisure.* Twentieth Century Fund, New York, 1962.

Durkheim, E.: *L'education morale.* Librairie Felix Alcan, Paris, 1925.
Quoted and translated in Everett Wilson: *Sociology: Rules, Roles, and Relationships.* Dorsey Press, Homewood, Ill., 1966.

Evan, W. M.: Cohort Analysis of opinion data: a procedure for studying long-term opinion change. *Publ. Opin. Quart., 23:* 63–72, 1959.

Glick, P., and R. Parke: New approaches in studying the life cycle of the family. *Demography, 2:* 187–202, 1966.

Handlin, O.: *The American people in the twentieth century.* Harvard University Press, Cambridge, Mass., 1954.

Hoffman, F. J.: *The Twenties: American writing in the postwar decade* (rev. ed). The Free Press, New York, 1965.

Lenski, G.: *The religious factor.* Doubleday and Co., Garden City, N.Y., 1961.
New York Times, July 11, 1966.

Ryder, N. B.: The cohort as a concept in the study of social change. *Amer. Sociol. Rev., 30:* 843–861, 1965.

Terman, L. M.: *Psychological factors in marital happiness.* McGraw-Hill, New York, 1938.

U.S. Bureau of the Census: *Current population reports,* Series P-20, No. 46 Dec. 31, 1953.

U.S. Department of Labor, Bureau of Labor Statistics: Bulletin No. 482, 1929.

Whelpton, P. K.: *Cohort fertility.* Princeton University Press, Princeton, N.J., 1954.

Whelpton, P. K., A. A. Campbell, and J. E. Patterson: *Fertility and family planning in the United States.* Princeton University Press, Princeton, N.J., 1966.

Wiggins, J. W., and H. Schoeck. A profile of the aging: USA. *Geriatrics 16:* 336–342, 1961. (Paper originally presented at the International Gerontological Congress, San Francisco, August 10, 1960.)

Socialization

3

Socialization, a key concept in social psychology, is a general term that refers to several processes which develop individuals into fully functioning social beings. Because socialization processes are learning processes, socialization can never be complete, particularly in a rapidly changing society. To the extent that a person knows and understands the social world and has the skills required by it, he or she can gain much from the social world. If a person does not understand the social system, life can be confusing and unpredictable.

However, it is not enough simply to learn one's culture. Society and culture change, and the individual must continue to learn or face a decline in the ability to function socially. In the absence of continued learning, aging can mean obsolete and ineffective social knowledge and skills. Aging also brings changes in roles, and people need preparation for these changes. A few formal mechanisms for adult socialization exist, but the bulk of it is informal, and much of it must be initiated by the individual.

Negotiation is a central aspect of adult socialization. Sociologists have tended to view socialization as imparting social demands to the individual. But people do not merely passively receive; they also *react*. This is true for children as well as adults. However, two crucial differences exist between the socialization of children and the socialization of adults. First, children usually cannot negotiate as equals with people in the outside world—adults often can. Second, adults have more freedom to select with whom they will negotiate. Also, adults probably initiate a great deal more of their socialization than children do. It might be a mistake, therefore, to borrow too heavily on the traditional socialization literature in sociology because this literature was developed mainly from the study of children. Adult socialization is different, and new concepts must be developed if we are to understand it.

In "Adult Socialization," Orville G. Brim, Jr., focuses on the acquisition of social roles by adults. Motivation for change comes from demands from the social environment and from desires and initiatives from *within* the individual. The major external demands on the individual come from the work place, the family, and the community at large, perhaps in that order. Changes in external role demands usually result from a changing situation—a business failure, the death of a spouse, the coming of age of a child. Aging and age grading also lead to changes in external role demands. But people also want to change *themselves.* Most sociologists have viewed socialization as society's way of training people, but it can also be viewed as a mechanism through which the individual can actively *seek* knowledge or skills. People may want to become better performers in the roles they play, or they may aspire to new roles, or they may anticipate future roles, such as that of widow. Brim suggests that as adults become better educated, they become more capable of self-initiated socialization.

Brim sees adult socialization as mainly an informal process, and fully mature adults as having many resources for informal socialization. They often have the power to select the experiences they want, the groups they will join, and the ideas they will seek. They have many relationships with other adults, which gives them many figures to emulate. This leads Brim to conclude that the outside world neither demands nor encourages adult socialization; it simply creates the conditions under which people can pursue their own development.

In "Interaction and Adaptation: Intimacy as a Critical Variable," Marjorie F. Lowenthal and Clayton Haven explore the importance of interpersonal supports to the process of adult socialization. They are particularly concerned with the *closeness,* or intimacy, involved in these interpersonal supports. They found that to older adults, a continuing intimate relationship with someone is more important than the mere number of roles played or the amount of social interaction in helping them to cope with sizable changes such as retirement and widowhood.

Lowenthal and Haven also found that the type of person who was likely to have a confidant varied considerably. Particularly in the working class, women are more apt to have learned to develop and sustain intimate relationships. Lowenthal and Haven imply that the early socialization of women may give them an edge in interpersonal resources for socialization later in life.

Adult Socialization

Orville G. Brim, Jr.

Introduction

One may be surprised at the lack of study given to adults by scholars in the area of socialization. After all, most of the world's great drama and literature is about adults, not children, and most of it describes the passage of adults from one role to another—how it happened, who demanded it, how one meets the new demands or avoids them. "One man in his time plays many parts," wrote Shakespeare; husband, father, old man, widower, soldier, employee, colleague, leader—these and many other roles are required of a person during the course of his adult years.

Socialization is continuous throughout life, for though individuals enter the adult world with some anticipatory socialization, the socialization experienced in childhood is not enough to meet the demands of the later years. This is especially true in modern industrialized societies and particularly so in the United States. In these rapidly changing societies, the lives of the new wave of twenty-one-year-olds who each year join the ranks of adults do not follow those of their predecessors. The younger adults must find new models or develop new styles of life without them; meanwhile, the older adults try to adjust to the conflicts created by the rapid rate of ideological and technological change.

Among those roles for which anticipatory socialization might take place, some require intolerable demands upon the person to practice, so to speak, the role which lies ahead. Lawyers and insurance men know how difficult it is to get most wives even to contemplate life as a widow, much less think through carefully what the role will require, and even perhaps to practice on occasion living alone and being independent while the husband is still alive. Downward mobility is a fact of many adult lives, but it is not reasonable to expect one, ahead of time, to practice life at a lower standard of living.

Adults must change and must be socialized into new roles. This essay presents an informal overview of some of the things the American adult will confront in occupations, in the family, and in the community, as he lives through a fifty-year period. It is a selective survey of contexts and types of adult socialization experiences and an identification of certain research and theoretical topics of adult socialization. What will others demand of him, and what will he come to demand of himself? How will he be able to meet these demands for change, and how can he reconcile his own wishes with those of society?

The review deals with the non-deviant adult—the average person and his experience. A good portion of what little research has been done on socialization of adult life has been concerned with the deviant individual. This well-known body of work includes the sociological analyses of the attempts by society through its institutions to socialize the delinquent or criminal in order to return him to a non-criminal way of life. Another major body of studies deals with socialization of the addicted, that is, the alcoholic or the drug addict. A third group of studies is concerned with the processes and effects of various therapies for the emotionally ill. The literature on these types of deviant behavior and the attempts to alter it through adult socialization are available in good recent reviews such as those by Wolfgang, Savitz, and Johnston (1962), or Becker (1964).

The studies of life changes associated with the changing physical state of the adult constitute another important body of socialization research, even though most were not made from this viewpoint. It is fairly obvious that important changes in socialization prescriptions for the adult will accompany changes in his health or the onset of a disability. Discussion of such studies is omitted from this chapter because much of the material is familiar to the reader and is readily available. Accidents which are disabling in minor or major ways render the adult unable to carry out his ordinary roles and require him to learn new roles. The adjustment of the disabled, of the physically handicapped, and of the blind have been analyzed and reviewed in some well-known sociological studies (Barker, 1953; Scott, 1968; Sussman, 1965). Other important work includes analyses of the impact of illness on the person (Davis, 1963) and of the consequences of physical stigma (Goffman, 1963). Aging itself, of course, is associated with changed demands for behavior because of the various increased disabilities which are correlated with the aging organism. Beginning with the middle years there frequently is a decline in strength, vigor, and memory, which leads to inability to carry out satisfactorily some of the customary roles the adult performs, which in turn leads to a readjustment of expectations and of performance levels. Socialization in later years that is a direct consequence of changed physical states can be reviewed in Riley (1968), and in Williams, Tibbitts, and Donahue (1963).

Individuals and groups differ greatly in the evenness of their lives, that is, in the degree to which they are under pressure to change as they move through the stages of the adult years. Some live very simply and have undemanding lives, with little change in their environments or their personalities. Even though socialization in later life is more characteristic of modern societies, with their increased rate of change and customs, their greater rates of social mobility, and their more rapid obsolescence of information, the quiet life still is the rule for most adults. In later sections of this chapter many life episodes in the family, work, and community are noted which cause socialization. We must stress that no single person will experience all of the episodes; for instance, except in unusual cases, one is not highly mobile both upward and downward in his lifetime. For the typical adult in the United States, most days ask very little in the way of change, and most people seem to like it this way. But other persons are beset by a wide array of demands, from society or from themselves, far exceeding those that the normal person faces. The life-spans of some are broken into separate phases by the demands upon them for radical change arising from divorce, family deaths, illness, loss of job, etc. It seems certain, also, that different categories of people face different types and degrees of adult socialization—for example, men versus women, rich versus poor. In this review we note many such differences in which sex, ethnicity, or social class seem to be correlated with the kind of demands for change which adults face.

The Demands of Self and Others

In our view socialization is the process by which one learns to perform his various roles adequately, and our concern here is with the acquisition of social roles. This may not encompass the whole of socialization, but role acquisition is an extremely important, if not the most important, component of adult socialization. In each instance of socialization a key element is the role prescription or expectation that someone else has for the person in question, which involves a change in, or addition to, that person's beliefs, attitudes, or behavior, or motives or values, with reference to some social situation. But the prescriptions by members of society for how an adult should change—that is, the demands of others—are only part of the picture. The person himself has many self-initiated ideas and prescriptions for his own personality and behavior change, and in many cases the self-initiated socialization is a greater source of adult personality change than are the demands of other persons.

The Demands of Others   Individuals or groups have an interest in changing the behavior of an adult so that his behavior will be more in accord with the wishes of the individual or group. In a complex, pluralistic society, such as the United States, many persons and groups compete for effective influence over the behavior of an adult and seek to alter the adult's personality in large or small ways to accommodate their own desires. The differences and conflicts between the objectives of these various persons are manifest in the efforts at adult socialization. The employer, the wife, the child, the advertiser, the physician, the politician—each in his or her own way has an interest in the adult's personality and behavior and seeks to remake it to his own advantage. The fashion industry conflicts with the husband's wishes about his wife's behavior, while the liquor industry competes with the wife in attempting to change her husband's habits. Each group has its own modes of attempted influence, and each has its relative persuasive power. The control over powerful rewards and punishments in the hands of the employers and family members make them especially effective in socialization efforts, while on the periphery of influence are neighbors, political groups, advertisers, and others.

We do not consider here the relative effectiveness of different "methods" of adult socialization. Much research has been done (Mann, 1965) on the effectiveness of various methods—including the one-minute radio talk and the use of drugs and other devices to influence prisoners of war—in inducing attitude and behavior change. In the sophisticated studies, the interactions of methods with the social conditions under which the effort at change is made and with adult personality characteristics are considered. Conceptually, these must be classed as studies of adult socialization, with a special focus not on content but on the efficacy of different procedures.

The focus of this chapter, as indicated earlier, is the substance of the demands made upon the adult, classified roughly according to the work situation, the family, and the community as the setting of the demands. We can say generally that in any of these adult socialization contexts those persons making the socialization effort can, and often do, make use of a whole range of procedures to induce attitude change and behavior. These persons seeking to socialize the adult employ various mass media to influence him and also engage in direct face-to-face interaction, the manipulation of group pressures, the use of economic sanctions in some instances, and other techniques to bring about change.

The cause of changed prescriptions for an adult's role performances are the more basic changes in economic resources, population pressures, density of and proximity to other kinds of persons, physical and emotional makeup of persons with whom the adult is closely associated, and other facts of life. The changes demanded of the adult may be at a very general or societal level, entailing alterations in the law, in the formal sense, on a regional or national basis. The demand that one desegregate his store, inn, restaurant, theater, or private club requires for many white Americans, both southern and northern, a change in beliefs and attitudes that contrasts sharply with earlier and deeply learned views toward the Negro. Changes in laws in a complex society follow from the more basic changes in the economy, from the available pool of trained talent, the need for men to fight the country's war, the growth or decline in population, the obsolescence of certain occupations, and so on.

The demands from others for change occur more frequently at the immediate level of social interaction than as a result of a change in the nation's laws. A person's occupational role, for example, may alter. The owner of a private filling station may no longer be able to compete with others and may be forced to join a larger petroleum company chain; as a consequence, his relation to his suppliers and his clients will no longer be the same. A man may be told that he has risen as high as he can go in his place of work and that his present position must be accepted by him as the achievement level for his lifetime; thus it is demanded that he deal in some way with his achievement motivation—his orientation toward success—and do so without displacing frustration upon something else or making a desperate and unwise change of occupation. The wealthy person who loses his money must adjust to a new place of residence, to new social groups, and to new consumption patterns, and, the impact of downward mobility being what it is, must also handle the deeper adjustment involving his self-esteem. Or change may result in the family because the increasing strength and knowledge of the eldest son enables him to challenge effectively the authority of the mother and father and to force a realignment of customary relationships within the family. The married woman who is widowed is faced with demands to substitute autonomy in decisions and actions for the customary dependency which characterized her relationship with her husband. Some women make this transition while others reestablish the familiar relationship through remarriage or alliance with a more autonomous woman friend.

The socialization of an adult is tied to the characteristics of that person, apart from changes in the outer world which lead to altered prescriptions on the part of others. Aging, in particular, is a source of changed demands on the adult. As one ages he progresses through the age-graded positions in society, from marriage to parenthood, through increased responsibilities in the community, and through positions of authority and leadership in employment, into a period of declining responsibility. There is, of course, nothing mystical about the fact that aging is associated with such progression. The natural accumulation of experience and power through maturation enables a member of society to assume roles which he could not take on before. The successful fulfillment of these more important roles is desirable from the viewpoint of society because of the contribution made to the general welfare. Hence there is strong pressure upon an adult to take on such roles and, indeed, to be enthusiastic about his progression "upward" and the chance to discharge his adult responsibilities to society. In the area of the family one is expected to marry and have children and rear them to maturity. In the occupational world, as one progresses he is expected to accept the advancements, along with increased rewards, of course, and not to refuse promotion. Senior professors who turn down deanships are frowned upon, and it is not easy to find a college where one can be a lifetime assistant professor, much as one might wish to. Thus the demands of the outer world are fitted to the perceived abilities of the adult, and these are closely associated with age grading in most societies; maturation itself leads to changes in the demands of others and to pressures toward socialization for new responsibilities (Riley, 1968; Williams, Tibbitts, and Donahue, 1963; Williams and Wirths, 1965).

Self-Initiated Socialization Many people have characteristics of their personalities—some aspects of their behavior and life styles—which are not what they wish them to be. Of these, a large number, perhaps larger than is commonly recognized, seek to change themselves to become more acceptable in their own eyes. Most analyses of socialization, whether of children or adults, view the process as one in which social groups or persons are training the child or adult for some role. Little attention has been given to the quite obvious self-initiated attempts by a person to change and improve his performance of certain roles in his life. As far as we have been able to find out, no major investigation has ever been made of the kinds of changes adults may be seeking to make in their personalities; that is, evidently no one has systematically asked adults about this, even though adults, clearly more than children, are able to, and surely do, initiate their own socialization. For some adults one could even say that most of their personality change is the result of their own efforts rather than the result of the demands of others. And it appears that self-initiated socialization may be on the increase because of the greater affluence of the average adult and the greater leisure for experimenting in new areas of life.

Some of the drive toward change is economic in origin. One attempts to improve upon his performance in the world of work so that he can rise in the occupational world and live better. The economic source of this striving for improvement may be more important for those from lower-income levels. At the upper-income levels, other motives may underlie the desire for change. Dreams of power, of recognition and fame, of nobility of character, or the wish to create something of one's own, or to contribute in some larger way to the common pilgrimage of man may motivate a person to change.

To speak of self-initiated socialization and contrast it with demands coming from others suggests that the former is independent of the influence of other persons. This is not true, of course. Theoretically, self-initiated socialization has its roots in the expectations that significant others have had for the individual's performance. The distinction really is between whether the demands are current, immediate, and from persons real and present, or whether the "others" involved are distant and symbolic. In the drive toward change, the person is always trying to please someone, but in self-initiated socialization, it is he who is the significant judge of his performance. We all have made or heard statements such as "I am not happy about the way I did that," and "I should be able to do better than that," and even, more rarely, "I think that was about as well as I could do." How does this "I-me" component of personality, in which the individual views himself as if he were another person observing himself, develop?

The individual, when looking or acting toward himself as an object, must initially do so from the point of view of some significant other person. This viewpoint gradually becomes disassociated from any specific person so that the individual is no longer able to recall or identify the other person in the interpersonal relation. How does this happen?

It appears that both generalization and the inability to discriminate are the sources of the "I-me" type of relationship. The "I-me" relationship is the product of a body of learning generalized from interaction with a number of reference figures now nameless because their identity has been lost in countless learning trials. In the most frequent case the information derived about one's self from interaction with others has been given by a great many people so that no specific individual remains linked to this self-other relationship. This is true about basic components of the self such as size, sex, ability, or appearance, and also one's conformity to and deviance from norms widely shared in society. . . . Secondly, there is a companion process also leading to generalization, namely, a lack of ability to discriminate on the part of the child in his early interactions with his parents. In these interactions a child's experience has been so limited that he has no basis for differentiating (discriminating) between the reactions of his parents and their demands upon him and the reactions and demands of the entire objective world. In largest part this inability to discriminate exists because communication between parent and infant is preverbal, and the infant lacks symbolic tools to facilitate discrimination between different sources of reward and punishment. What is learned from parents thus is viewed as inherent in the world at large, that is, in the generalized social order. It follows that elements of personality thus acquired provide a good foundation upon which the further process of generalization mentioned above may proceed. (Brim, 1966).

Adult Socialization

Thus we see that the "I" to which one refers his beliefs and behavior for approval is a product of early and still continuing learning and generalizing of the expectations of important others for his own behavior, and that as the "I" is gradually established, the demands one places upon himself become just as powerful as if the parental and other early influential figures were the source (Brim and Wheeler, 1966).

The role prescriptions which come from the self may change under the impact of new experience. Experience provides the raw material from which the self grows; it leads to the introduction of new elements in one's conception of a desirable style of life. The adult meets new people and gets ideas from books, conversations, travel, or from observation of others' lives. A person's changing health and strength may cause conflict in his existing self. New ideal states for an individual's personality evolve and can be seen just ahead; thus the individual directs himself toward these new ends.

Certain persons may have more initiative toward change than others. . . . Analyses of the organization of personality and the role of the motivation for "self-actualization," such as Maslow has presented (Maslow, 1954), stress individual differences in this kind of behavior. We do not know whether there are group differences in self-initiated socialization, and in the absence of data we can do no more than raise the question for further consideration.

We emphasize here that self-initiated socialization need not involve less significant changes in personality than those which result from demands of the outside world. Large changes in personality have been demonstrated to come from within. Dramatic religious conversions, perhaps the most familiar example, have been described in recent articles (Lofland and Stark, 1965) and, of course, in the analysis by William James (1902), and also in Frank's recent book (1963).

Other changes in personality, not so abrupt or dramatic but still deep and important, result from self-initiated socialization. Behavior, motives, and beliefs can be transformed gradually through a process of "personality drift." Minor changes in expectations that an individual holds for himself may occur over a period, without there being any noticeable demarcation. There may be small but incremental shifts from time to time in what an individual asks of himself, and the resultant day-to-day alterations in his behavior, rewarded by himself, lead to a cumulative change which over the years makes him much different from what he was when younger. Thus what a person proposes to do with his life—both where he would like to arrive and how he wants to live along the way—can be substantially affected by these successive minor alterations, until one day he finds himself a person quite different from that of a decade earlier, without knowing how the change occurred.

Some Theoretical Aspects

Role and Status Changes   Demands from others or from oneself are the same in certain respects. Both encompass two theoretical kinds of changes: an alteration of a role associated with a continuing status or social position and the assumption of a new status and the learning of a new role related to that status. In the first case, the new socialization demand may come from someone with whom the adult has had a continuing relationship, such as a spouse, employer, or friend. Here we might say that new and different demands are made upon the adult in the same old relationship. In the second case, socialization involves new and different persons and new types of social relationships; here the adult must learn to meet the new demands issuing from a new relationship, for example, from working with a new employer, being married to a new husband or wife, or having a new child.

Conflict and Congruence in Socialization Demands   As we see, many persons and groups compete to influence the adult's behavior, and the adult himself has his own ideas about the way in which he wishes to change. The inevitable result is frequent conflict between the direction in which the adult wishes to move, with respect to his career, family, or role in the community, and the direction in which others wish him to change, or not to change.

Where the same change is desired on both sides, there can be cooperative effort between the person and society. In some roles, such as the profession of medicine or the law, one's colleagues and clients as well as the professional person himself expect a continuing growth on his part, manifested in the acquisition of new techniques and knowledge. Joint development of the social skills of both the husband and wife in a marriage, as in the instance where both take dancing lessons, and the joint effort to save a marriage itself, as when a husband and wife together decide to seek marriage counseling, are illustrations.

Where the demands of the society for change truly are counter to the wish of the individual to stay the way he is, then resistance, antagonism, evasion, and outright revolt may ensue. Rare is the person who does not have many experiences as an adult in which pressure is exerted on him to change when he would rather not. From young adulthood to older age, the conflict between the demands for socialization and the wishes of the individual leads to draft evasion, avoidance of marriage, quitting a job, staying away from home, and in extreme cases self-imposed isolation from society.

Where the reverse is true—the adult seeks to change himself but those with whom he lives or works want him to stay the same—he must find a way to move ahead against the resistance. It may be that the friend or the husband or wife fears that the other is moving out of his reach, or the employer or the community may be threatened by the innovations sought by the person. Family controls, economic sanctions, or bureaucratic controls in the work situation, or community legal and informal controls may be used to thwart the attempts of an adult to change himself when this change is not acceptable to others. Wanting an early marriage, wanting to enlist in the military service but being rejected, trying to move an organization ahead but meeting opposition, trying to alter a habitual pattern in a marital relationship or in the parental role are common experiences of this type.

Unmarried young adults have more freedom to leave home, to change jobs, or even not to work at all, because they are not yet locked in with responsibilities and they have not been fully socialized into the values of adult roles. Still, on balance, it would seem that adults more frequently than children can select the kind of socialization experiences they want, and have greater power to resist external demands, through deciding whom they will expose themselves to, what groups they will join, what teachers they will have, and what ideas they will examine. For example, the mass media research shows that adults routinely select confirming evidence from the mass media to substantiate their existing attitudes and beliefs. Moreover, adults have financial and other resources with which to fight back, even though we recognize that there are differences in power between certain groups to resist the influence of others, depending on one's wealth, social status, and political influence.

Most important is that adults have a wider set of reference figures to draw upon for counteracting sets of values and opinions. Resistance to the immediate local demands for conformity springs from reliance on non-immediate significant others in one's life, so that the person is not necessarily concerned with approval and acceptance at this time and place. The increased number of interpersonal relationships, that is, the richness of the gallery of significant others, gives the adult greater autonomy and independence from many groups. The extreme instance is the adult martyr who can pursue his distinctive purpose even though strong coercive measures may be used against him by many groups in society, because he is supported by others whose approval is of higher significance to him and so sustain him in his independent course, whether they be future generations of men, the host of dead poets, his father or his mother, or perhaps his God.

Aids to Socialization   . . . A great many social institutions have developed to aid the adult in socialization. Most of these are familiar and include a wide variety of forms: the citizenship class for the immigrant, the programs of employers to retrain their employees to handle a new technology, family-life education and parent-education programs for newlyweds and first-time parents, college programs for women reentering the labor force or entering it for the first time, etc. Some of these express the demands of society that the individual be changed, as in the various correctional institutions supported by society to which persons are remanded. Others express the collective desires of individuals to change their lot, as seen in the creation of continuing education programs for physicians sponsored and paid for by the participants themselves.

Usually overlooked in adult socialization are the many informal ways, as opposed to the above-mentioned institutional aids, in which socialization is aided. An adult customarily will seek out, informally, people with similar experiences so that he may learn from them. He restructures his friendships and primary groups to fit the particular growing edge of his interests: pregnant women find each other and discuss their progress, newly elected departmental chairmen chat informally about their common problems and how they handle them in this new role, and army recruits socialize each other in a way that the formal institutions of the military service could never achieve (Brim and Wheeler, 1966). We cannot really, of course, say that most adult socialization occurs in informal primary-group relationships rather than in the formal and tutorial organizations, but certainly it must be stressed that if we look only at what goes on in the institutions, we will miss a substantial portion of the continuing day-to-day, hour-by-hour socialization of adults in informal primary-group relationships.

This leads us to recognize an important fact about the relationship between a person and his world with reference to adult socialization: in many cases other persons do not demand that the adult change, nor do they actively collaborate with him as he seeks his own change. Rather they provide conditions in which he can pursue his own development. In seeking change, the individual frequently is dependent on a group, and by his own initiative he must find and get into the groups which provide him with the socialization experiences that he needs. The alcoholic who wants to quit drinking and searches for Alcoholics Anonymous is an illustration, as is the person entering into a relationship with a psychotherapist to bring about the change in his personality that he desires. The good teacher or the good guidance counselor, adviser, friend, spouse, or parent can provide a human relationship in which his information and emotional support and expectations will encourage and stabilize the adult's own efforts to change.

We see that in these cases of adult socialization the distinction between the inside and the outside becomes blurred and the adult, in order to achieve his own socialization ends, must find a supportive social relationship. We know quite a bit, at an abstract, general level, about how and why such supportive relationships should exert their influence. The story we have not been told is how adults search and find among the variety of groups in society those which can aid them in completing the changes they want to fashion in their own personalities. Nor have we been told how many persons, in their attempts to change, are defeated by the absence of the human relationships necessary to sustain them in their efforts. . . .

Conclusion

Adult socialization has not been a familiar and common object of study in the workshops of social scientists. The main theoretical and research questions here derive from, and in due course will contribute to, our knowledge of the variable consequences of childhood socialization. They also derive from, and in time will enrich, our insight and theory concerning the relationships between personality and social structure—how the former transforms the latter, and how the latter channels and regulates the former. From the many items noted in this chapter we call attention here to a few from different facets of the adult socialization process that need study.

The depth of personality change in adulthood had never been charted in a systematic way; individual cases of fundamental alteration of personality are familiar to most of us, but the frequency of these changes and their distribution by types of persons is not known, nor do we know very much about the social episodes, whether external or internal, which produce these changes. We noted also the importance of studying the adult seeking personality change and his need for a supporting environment (that is, social, interpersonal, immediate, and real) during his attempt to change; otherwise he must fall back upon symbolic reference figures who support him with rewards and punishments in a more distant and necessarily less organic manner. But at the same time, we noted that symbolic reference figures on many occasions provide the support the individual needs to change, for they can be a counteractive force to the real, immediate reference figures. The parameters of these complicated processes, not to speak of systematic analyses, are still to be established.

In the world of occupations we called attention to the importance of studying career socialization of adults whose earlier lives left much room for adult learning, such as Negroes entering the executive world. In the same vein we noted the need for more study of post-child-rearing female participation in the labor force, with attention given to the fit of earlier socialization to the new occupational demands and with more attention than has been heretofore devoted to the reasons for this change of status. And interpersonal relationships change in one's job—familiar faces disappear, new colleagues or employees or supervisors arrive. How one learns to get along with the new personalities and the new styles of life, and the impact of this learning on work or the family or on one's more secret aspirations deserve more study. So also does the process of reconciliation of achievement to aspirations in the middle-years period. The majority of men and women face a time in their lives when what they thought they could do proves to be unachievable. The varieties of adaptations to these middle-years realities are a social process, taken as a whole, which warrants more study than it has received.

In the institution of the family, the sizable adult socialization that takes place in new relationships (as between parent and child) and in the changes in continuing human relationships (as between parent and child) and in the change in continuing human relationships (as between husband and wife) demands study; the impact of the family upon the adult is evident if one takes the time, and perhaps has the courage, to reflect. Notable among the topics here are the influence of children upon adults over the span of child-rearing years and the influence of husband and wife upon each other.

Finally, downward mobility and its demands for behavioral, attitudinal, and motivational change pose problems for many women and men in the United States and have been neglected in contrast to the elaborated concern of American social scientists with upward mobility. The social analysts and artists of England, for example, have been sensitive to, and concerned with, the causes and impact of downward mobility, but this country's social scientists and its artists and novelists still look mostly upward.

References

Barker, R. G., *et al.* Adjustment to physical handicap and illness. *Social Science Research Council Bulletin*, No. 55. Rev. ed., 1953.

Becker, H. S. (Ed.) *The Other Side; Perspectives on Deviance.* Glencoe, Ill.: The Free Press, 1964.

Brim, O. G., Jr., and Wheeler, S. *Socialization After Childhood: Two Essays.* New York: John Wiley & Sons, 1966.

Davis, F. *Passage Through Crisis.* Indianapolis: The Bobbs-Merrill Co., 1963.

Frank, J. D. *Persuasion and Healing.* New York: Schocken Books, 1963.

Goffman, E. *Stigma.* Englewood Cliffs, N.J.: Prentice-Hall, 1963.

James, W. *The Varieties of Religious Experience.* Modern Library Edition. New York: Random House, 1902.

Lofland, J., and Stark, R. Becoming a world-saver: a theory of conversion to a deviant perspective. *American Sociological Review*, 1965, 30, 862–75.

Mann, J. *Changing Human Behavior.* New York: Charles Scribner's Sons, 1965.

Maslow, A. H. *Motivation and Personality.* New York: Harper, 1954.

Riley, Matilda W. Socialization for the middle and later years. In D. A. Goslin and D. C. Glass (Eds.), *Handbook of Socialization Theory and Research*. New York: Rand McNally & Co., 1968.

Scott, R. A. *Social Science and Work for the Blind*. New York: Russell Sage Foundation, 1968.

Sussman, M. B. (Ed.) *Sociology and Rehabilitation*. Washington, D.C.: American Sociological Association, 1965.

Williams, R. H., Tibbitts, C., and Donahue, Wilma (Eds.). *Processes of Aging: Social and Psychological Perspectives*. Vols. I and II. Behavioral Science Series. New York: Atherton Press, 1963.

Williams, R. H., and Wirths, Claudine G. *Lives Through the Years*. New York: Atherton Press, 1965.

Wolfgang, M. E., Savitz, L., and Johnston, N. (Eds.) *The Sociology of Crime and Delinquency*. New York: John Wiley & Sons, 1962.

Interaction and Adaptation: Intimacy as a Critical Variable

Marjorie Fiske Lowenthal and Clayton Haven

Introduction

This paper is a sequel to previous studies in which we noted certain anomalies in the relation between traditional measures of social deprivation, on the one hand, and indicators of morale and psychiatric condition, on the other, in studies of older populations. For example, lifelong isolates tend to have average or better morale and to be no more prone to hospitalization for mental illness in old age than anyone else, but those who have tried and failed to establish social relationships appear particularly vulnerable.[1] Nor, with certain exceptions, do age-linked trauma involving social deprivation, such as widowhood and retirement, precipitate mental illness.[2] While these events do tend to be associated with low morale, they are by no means universally so. Furthermore, a voluntary reduction in social activity, that is, one which is not accounted for by widowhood, retirement or physical impairment, does not necessarily have a deleterious effect on either morale or on professionally appraised mental health status.[3]

In analyzing detailed life histories of a small group of the subjects making up the samples for these studies, we were struck by the fact that the happiest and healthiest among them often seemed to be people who were, or had been, involved in one or more close personal

From the *American Sociological Review*, Vol. 33, No. 1, February 1968. Reprinted by permission of the American Sociological Association and Marjorie Fiske Lowenthal.

relationships. It therefore appeared that the existence of such a relationship might serve as a buffer against age-linked social losses and thus explain some of these seeming anomalies. The purpose of the present study is to explore this possibility. In doing so, we shall first illustrate how two rather conventional measures of interaction and role status are related to three measures of adaptation which represent different frames of reference. Taking advantage of the panel nature of the data, we shall further document these relationships by analyzing the effect of social gains and losses on adaptation. We shall then show how the presence or absence of a confidant serves as an explanatory variable in the overall trends and deviations noted in the relationships between the more conventional social measures and adaptation. Finally, we shall describe briefly the characteristics of those who do and do not have a confidant, and discuss the implications of these findings for adult socialization and adaptation.

The Concept of Intimacy   As we explored the literature prior to analyzing our own material on intimacy, we were struck by the paucity of references to the quality, depth or reciprocity of personal relationships in social science materials. In their studies of the relationship between social interaction and adjustment, sociologists traditionally have been concerned with the concepts of isolation and anomie, often gauged or inferred from low rankings on quantitative indicators of social roles and contacts; that is, with questions such as how many roles a person fills, how much of his time is spent in interaction with others, and the relationship to the subject of persons with whom this interaction takes place. Several of these studies have established a modest relationship between social isolation and maladjustment.[4] With a few exceptions noted below, they have not taken into account the quality or intensity of the individual's relationships with others.

Psychologists have been concerned with dyadic relationships, including the parental and the marital, but although there are references in the literature to Freud's possibly apocryphal mention of the capacity for love as a criterion of mental health, one finds little research directly related to qualities or behavior reflecting the capacity for intimacy or reciprocity. Nor do the traditional personality tests often tap characteristics relevant to such concepts. Some research on animal and human infants, however, has explored this dimension. Harlow and Zimmermann[5] have shown that infant monkeys spend a great deal more time with a cloth mother surrogate than with a wire surrogate, regardless of which mother provides the milk. They conclude, as have Spitz and Wolf in their studies of human infants,[6] that the need for love is instinctual. Ferreira,[7] drawing on his own research and that of Bowlby,[8] concludes that the need for intimacy is "primary and of an instinctual nature . . . the intimacy need may represent a more basic instinctual force than oral or even nursing needs."

It is primarily the psychoanalysts and the analytically-oriented psychologists who, largely on the basis of clinical insights, have stressed this capacity or need, often implying that from its development and fulfillment grow all other forms of social growth and constructive social action. One of the fundamental precepts of Angyal's theory[9] is that "existing in the thought and affection of another really is a very concrete level of existence. . . ." He goes on to say that the establishment and maintenance of such a close relationship is "the crux of our existence from the cradle to the grave." Erikson postulates the capacity for intimacy as one of the major developmental tasks of life, ideally to be achieved in the establishment of a close relationship with a person of the opposite sex in late adolescence and early adulthood.[10] While our data support this view, it seems clear that there are other viable forms of intimacy which are not necessarily experienced as substitutes for, or supplements to, a stable heterosexual relationship.

In the light of the general paucity of research on the problem of intimacy, it is not surprising that it has not been systematically explored in relation to older populations. Rosow's important study of friendship patterns under varying age-density conditions[11] does not take the depth of these relationships into account. Arth,[12] in his study of friendships in an aging population, is concerned with "close" friendships, but he does not define closeness. Blau's pioneering study of structural constraints on friendships of the aged[13] documents the importance of prevailing age-sex-marital status patterns in the establishment of friendships, but it does not discuss the quality or intensity of these relationships.

Obviously, this is a delicate area to explore with field research methods, and our own approach was a simple—if not crude—one. The analysis rests largely on responses to the question: "Is there anyone in particular you confide in or talk to about yourself or your problems?" followed by a description of the identity of the confidant. Still, the findings tend not only to confirm the insights of clinicians and the rather sparse observations of other researchers, but also to clarify some of the puzzling deviations we have noted in our own work in regard to the relationship between social measures, on the one hand, and adaptation, on the other.

The Sample

The sample on which this report is based consists of 280 sample-survivors in a panel study of community-resident aged, interviewed three times at approximately annual intervals. The parent sample included 600 persons aged sixty and older, drawn on a stratified-random basis from 18 census tracts in San Francisco. The sample of 280 remaining at the third round of interviewing is about equally divided in terms of the original stratifying variables of sex, three age levels, and social living arrangements (alone or with others). As might be expected, the panel differs from elderly San Franciscans (and elderly Americans), as a whole, by including proportionally more of the very elderly, more males, and more persons living alone. Largely because of the oversampling of persons living alone, the proportion of single, widowed, and divorced persons, and of working women, is higher than among elderly Americans in general. Partly because of the higher proportion of working women, their income level was higher than average (44 percent having an income of over $2,000 per year, compared with 25 percent among all older Americans). The proportion of foreign born (34 percent) resembles that for older San Franciscans in general (36 percent), which is considerably more than for all older Americans (18 percent). While some of these sample biases may tend to underplay the frequency of the presence of a confidant, we have no reason to believe that they would influence findings from our major research question, namely the role of the confidant as an intervening variable between social resources and deprivation and adaptation.

Measures of Role, Interaction and Adaptation   The two conventional social measures to be reported here are number of social roles[14] and level of social interaction.[15] Men tend to rank somewhat lower than women in social interaction in the younger groups, but up through age 74, fewer than 17 percent of either sex rank "low" on this measure (defined as being visited [only] by relatives, contacts only with persons in dwelling, or contacts for essentials only).[16] Isolation increases sharply beginning with age 75, however, and in that phase women are slightly more isolated than men (32 percent compared with 28 percent), possibly because of the higher proportion of widows than of widowers. In general, because they are less likely to be widowed and more likely to be working, men have more roles than women at all age levels, and this discrepancy becomes particularly wide at 75 or older, when 40 percent of the men, compared with only 15 percent of the women, have three or more roles. Among men, a low level of social interaction and a paucity of social roles tend to be related to low socioeconomic status, but this does not hold true for women.

The principal measure of adaptation in this analysis is a satisfaction-depression (or morale) score based on a cluster analysis of answers to 8 questions.[17] For a subsample of 112, we shall also report ratings of psychiatric impairment by three psychiatrists, who, working independently, reviewed the protocols in detail but did not see the subjects.[18] We thus have a subjective indicator of the sense of well-being, and a professional appraisal of mental health status. A third measure, opinion as to whether one is young or old for one's age, is included to round out the adaptation dimension with an indication of what might be called the respondent's opinion as to his relative deprivation—that is, whether he thinks he is better or worse off than his age peers.

As is true for the social indicators, there are age, sex, and class differences in regard to these adaptation measures which we shall have to bear in mind in analyzing the relationship between these two dimensions. Among men, morale deteriorates evenly with advancing age, from somewhat over one-third "depressed" among those under 65 to about three-fifths among those 75 or older. The youngest women are more depressed than the youngest men (47 percent depressed), but there is no increase—in fact there is a slight decrease—in depression among the 65–74 year old women. The oldest women, however, are nearly as depressed as the oldest men. There are no consistent age or sex trends in regard to whether the subject thinks he is young or old for his age—a slight majority of both sexes at all age levels consider themselves young.

Mental health status, as judged by psychiatrists, indicates that if all age groups are combined, men are psychiatrically more robust than women. This is especially true for the oldest group (75 or older), where four-fifths of the men, compared with only two-fifths of the women, are considered unimpaired. The sex difference is reversed, however, in the middle age-range (65–74), where men are judged to be more impaired than women (44 percent, compared with 29 percent rated impaired). While at first glance this discrepancy might be interpreted as a consequence of psychic crises relating to retirement, detailed analysis of a large psychiatrically hospitalized older sample[19] indicates that retirement rarely precipitates psychiatric disorder. But this same analysis does demonstrate clearly that physical deterioration in the elderly is frequently accompanied by psychiatric impairment. The sharp reversal of sex differences in mental health status in the middle age group may, therefore, be associated with the earlier onset of physical impairment among men. The fact that the death rate for men between 65 and 74 is considerably greater than for women may, in turn, on the principle of survival of the fittest, account for the oldest men's (75 or more) again being judged of more robust mental health than women.

In view of the association between physical and mental health in the elderly, and of the association between poor health and low socio-economic status, it is not surprising that there is also some relationship between low socioeconomic status and psychiatric impairment, though this association is more marked for men than for women. Low morale, on the other hand, is related to low socioeconomic status among both men and women.[20]

Relationship between Social Measures and Adaptation As Table 1 indicates, there is a clear and consistent relationship between social resources and good morale, and between social deprivation and low morale. Low social interaction, in particular, is strongly related to depression. While high ranks on both social measures contribute to the sense of relative privilege (feel young for age), a low rank is not related as consistently to a sense of relative deprivation as it is to poor morale. A high rank on the two social measures is more closely associated with professional ratings of good mental health than with the respondents' own reports on mood and sense of relative advantage or deprivation. A low rank on social measures, however, is not consistently or markedly related to a rating of impairment. In other words, social resources and social deficits appear to influence self-appraisals of mood, comparison of self with others, and professional appraisals of adaptation in different ways. Social roles and high interaction are apparently considered to be indicators of, or associated with, mental health—but their absence is not necessarily construed as indicative of impairment. The pattern of association between the social indicators and morale is just the reverse. Social deficits—at least as indicated by the social interaction measure—are more highly correlated with a depressed state than are social resources correlated with a satisfied state. The sense of relative privilege is enhanced by social advantage, but social disadvantage does not necessarily evoke a sense of relative deprivation, at least insofar as this sense is reflected by feeling average or old for one's age.

Table 1 Social Indicators and Adaptation

	Social Interaction		Role Status	
	High	Low	High	Low
	%	%	%	%
Psychiatric status				
Unimpaired	73	42	90	61
Impaired	27	58	10	39
Opinion of own age				
Young	65	39	67	57
Not young	35	61	33	43
Morale				
Satisfied	58	15	60	46
Depressed	42	85	40	54

If we compare these social indicators, as reported at the second follow-up, with those reported at the first follow-up approximately one year earlier [Table 2], we find that several changes took place. These trends were on the order of those noted for other variables used in the panel questionnaire.[21] Social interaction and role status closely resemble each other with respect to change, with 14 and 15 percent, respectively, "improving," and 20 and 21 percent, respectively, "deteriorating." The broad patterns of relationship between change in social resources and the three indicators of adaptation resemble those which emerged in the more static picture shown in Table 1. Social losses are related to poor morale, but gains are not related to high morale. Gains are, however, highly correlated with good psychiatric status, though again decrements are not so strongly associated with poor status. Improvements in role and social interaction are related to a sense of relative advantage, as indicated by feeling young for one's age, but losses do not markedly contribute to a sense of relative deprivation (feeling old). This again suggests that a professional's judgment of mental impairment rests on factors other than the absence of indicators of health; an individual's subjective sense of well-being does not automatically result from supplying the role and interaction deficits that often are associated with low morale.

On the other hand, maintaining the status quo in social interaction and role is related to good adaptation, regardless of which indicator of adjustment is used. In fact, on four of the six correlations, stability proves to be more highly associated with good adaptation than does "improvement." At the same time, we note that sizeable proportions of those who suffered social decrements are well-adapted, ranging from one-third to over half, depending on the adaptation measures used. Clearly, our conventional measures alone do not fully

Table 2 The Relation Between Change in Social Measures and Adaptation

	Social Interaction			Role Status		
	More	Less	No Change	More	Less	No Change
	%	%	%	%	%	%
Psychiatric status						
Unimpaired	(32)	42	30	(11)	(45)	35
Impaired	(68)*	58	70	(89)	(55)	65
Opinion of own age						
Young	70	49	63	53	55	63
Not Young	30	51	37	47	45	37
Morale						
Satisfied	47	35	58	50	47	53
Depressed	53	65	42	50	53	47

*Percentages are placed in parentheses when the numbers on which they are based are less than 20; the N's for the percentages in parentheses range from 14–19.

explain the relation between the individual's position and behavior in his social milieu, on the one hand, and his adjustment, on the other.

Pursuing our hypothesis with regard to the potential importance of a confidant as a buffer against social losses, we turn to Table 3, which shows the current presence or absence of a confidant, and recent losses, gains, or stability in intimate relationships, in conjunction with the three adaptation measures. As the first column shows, the presence of a confidant is positively associated with all three indicators of adjustment. The absence of a confidant is related to low morale. Lack of a present confidant does not, however, have much bearing on the individual's sense of relative deprivation, or on the psychiatric judgments of mental impairment. We suggest, though with the present data we cannot fully document, two possible explanations for these findings. First, as we have previously noted,[22] there are some lifelong isolates and near-isolates whose late-life adaptation apparently is not related to social resources. The sense of relative deprivation, at least for older persons, no doubt applies not only to current comparisons with one's peers, but also to comparisons with one's own earlier self. This would contribute to an explanation of the fact that some older people without a confidant are satisfied. They do not miss what they never have had. Our second explanation echoes the old adage that it is better to have loved and lost than never to have loved at all. The psychiatrists, in rating mental health status, may take *capacity* for intimacy into account, as indicated by past relationships such as marriage or parenthood. The respondent, in a more or less "objective" comparison of himself with his peers, may also take these past gratifications into account. However, such recollections may well be less serviceable on the more subjective level of morale and mood.

Table 3   The Effect of a Confidant on Adaptation

| | Current Presence of Confidant | | Change in Confidant Past Year | | |
	Yes	No	Gained	Lost	Maintained same confidant
	%	%	%	%	%
Psychiatric status					
Unimpaired	69	60	(60)	(56)	80
Impaired	31	40	(40)	(44)	20
Opinion of own age					
Young	60	62	42	49	61
Not young	40	38	58	51	39
Morale					
Satisfied	59	41	44	30	68
Depressed	41	59	56	70	32

Interaction and Adaptation

The right side of the table, showing change and stability in the confidant relationship, dramatically exemplifies the significance of intimacy for the subjective sense of well being: the great majority of those who lost a confidant are depressed, and the great majority of those who maintained one are satisfied. Gaining one helps, but not much, suggesting again the importance of stability, which we have noted in relation to the other social measures. Maintenance of an intimate relationship also is strongly correlated with self-other comparisons and with psychiatrists' judgments, though losses do not show the obverse. This supports our suggestions that evidence of the *capacity* for intimacy may be relevant to these two more objective indicators of adaptation.

The great significance of the confidant from a subjective viewpoint, combined with the fact that sizeable proportions of people who showed decrements in social interaction or social role nevertheless were satisfied, raised the possibility that the maintenance of an intimate relationship may serve as a buffer against the depression that might otherwise result from decrements in social role or interaction, or from the more drastic social losses frequently suffered by older persons, namely widowhood and retirement. To test this hypothesis, we examined the morale of changers on the interaction and role measures in the light of whether they did or did not have a confidant.

The Intimate Relationships as a Buffer Against Social Losses As Table 4 shows, it is clear that if you have a confidant, you can decrease your social interaction and run no greater risk of becoming depressed than if you had increased it. Further, if you have no confidant, you may increase your social activities and yet be far more likely to be depressed than the individual who has a confidant but has lowered his interaction level.[23] Finally, if you have no confidant and retrench in your social life, the odds for depression become overwhelming. The findings are similar, though not so dramatic, in regard to change in social role: if you have a confidant, roles can be decreased with no effect on morale; if you do not have a confidant, you are likely to be depressed whether your roles are increased or decreased (though slightly more so if they are decreased). In other words, the presence of an intimate relationship apparently does serve as a buffer against such decrements as loss of role or reduction of social interaction.

What about the more dramatic "insults" of aging, such as widowhood or retirement? While a few people became widowed or retired during our second follow-up year (and are therefore included among the "decreasers" in social role), there were not enough of them to explore fully the impact of these age-linked stresses. We therefore have checked back in the life histories of our subjects and located persons who retired within a seven-year period prior to the second

Table 4 Effect on Morale Changes in Social Interaction and Role Status, in the Presence and Absence of a Confidant

Social Interaction

	Increased		Decreased	
	Has Confidant	No Confidant	Has Confidant	No Confidant
	%	%	%	%
Morale				
Satisfied	55	(30)	56	13
Depressed	45	(70)	44	87

Role Status

	Increased		Decreased	
	Has Confidant	No Confidant	Has Confidant	No Confidant
	%	%	%	%
Morale				
Satisfied	55	(42)	56	(38)
Depressed	45	(58)	44	(62)

follow-up interview or who became widowed within this period. Though our concern is primarily with social deficits, we added persons who had suffered serious physical illness within two years before the second follow-up contact, since we know that such stresses also influence adaptation.

Table 5 indicates that the hypothesis is confirmed in regard to the more traumatic social deprivations. An individual who has been widowed within seven years, and who has a confidant, has even higher morale than a person who remains married but lacks a confidant. In fact, given a confidant, widowhood within such a comparatively long period makes a rather undramatic impact on morale. Among those having confidants, only 10 percent more of the widowed than of the married are depressed, but nearly three-fourths of the widowed who have no confidant are depressed, compared with only about half, among the married, who have no confidant.[24] The story is similar with respect to retirement. The retired with a confidant rank the same in regard to morale as those still working who have no confidant; those both retired and having no confidant are almost twice as likely to be depressed as to be satisfied, whereas among those both working and having a confidant, the ratio is more than reversed.

Although relatively few people (35) developed serious physical illness in the two-year period prior to the second follow-up interview, it is nevertheless amply clear that a confidant does not play a mediating role between this "insult" of aging and adjustment as measured by the depression-satisfaction score. The aged person who is (or has recently been) seriously ill is overwhelmingly depressed, regardless of whether or not he has an intimate relationship. Superficially, one

Table 5 Effect of Confidant on Morale in the Contexts of Widowhood, Retirement and Physical Illness

	Satisfied %	Depressed %
Widowed within 7 Years		
Has confidant	55	45
No confidant	(27)	(73)
Married		
Has confidant	65	35
No confidant	(47)	(53)
Retired within 7 Years		
Has confidant	50	50
No confidant	(36)	(64)
Not retired		
Has confidant	70	30
No confidant	50	50
Serious physical illness within 2 Years		
Has confidant	(16)	(84)
No confidant	(13)	(87)
No serious illness		
Has confidant	64	36
No confidant	42	58

might conclude that this is a logical state of affairs. A social support—such as an intimate relationship—may serve as a mediating, palliative or alleviating factor in the face of social losses, but one should not expect it to cross system boundaries and serve a similar role in the face of physical losses. On the other hand, why doesn't one feel more cheerful, though ill, if one has an intimate on whom to rely for support, or to whom one can pour out complaints? At this point we can only conjecture, but one possible explanation is that serious physical illness is usually accompanied by an increase in dependence on others, which in turn may set off a conflict in the ill person more disruptive to his intimate relationships than to more casual ones. This may be especially true of dependent persons whose dependency is masked.[25] A second possibility is that the assumption of the sick role may be a response to the failure to fulfill certain developmental tasks. In this event, illness would be vitally necessary as an ego defense, and efforts of intimates directed toward recovery would be resisted.[26] A third possibility is that illness is accompanied by increased apprehension of death. Even in an intimate relationship, it may be easier (and more acceptable) to talk about the grief associated with widowhood or the anxieties or losses associated with retirement than to confess one's fears about the increasing imminence of death.

Characteristics of Persons Having a Confidant; Confidant Identity In turning to the question of who does, and who does not, maintain an intimate relationship, we found sex and marital status differences that were not unexpected, and some discrepancies with respect to age and socioeconomic status that seemed, at first glance, puzzling [see Table 6]. Despite the fact that there were about twice as many widows as widowers in this sample, women were more likely to have a confidant than were men (69 percent, compared with 57 percent). Age trends are irregular. Both persons under 65 and those 75 and older were less likely to have a confidant than the 65 to 74 year olds. Women are more likely than men to have an intimate relationship at all age levels, and the differences between the sexes are especially pronounced in those under 65, where nearly three-fourths of the women and only half the men reported that they have a confidant. These findings tend to support those of Arth[27] and Blau[28] in regard to the social capacities and advantages of women. The married are notably more likely to have a confidant than those who are not; single persons are most deprived on this score, and the widowed fall between. Persons above the median on our socioeconomic measure are consider-

Table 6 Characteristics of Persons Having a Confidant

	Percent with Confidant		
	Men	Women	Total
Sex			
Men			57
Women			69
Age			
60–64	50	72	62
65–74	68	75	72
75+	55	59	57
Marital status			
Single	36	67	46
Married	74	81	77
Separated/Divorced	50	57	54
Widowed	50	65	62
Socioeconomic status			
High	69	77	73
Low	38	56	47
Educational level			
Less than 8 years	51	67	56
8 years	58	62	60
More than 8 years	61	70	67
Occupational level			
Blue collar	48	67	55
White collar	65	69	67
Social interaction			
High	62	72	68
Low	39	50	44
Role status index			
3–5 roles	71	84	76
0–2 roles	45	62	55

ably more likely to have a confidant than those below it, and the differences are more marked for men than women. Education makes surprisingly little difference for either sex, but occupational differences are marked for men.

As to the identity of the confidant, among the nearly two-thirds of the sample who do have a confidant, the identity of this person is fairly evenly distributed among spouse, child and friend. Siblings or other relatives as confidants are comparatively rare. Among women in general, husbands are least frequently mentioned, while wives are the most important for men. This is not only because women are more likely to be widowed, for if we look only at those who are married, or still married, men at all age levels are more likely to report a spouse than are women. Women are about twice as likely as men to mention a child or another relative, and more likely to name friends.

In view of the frequently noted class differences in social interaction,[29] it does not surprise us that more than half again as many of those above the median on our socioeconomic measure have a confidant than do those below the median. The generally reported wider range of friendship patterns among the higher socioeconomic groups does not prepare us for the class differences in the identity of confidants reported by this older sample, however. More than three times as many of the higher class report a spouse than do those of lower socioeconomic status (28 percent compared with 8 percent). While this tendency holds among both sexes, the discrepancies are most dramatic among men (36 compared with 2 percent). Conversely, more than twice as many of the low socioeconomic group report a friend, and again it is men who account entirely for the discrepancy. Women of higher status are slightly more likely to have a friend as confidant than are women of lower status. Analysis of detailed life history interviews available for a subsample provide some evidence that the lesser importance of the spouse as confidant among the men of the lower socioeconomic group is connected with problems of masculine role and identity, low-status males considering close association with women a sign of male weakness. This he-man theory gains some support in the fact that among men, not having a confidant is more related to blue collar occupational status than it is to little schooling. Men in the blue collar occupations, whether skilled or unskilled, would obviously—at least in the United States—have less opportunity to associate with women than would white collar males.

In these same life history studies, we have noted some examples of "a regression or escape into intimacy" with advancing age. That is, people who have maintained both intimate and other types of social relationships may, on retirement, for example, or after the departure of children from the home, withdraw to a situation where a close relationship is, in effect, the only social contact. But this is by no means the rule. In general, the more complex the social life, the more

Socialization

likely is there to be an intimate relationship, no doubt, in part, because of the larger pool of social resources from which a confidant may be drawn. Among persons having three or more social roles, for example, three-fourths have a confidant, whereas among those having two or fewer social roles, only slightly more than half have a confidant. Similarly, two-thirds of those on the highest level of social interaction have an intimate relationship, while the majority of those whose interaction is limited to being visited by relatives do not. Such resources, however, are more important for men than for women.

Implications

This study indicates that when two conventional indicators of social role and interaction are used, the significance for adaptation of being socially deprived or advantaged varies in accordance with the degree of subjectivity of the adjustment measure used. Social resources are more related to professional appraisals of good health than to subjective appraisals of high morale; social deprivation, on the other hand, is associated with subjective reports of poor morale, but not with professional assessments of poor mental health. A more objective self-report involving comparisons with others resembles the psychiatrists' judgments; that is, being socially privileged enhances one's evaluation but being socially underprivileged does not deflate it. Regardless of the indicator of adaptation which is examined, however, the deviant cells are sizeable.

To help explain these variations, we went on to show that the maintenance of a stable intimate relationship is more closely associated with good mental health and high morale than is high social interaction or role status, or stability in interaction and role. Similarly, the loss of a confidant has a more deleterious effect on morale, though not on mental health status, than does a reduction in either of the other two social measures. We suggested that while psychiatrists may take the capacity for an intimate relationship into account in their professional judgments, awareness that he has such a potential does not elevate an individual's mood if he has recently lost a confidant. Finally, we have noted that the impact on adjustment of a decrease in social interaction, or a loss of social roles, is considerably softened if the individual has a close personal relationship. In addition, the age-linked losses of widowhood and retirement are also ameliorated by the presence of a confidant, though the assault of physical illness clearly is not.

In view of the apparently critical importance of an intimate relationship, the sex and class differences we have noted in the reporting of the presence or absence of a confidant provoke speculation. In the youngest age group (those between 60 and 64, presumably a period where the pool of potential confidants is greatest), nearly half again as many women as men reported an intimate companion. We are reminded, in this connection, of the observations of psychoanalyst Prescott Thompson in regard to age trends in the significance of interpersonal communication among spouses. In early periods of the adult life span, he suggests, communication problems may well have been obscured by the pressures and distractions of job and children; as the empty nest and retirement phases approach, awareness of deficiencies in this respect may become acute.[30] Significantly, it is the wives who are most likely first to become conscious of the problem, and to be able to talk about it.[31]

There seems little doubt that, to some extent, marital status is an indication of the capacity for intimacy. We have seen that the married are most likely to have a confidant, whether spouse or some other. Among those not married and living with spouse when we interviewed them, widows and widowers were most likely to have a confidant, single persons least, and the divorced and separated fell between. Finally, the class and sex differences we have noted suggest that the lower class men may harbor a concept of virility which discourages the development of types of intimacy other than the purely sexual. Thus, with the waning of sexual potency or the loss of a partner with advanced age, they are left with fewer alternatives for an intimate relationship than are women.

At this stage of our knowledge, we can only wonder whether women's greater sensitivity to close relationships, and, as we have seen, their greater versatility in the choice of objects for such relationships, has any causal connection with their greater adaptability for survival. Not only is the overall death rate higher among men, but among them, and not among women, the suicide rate increases rapidly with age. And despite their greater potentiality for remarriage, it is among men, not women, that widowhood is more likely to trigger mental illness. Conversely, the few instances where retirement precipitates mental disturbance tend to be found among working women rather than men, suggesting that an important source of frustration and conflict may lie precisely in the incapacity, or lack of opportunity, to carry out the special feminine task of developing and sustaining intimate relationships.[32] We are reminded once more of Angyal's guiding thesis,[33] that the maintenance of closeness with another is the center of existence up to the very end of life.

[1]Marjorie Fiske Lowenthal, "Social Isolation and Mental Illness in Old Age," *American Sociological Review*, 29 (February 1964), pp. 54–70.
[2]Marjorie Fiske Lowenthal, "Antecedents of Isolation and Mental Illness in Old Age," *Archives of General Psychiatry*, 12 (March 1965), pp. 245–254.

Socialization

[3]Marjorie Fiske Lowenthal and Deetje Boler, "Voluntary vs. Involuntary Social Withdrawal," *Journal of Gerontology*, 20 (July 1965), pp. 363–371.

[4]For a selected review of this literature, see Lowenthal (1964), *op. cit.*

[5]Harry F. Harlow and Robert R. Zimmermann, "Affectional Responses in the Infant Monkey," *Science*, 130 (1959), pp. 421–432.

[6]Rene A. Spitz and Katherine M. Wolf, "Anaclitic Depression," *Psychoanalytic Study of the Child*, 2, New York: International Universities Press, 1946, pp. 313–342.

[7]A. J. Ferreira, "The Intimacy Need in Psychotherapy," *American Journal of Psychoanalysis*, 24 (November 1964), pp. 190–194.

[8]John Bowlby, "The Nature of the Child's Tie to His Mother," *International Journal of Psychoanalysis*, 39 (September–October 1958), pp. 350–373.

[9]Andras Angyal, *Neurosis and Treatment: A Holistic Theory*, New York: John Wiley and Sons, 1965, p. 19.

[10]Erik H. Erikson, "Identity and the Life Cycle," *Psychological Issues*, [Monograph 1], New York: International Universities Press, 1959.

[11]Irving Rosow, *Social Integration of the Aged*, New York: Free Press of Glencoe, 1967.

[12]Malcolm Arth, "American Culture and the Phenomenon of Friendship in the Aged," in Clark Tibbitts and Wilma Donahue, eds., *Social and Psychological Aspects of Aging*, New York: Columbia University Press, 1962, pp. 529–534.

[13]Zena Smith Blau, "Structural Constraints on Friendships in Old Age," *American Sociological Review*, 26 (June 1961), pp. 429–440.

[14]Roles include parent, spouse, worker, churchgoer and organization member.

[15]Ranging from "contributes to goals of organizations" to "contacts for the material essentials of life only." All measures of interaction and adaptation reported here pertain to the second round of follow-up.

[16]Only a few of the tables drawn upon for this paper are presented in the text; others are available on request.

[17]The distribution of individual cluster scores was dichotomized at the median: persons falling below the median are called "depressed," and persons falling above the median are called "satisfied." Questions pertained to the sense of satisfaction with life, happiness, usefulness, mood and planning.

[18]One-third (38 persons) were judged impaired, the majority (30 persons) only mildly so. Seven were rated moderately, and one severely impaired.

[19]Marjorie Fiske Lowenthal, Paul L. Berkman and Associates, *Aging and Mental Disorder in San Francisco: A Social Psychiatric Study*, San Francisco: Jossey-Bass, Inc., 1967; Alexander Simon, Marjorie Fiske Lowenthal and Leon J. Epstein, *Crisis and Intervention* (working title), New York: Basic Books, pending.

[20]The index of current economic position is based on a combination of monthly rent, annual income, and the Tyron Index of San Francisco census tracts. The Tryon Index, with scores ranging from zero (low) to 10 (high), is based on proportions of persons in professional or managerial occupations, with college education, and self-employed, the proportion of dwelling units with one or fewer persons per room, and the proportion of domestic and service workers. See Robert C. Tryon, *Identification of Social Areas by Cluster Analysis*, Berkeley: University of California Press, 1955. The lowest quartile consists of persons who scored below the median on all three measures (the medians were: income, $2,500; rent, $60; Tryon score, 4.5), and the highest quartile consists of persons who scored above the median on all three socioeconomic measures.

[21]Lowenthal and Berkman, *op. cit.*

[22]Lowenthal (1964), *op. cit.*

[23]Parallel analyses of the other two adjustment measures are not included here. The psychiatric ratings are available for only a subsample of 112 (and cells would become too small). The indicator of opinion of own age reflects trends similar, though not so marked, as those shown here, except for increase in role status, where the absence of a confidant does not contribute to a negative opinion.

[24]This finding suggests the need for far more detailed questioning on the confidant relationship than we were able to undertake. It may well be that some married persons assumed that the question pertained to confidants other than spouses.

[25]Alvin Goldfarb, "Psychodynamics and the Three-Generation Family," in Ethel Shanas and Gordon F. Streib, eds., *Social Structure and the Family: Generational Relations*, Englewood Cliffs, New Jersey: Prentice-Hall, 1965, pp. 10–45.

[26]Lowenthal and Berkman, *op. cit.*

[27]Arth, *op. cit.*

[28]Blau, *op. cit.*

[29]*Ibid.*; Rosow, *op. cit.*

[30]Prescott W. Thompson and Ronald Chen, "Experiences with Older Psychiatric Patients and Spouses Together in a Residential Treatment Setting," *Bulletin of the Menninger Clinic*, 30 (January 1966), pp. 23–31.

[31]Prescott W. Thompson, *Personal Communication*, 1966.

[32]Lowenthal and Berkman, *op. cit.*

[33]Angyal, *op. cit.*

The Family   4

Some of the more persistent gerontological myths concern the family. We commonly hear: "Why don't we take care of older people like we used to in the good old days?" Or "Three generations used to be able to live in the same house in the 'good old days'; why can't they now?" Or "They used to be able to look after each other—why don't they now?" Such romantic images of the past reflect misinformation about how things were. In fact, the three-generation household was a rarity in the United States except for a short period early in the twentieth century, when housing was in short supply. Because of low life expectancies and high residential mobility in an expanding society, American families were seldom composed of more than two generations. In fact, the current situation is perhaps more like what today's pessimists say the past was like.

"Integration and Family," by Peter Townsend, is taken from *Older People in Three Industrial Societies,* a book that describes the lives of older people in Great Britain, Denmark, and the United States. The topics considered included the nature of family relationships, the extent to which older people are isolated from or integrated into the broader society, and the participation of older people in family life. The three-generation family living together is not typical in any of these countries, but 28 percent of older Americans with children live within half an hour's trip of one or more of their children. Older Americans generally see at least one child fairly frequently, and those who have no children turn to their siblings for relationships.

In contrast with the stereotypes, Townsend shows that assistance goes both up and down the generational ladder. Older people help their children and grandchildren with money and services, and older people receive help from younger family members. In the three countries studied, a large minority of older people depend on children and other relatives as the chief source of help when they are ill. Between 80 and 90 percent of older people who are bedfast in their own homes depend primarily on family members for help.

The heterogeneity of family structures to which older people are attached and the variety of functions performed by the family mirror the tremendous heterogeneity among older people. Family situations range from those in which older people are part of closely knit extended families to isolated individuals without any family ties at all, but isolation is by far the rarer pattern.

Townsend also calls attention to the increasingly common four-generation family. While we know little at this time about intergenerational relationships in four-generation families, the fact that it is becoming a commonplace phenomenon requires that we investigate it more fully. Certainly more generations in a family mean a greater number of potential sources of help. To some extent the four-generation family may compensate for the fact that future generations of older people will have fewer siblings.

Despite the folk saying "A son is a son 'til he gets him a wife; a daughter is a daughter all of her life," Townsend found that the difference between sons and daughters in their contact with parents was less than they had anticipated, and a large proportion of old people had frequent contacts with at least one of their sons. The importance of children in the lives of older parents, particularly widowed parents, is great. Older people who had no children used sibling relationships as substitutes. The marital bond appeared to be the most salient one for older people. The norms of parent-child relationships encouraged separate households for the parents and for the children, but in an emergency, children are expected to help their older parents, and older parents expect this help.

Townsend concludes with a section on social services and formal organizations. He notes that social services are integrating forces for the older person—supplementing, or substituting for, the informal services and activities often provided by the family.

Gordon F. Streib's selection, "Older Families and Their Troubles: Familial and Social Responses," deals with the theory of shared functions. Based on an idea developed by Eugene Litwak and his colleagues, *shared functions* refers to the necessity for formal organizations and families to coordinate their efforts if they are to achieve their goals in a highly industrialized and urbanized society. Bureaucracy is characterized by impersonality, formality, affective neutrality, and universality, whereas the family is characteristically highly personalized, informal, affective, and particularistic. The articulation of the two organizational forms can help individuals solve their problems.

Streib distinguishes between the residential and the extended family. The former is the family in which one lives, whereas the latter refers to one's kinship network. He provides some demographic data about the living arrangements of older people and reinforces the Townsend findings about the number of three- and four-generation families. He emphasizes, as others have, that there is no such thing as a "typical family" in later life.

In addition to physical health, Streib says, three other major resources contribute to the strength of older families: emotional health, economic resources, and social resources. Relationships among these four variables are complicated. Various combinations result in five family types and four typical ways in which families deal with problems. A family's pretrouble level of organization has important implications for the forms of crisis intervention that are used.

Streib calls attention to a tendency among gerontologists to neglect the needs and rights of adult children and to blame these children if the aged parents are not happy. In a society that stresses the self-actualization of individuals, we are reminded once again that children have rights too—even when they are adult children. Adult children are often the generation caught in the squeeze play of intergenerational relationships—blamed for the problems of both their parents and their children.

Solutions that have been attempted are described by Streib. He refers to pseudofamily types of intervention such as Foster Grandparents and SERVE, in which the older person takes on fictive family roles. In other programs younger persons initiate such roles (for example, Adopt-a-Grandparent). Streib makes some concrete recommendations for ways in which the mass media can be used to increase the social resources and emotional health of older persons.

In the final selection in this chapter, Ruth S. Cavan offers "Speculations on Innovations to Conventional Marriage in Old Age." Older people maintain an interest in people of the opposite sex, the same sex, and in sex itself. The need for intimacy and for intimate relationships does not fade away; rather, it persists throughout the life cycle. Differential mortality heightens the frequency of widowhood among women in old age.

Cavan examines the applicability of sex relationship innovations usually considered to be limited to younger people. Her focus is essentially on peer relationships rather than on cross-generational relationships, particularly old-young sex relationships. She considers several kinds of innovation: nonmarital cohabitation, homosexual or lesbian companionships, group marriages, communes, and comarital contracts. As a result of their more traditional morality, many of today's cohorts of older people may be reluctant to become involved in one or more of the kinds of relationships Cavan discusses, but future cohorts may have a more secular attitude toward alternative forms of sexual relationships. It is interesting that Cavan emphasizes peer-oriented innovative sexual arrangements. She does not suggest breaking the age barrier and establishing sexual relationships of various kinds between persons who are not age peers. Perhaps she is dealing with the breakdown of less threatening taboos.

The selections in this chapter on the family once again stress the tremendous range of differences among older people. We are reminded that stereotypes are often not based on data and that no single, simple, perfect solutions exist. Further, an accurate description of today's older people will not necessarily be accurate for succeeding generations. This chapter contains many ideas that can be used for future research into the family lives of older people.

Integration and Family

Peter Townsend

Sharing a Household   A large part of this report is concerned with contacts between old people and their families. Are old people isolated or integrated? What are the tests of involvement with family—in the sense that they participate in the activities of the extended family? These seem to be sharing a household, geographical proximity, frequency of family contacts, and the exchange of services. First, sharing a household. From a fifth to a quarter of the elderly in the three countries live alone, and another one-third to one-half live as married couples on their own. But substantial minorities—27 per cent in Denmark, 45 per cent in Britain, and 35 per cent in the United States—live with others, mostly with unmarried or married children and brothers or sisters. Of those with children 20 per cent in Denmark, 42 per cent in Britain, and 28 per cent in the United States live with at least one of them. Rather more than half of these are living with unmarried children.

Family Proximity   Second, geographical propinquity. Of those with children there are, in addition to those who live with them, another 55 per cent in Denmark, 40 per cent in Britain, and 49 per cent in the United States who live within 30 minutes journey of one or more of their children. Altogether, three-quarters or more of old people with children live with, or within 30 minutes journey of, at least one of their children.

Frequency of Family Contacts.   Third, frequency of contacts within the family. The number of old people with children who report seeing a child the same day or the previous day is 62 per cent in Denmark, 69 per cent in Britain, and 65 per cent in the United States. Around another fifth report seeing a child within the previous week. In all

From *Old People in Three Industrial Societies*, chapter 14, by Shanas et al., Aldine Publishing Company, 1968. Reprinted by permission of the publisher and Peter Townsend.

three countries the great majority even of old people living alone have frequent contacts with their children; more than half report seeing a child the same day or the previous day and more than another quarter within the previous week. Again, from a third to nearly two-thirds of those living alone report staying with children overnight during the previous year; and rather smaller proportions report children staying overnight with them. Altogether more than a third of old people with brothers and sisters report seeing at least one within the previous week. Contacts with siblings are more frequent among those persons who lack children or who do not see their children weekly or daily.

Exchange of Family Services   Fourth, exchange of services. Our data take two forms—answers to general questions about patterns and kinds of help and answers to specific questions about source of help during a previous illness and with certain everyday personal and household tasks. From rather less than a half to substantially more than a half of old people in Britain and the United States report giving help to their children and grandchildren, including money gifts as well as such types of help as housekeeping services. Around two-thirds report receiving help from their families, including regular and occasional money allowances or gifts. Considerably fewer old people in Denmark, though still a substantial minority, report such services. In illness from a third to two-fifths rely for help with housework, meals, and shopping upon husbands or wives and a similar proportion upon children or other relatives. In all countries a considerable minority rely on children or other relatives outside the household as the main source of help. Only from a fifth to rather more than a quarter of the old people in the three countries rely on persons or agencies outside the family, such as social services, or have no source of help. Over a range of everyday personal and household tasks—for example, housework, meals, shopping, bathing, and dressing—the great majority of those old people who experience difficulty rely on husbands and wives, children, and other relatives for assistance. Between 8 and 9 in every 10 of the bedfast at home depend primarily on members of their families for meals, housework, personal aid, and so on.

Modifications of Theory   These were the principal measures of family involvement that we developed. We would not pretend that they are comprehensive. In various respects the data are limited. We are unable, for example, to explore the content or quality of family "contacts" and the total role and extent of extra-familial activities in relation to familial activities. We believe, however, that the statistical evidence cross-nationally of "integration" is sufficiently formidable to demand modification of much existing theory about the extended family and the relations between generations in industrial society. It also provides a useful framework for theories about the social process of aging.

Family Structure Integration, however, is neither universal nor consistent. There is great variety among the aged. A major thesis of this report is that family structure influences the organization and geographical distribution of the extended family and its sub-groups, and the character and intensity of different types of individual relationships. How could the family structure of the elderly be described? The survey showed that nearly a fifth of the elderly in Denmark and the United States and nearly a quarter in Britain are single or otherwise childless. Yet between a fifth and a seventh of those with surviving children have six or more. Around 90 per cent of those with children have grandchildren; and 23 per cent in Denmark and Britain, and 40 per cent in the United States, have great-grandchildren. Around 80 per cent of the elderly have surviving brothers and sisters, some of them five or more.

Diversity of Structure One important feature of the family structure of the aged in industrial society is its diversity. At one extreme there are from 3–5 per cent of the elderly, most of whom are single or widowed, who lack children and brothers and sisters. At the other extreme there is a large minority who have grandchildren and great-grandchildren as well as at least two children. Most of these old people also have surviving brothers and sisters. In Britain, for example, as many as 5 per cent of old people have five or more brothers or sisters *and* five or more children. The old person may therefore have no kin at all, or he may be knitted into a complex network of surviving kin spanning several generations.

Four Generations A second important feature of family structure is its frequent extension to the fourth generation. That the four-generation family is already a *common* phenomenon in industrialized societies is one of the more surprising facts to emerge from the cross-national survey. From a half to three-fifths of all old people in the three countries belong to an immediate family structure of three or four generations and also have more than one surviving child. These persons might be said to have good potential family resources for help in old age. Another fifth have resources in depth over two, three, or four generations, but either they have only one child, or, if they have two or more children, they lack grandchildren.

Sons or Daughters A third feature of family structure that we found to be important was the large proportion of "families" of children who are males only or females only. From a fifth to a quarter of the elderly have a single child. Around another fifth have families consisting of two or more sons or two or more daughters only.

Structure and Organization   How does family structure affect household composition? For example, we found that compared with widowed persons those who are married more commonly maintain households independent of married children. Single persons more often share a household with a brother or sister than do widowed persons—even than widowed persons who are childless. Widowed persons with sons only are more likely to be found living alone than widowed persons with daughters only. Divorced persons compared with widowed persons are less often found living with their children.

Structure and Geographical Distribution of the Family   Fewer widowed than married persons live at considerable distances from their children. The fewer the children, the more likely it is for old persons to be found living further than 30 minutes journey from their nearest child. This is much as one might expect. But the distribution by family size is by no means random. Children in small families tend to compensate. The chances of an only child's living with or near an old person, for example, are found to be much greater than those of an eldest or youngest or, at least for Britain, of any other child ranked in age-order. The sex of children has some but not a marked effect on family proximity. Although a higher proportion of nearest daughters than of nearest sons in Britain and the United States are to be found living in the same household as a parent, the difference is largely canceled out by the higher proportion of nearest sons than of nearest daughters who are living within 30 minutes journey of the old people. And in Denmark the differences in geographical distribution between sons and daughters are small. On a broad cross-national basis, then, there is no evidence of marked matrilocal family organization.

Structure and Individual Relationships within the Family   More of the widowed than the married, more of those with several children than with one child only, and more of those with daughters than with sons only, are found to have seen at least *one* child the previous day. Even when children live at comparable distances, contacts with daughters are found to be more frequent than contacts with sons. However, the difference between sons and daughters in their contact with parents is less marked than previously anticipated, and a large proportion of old people clearly have frequent contacts with at least one of their sons.

Structural Compensation   One important finding was the operation of a principle of compensation or substitution in family organization, distribution, and relationships. More widowed than married old people of comparable age live with single children. We would suggest that children sometimes postpone marriage if a father or mother, particularly a father, dies during their adolescence or early adulthood. Children in small families tend to live closer to and see more of their parents than do children in large families. Again, people without children see more of their siblings than do people with both children and siblings. Finally, those who do not share a household with a child tend to live near at least one of their children. This form of family compensation is particularly noticeable in Denmark, the country that has the lowest proportion of older persons living with children.

Structure and Social Norms   Such findings suggest a structural explanation for inconsistencies between existing patterns of family organization (including household composition), family "distribution" or family contacts, and social norms. The integrity of marriage is respected, partly by recognizing the right of a married couple to live in an independent household. Social distance between the adult generations is also observed. But it is the responsibility of adult children to provide comfort and care during a parent's infirmity or upon his or her bereavement. Preferment is given in family organization and management to relations with daughters over relations with sons. Preferment is given in relations with children over relations with siblings but if people do not marry, or if they marry and do not have children, relations with siblings can be maintained throughout life—especially if these siblings are childless or single.

Social Class and Family Relations   What effect has social class on family structure and relations? In this survey occupation was used as a rough indicator of class position and the elderly population was divided into four categories: white collar, blue collar, service workers, and agricultural workers. Compared with the elderly belonging to working class groups ("blue collar" and "service workers"), fewer belonging to middle class (or "white collar") occupations share a household with children or live within 10 minutes journey of them, and more of these middle class persons live further than one hour's journey distant. In Britain and the United States fewer middle class persons report seeing a child the same day or the previous day and slightly more report not seeing any child for more than a month.

Class Differences in Family Structure   The above statements of differences between middle class and working class elderly in their family relations have to be strongly qualified for two reasons. First, there are differences in marital status and size and *structure* of family between the classes, which to some extent "explain" differences in family relationships. Compared with working class old people (that is, those formerly belonging to "blue collar" and "service worker" categories), more middle class old people are single or childless or have only one or two children. Fewer have a surviving daughter and fewer have several surviving children. Fewer in Britain and the United States, but not in Denmark, are widowed. All this suggests why fewer of the middle class than of the working class elderly share households with children. Fewer among the middle class have a fourth, a fifth, or a sixth child who was born late in life and who is only now reaching the usual marrying age, and fewer are widowed and therefore fewer are likely to live with a married child in old age. These differences also suggest why the interdependence of the elderly middle class man and wife tends to be contrasted in sociological studies of family and community with the close relationship between daughter and elderly working class parent, particularly mother.

Similarity Between Classes in Family Relations Second, the difference between middle class and working class elderly in their family relations is far smaller than is generally supposed—at least in terms of the rough indices adopted in this study. Although there is a tendency for more working class than middle class elderly to live with or near at least one of their children, nevertheless the over-all differences between the classes in frequency of contact and patterns of help are small. For example, the percentages of persons of "white collar" background who share a household with a child or report seeing one the same or the previous day are 60 in Denmark, 62 in Britain, and 61 in the United States. The comparable percentages for persons of "blue collar" background are 59, 71, and 65 respectively. There are, indeed, indications that more of the elderly from "white collar" than "blue collar" backgrounds have certain kinds of relationships with their children. For example, more stay overnight with their children and more have children to stay with them during a year. In Britain and the United States more give help to their children and grandchildren, though about the same proportions *receive* help from their children.

The Family Relations of Farmers and Farm Workers In all three countries more persons from a background of agricultural work than from a background of "blue collar" or "white collar" work are likely to report seeing their children the same or the previous day. This class difference is fairly pronounced for Denmark, where a much larger proportion of the former category than of the latter two either live in the same household with children or have seen them the same or the previous day. The difference between those with agricultural and other backgrounds is not so pronounced as is commonly assumed.

Integration, Social Services, and Formal Associations

Functions of Social Services It is often supposed that in the course of time social services and other formal organizations and associations have "taken over" the functions previously performed by the family and the local community and that as a result many of the elderly live in a kind of comfortable seclusion provided by the health and welfare services, special housing services, and clubs and centers—or, in short, by "the Welfare State." This is a misrepresentation of social change. In some important respects these services and associations integrate the elderly into society by supplementing, or substituting for, the informal services and activities of the family. They may, for example, furnish expert professional help which the family cannot supply, or help persons who lack families altogether. Theorists who have postulated the loss of functions by the family, the dispersion of the extended family, and the segregation of the aged during urbanization and industrialization tend to discount such positive developments.

Services for Those without Families The information about aid that was collected in the cross-national survey had to be limited in scope, but we found that the community social services are concentrated overwhelmingly among those who have neither the capacities nor the resources to undertake the relevant functions alone and that these services primarily reach those people who lack relatives or who have only slender family resources. Of the 4–6 per cent in institutions in the three countries, from a third to over a half are in a hospital. Institutionalized persons tend to be people of advanced age, many of whom are 80 and over. In the United States and Britain, for example, about two-fifths are aged 80 and over. A disproportionately large number of them are single or widowed. Of those receiving domiciliary services we also found, at least in Britain, that a disproportionately large number are moderately or severely incapacitated, live alone, and are single or, if married or widowed, childless. The evidence therefore suggests that the social services tend to complement rather than replace informal community and family associations and that they tend to reach those in genuine "need." But the total role of the domiciliary and residential social services is small. The number of old people actually helped in their housework, provision of meals, and care during illness is dwarfed by the numbers being helped by husbands and wives and relatives. The services are also generally acknowledged to be functionally inadequate.

Older Families and Their Troubles: Familial and Social Responses

Gordon F. Streib

The assertion is frequently made that the American family is declining. One piece of evidence offered is that the American family is not meeting its traditional obligations, particularly in the care of its older members. The idea that the family alone should be primarily responsible for the health and welfare of older persons is a vestigial attitude from an earlier historical period. The conception of the family as an autonomous social unit which is supposed to solve all of the basic problems of living is, in some ways, a carry-over of thinking about the family retained from the agrarian and early phases of industrialization.

Many families do have considerable autonomy, and this is a goal desired by most family units. However, when we consider the family in the latter part of the life cycle, there is a need to rethink the notion of the autonomous family—independent, self-regulated, and able to take care of itself as a group. Family autonomy and independence are very congruent with American goals and values in the spheres of the political, the economic, and the educational. But family autonomy must be more than a shibboleth, particularly when one studies families in trouble at any stage of the life cycle. Independence and autonomy may be desired by families, but in reality they are sometimes hard for some families to attain, particularly under conditions of economic or medical crisis at the end of life. It is during the latter phases of the life cycle that some notion of shared function must be brought into the analysis of the situation of older families and into the thinking of persons involved as practitioners with older families.

What is the theory of shared functions? It is the notion that formal organizations and families must coordinate their efforts if they are to achieve their goals. The idea of shared functions was developed by Eugene Litwak who with several colleagues explicated and tested the implications of the theory in a series of stimulating papers. (Litwak, 1965; Litwak and Meyer, 1966; Litwak and Figueira, 1968; Litwak and Szelenyi, 1969)

The ways in which bureaucratic structures and family groups are articulated is a crucial matter in urban-industrialized societies. Although the theoretical analysis is still incomplete and many of the applications must be worked out, the basic idea of shared functions is sound.[1]

This paper will explore some of the ways in which various kinds of primary groups and bureaucratic organizations may share functions in meeting problems or crises which older families face. Bureaucracies are social structures which have an instrumental basis for operation, emphasize impersonality, are organized on the basis of formal rules, and stress professional expertise. On the other hand, a family as a prototype of primary groups is characterized by face-to-face contacts, employs affective bases for judgments, stresses diffuse demands and expectations, and so on.

One primary assumption which needs to be emphasized is that family groups and bureaucratic organizations are not to be considered in competition with each other. The two types of structures have multiple goals and tasks which in many instances may overlap. Furthermore, it is assumed that the family has not "failed" when it utilizes formal organizations for assistance. There is a range or a continuum of groups from a "pure" primary group—the nuclear family—to the monocratic bureaucracy, and there is a variety of mixed types of groups or organizations which may be located on the continuum.

There are writers who describe the United States as a post-industrial society (Bell, 1967), and there are others who write about American society as being in the mature—not the developmental—phase, of industrialization. (Litwak and Figueira, 1968) Clearly a society whose urban-industrial structure is as developed as is that of the contemporary United States is markedly different from the society emerging at the turn of the century or even the society which America's senior citizens lived in just a generation ago at the beginning of World War II. Technology has changed; some phases of private and governmental bureaucracies have changed, and primary groups—such as the family—are changing. But as Litwak and Szelenyi state: "It would be an error to say that, because a primary group structure changes from one stage of historical development to another, it is moving to destruction." (Litwak and Szelenyi, 1969, 480)

Two Kinds of Families: Residential and Extended

One of the first steps which is necessary in order to understand the notion of shared functions is to clarify what is meant by the family. A major distinction must be made between: (1) the residential family or the family in which one lives, and (2) the extended family or the kin network to which a person belongs by blood ties or marriage.

Residential families are diverse because of their intrinsic structure and also because of two other important considerations, age and sex. Whether a person is 65 or 85 makes a great deal of difference in

The Family

terms of family relations and the need for assistance. Sex is a factor because of the differential death rates; the proportion of widowhood is much greater among women than among men. About ten percent of the men in the age category 65 to 69 are widowed, in comparison to 38 percent of the women. (Riley et al., 1968) Considering all persons over 65, about a fifth of the males are widowers and about half of the women are widows. This means that a man is much more likely to have another person in his household to help in times of trouble or crisis, while a woman is more likely to need to turn to outsiders or bureaucratic organizations for assistance.

Most older people—70 percent of men and women over 65—live in families (living arrangements) with two or more members. Twenty-one percent of older persons over 65 live alone and only four percent live in institutions or other kinds of group quarters. (Riley et al., 1968)

A more detailed examination of the kinds of persons who live in a household of one person accentuates the differentiation by sex: only sixteen percent of the males compared to 32 percent of the women live in households entirely alone or with nonrelatives. (Riley et al., 1968) These proportions increase for subcategories of the older persons, for living alone is a characteristic of the later rather than the earlier phases of the life cycle.

An examination of the facts about kin networks in Table 1 shows that the great majority of older persons in the United States belong to kin networks of three or four generations. A nationwide survey conducted by Shanas and her associates revealed that about one older person in five was a part of a one generation kin network and almost one-third of the older persons in the United States were members of three or four generation networks.

Thus the analysis of the older family in situations of trouble and stress encompasses a tremendous variety of family structures based on the variation in residential types of families and the way they are not tied in with kin networks of varying complexity. There are, for example, three generation families living in one household, older couples with young children, single-person families, and newly-weds

Table 1 Kin Networks of Older Persons in the U.S.

Number of Generations in Family	Percentage of Older Persons
One	18
Two	6
Three	44
Four	32
Total number of families	2,436

Source: Shanas, et al., 1968, 143.

Older Families and Their Troubles

in post-retirement families, to mention a few of the variations. Thus it is important to stress: there is no "typical family" in later life, for there are many patterns.

This great variation in family structures and relations is the result of a complicated set of factors and of decisions which go back much earlier in the life cycle. To understand those families which are most vulnerable, have the fewest resources to draw upon, and probably require the most attention from health and other helping agencies, one must realize that many of these families have been limping along through most of life. In addition, there are some families which are in trouble for the first time in later life. Many families which have met the vicissitudes of child rearing, have dealt successfully with intermittent economic distress, and have been able to solve previous medical emergencies now find the dilemmas of later maturity too much of a challenge to cope with.

Family Resources and Family Problems

Attention to the major factors that create problem families in later maturity follows. There are four major resources which contribute to the strength of older families. They are:

1. Physical health
2. Emotional health
3. Economic resources
4. Social resources—family, kin, friends.

The interrelationship between these four factors is very complex, as one can see in Table 2, and the absence of one or more can bring about severe dislocation in the life of the older person. On the other hand, an abundance of any of the resources can greatly alleviate the stress caused by the absence of the others. For example, a warm, supportive family can help to ease the crises caused by failing physical and emotional health, and assist in supplying economic resources.

Table 2 Family Resources and Problem Proneness in Older Families

	Resources			
Family Types	Physical Health	Emotional Health	Economic Resources	Social Resources
I "Strong"—"Organized"	+	+	+	+
II	−	+	+	+
III	−	−	+	+
IV	−	−	−	+
V "Weak"—"Disorganized"	−	−	−	−

An examination of five types of families in terms of these major resources follows. Type I, the Golden Sunset Family obviously is not the concern of this paper. Fortunately, they constitute a significant number of older families in this society. These are the people in good health and spirits with a comfortable pension, warm family relations and friends.

At the other extreme are the "unfortunate families" who end their years in misery—the Totally Deprived. These families are the ones who present the most serious crisis in old age—indeed, many of them are in institutions for they lack *any* of the basic resources needed to meet their needs. When people talk about the family and a care crisis, it is this type of "family" that they have in mind, and from their knowledge or acquaintance of such tragic types, they may assume that there are more of these families than really exist. Between these two polar types there is a variety of combinations: in all there are sixteen different combinations considering the four resources.

An important and interesting question is how many families are there of the various types referred to in Table 2? At the present time only a rough estimate can be made of the numbers and proportions of the various types by fitting together items of information on single variables and isolated characteristics. A crude estimate is that about a quarter of the older population are "privileged aged" and about a half are "typical aged" and the remaining proportion, roughly 25 percent, are the "needy aged."[2]

These estimates are based upon facts of the following kind: About 95 percent of the United States' older population lives in the community, and of those who do about nine out of ten are ambulatory and perhaps two percent are bedfast. (Shanas et al., 1968, 24) Moreover, among the older persons living at home almost two-thirds scored zero on an incapacity scale; that is, they could perform six basic tasks without difficulty.

The economic resource variable is probably the one that has been surveyed more often and with greater precision than the others. For example, a recent U.S. Senate Committee reported that one out of every four individuals 65 and older lives in poverty. (Special Committee on Aging, U.S. Senate, 1971, 3) Poverty, like other characteristics, is differentially distributed in the population, for the same Senate document reported that among the elderly women who live alone about one-half fall below the poverty line; and the non-white older females are especially disadvantaged.

Another way to index economic resources is by the ownership of property. About two-thirds of the aged own their own homes, and of these thirteen million plus older American homeowners about 80 percent own their homes free and clear. Moreover, over six and half million (about 50 percent of the homeowners) have an equity of $25,000 or more in their homes. (Special Committee on Aging, U.S. Senate, 1971, 29)

Social resources are more difficult to ascertain than financial resources. What indices of social resources should one utilize? Presence or absence of children? Siblings? Neighbors? Membership in organizations? The presence of facilities like the telephone, radio, or television which may increase one's social contacts with the wider world? For example, about a third of the aged never married or have no living children.

The psychic or emotional resources are probably the most difficult resource to estimate. Gurin and associates in a nationwide survey of America's mental health, using five questions, found that among persons 55 and over about 27 percent reported themselves as "very happy," 55 percent as "pretty happy," and 18 percent as "not too happy." (Gurin et al., 1960) The same national survey found that if one employs "worry" as an index of emotional health, the elderly report themselves as not worrying any more than younger categories of the population. About a third of the persons over 55 years of age say they "worry a lot" or "worry all the time."

How can these complicated variables be grouped together into clusters or types? In a nationwide urban survey of males 60 and over conducted some years ago, four variables were grouped together in order to determine how health, socioeconomic status, and whether a person was working or retired were related to morale. (Streib, 1956) The three independent variables had a cumulative effect upon morale. For example, among those who were retired, in poor health, and had a low socioeconomic status 71 percent had low morale. Conversely, among the men who were employed, in good health, and had a high socioeconomic status, only 25 percent had low morale. And between the extreme categories low morale varied according to whether a positive or negative factor was present.

Some persons have argued that the way to solve the problems of families in old age is to give them more money. Yet they forget that some people can be rich in economic resources and poor in some of the other factors that make life meaningful. Some readers will recall the news accounts of the "richest girl in the world" who spent a recent Christmas sick in a luxury hotel suite in San Francisco and alone except for an entourage of servants. If one is to believe news reports, her circle of friends and relatives is small, she is in poor physical health, and she is unhappy. Yet she has tremendous economic resources at her command.

The most elusive and most difficult resource to identify and measure is the emotional or psychological health of the individual. Just as one person may have immense financial resources and lack the other three, there are some old persons who are lacking in health, financial and social resources and yet have sufficient psychological and emotional resources. These are the kinds of older people whom Dr. George Reader of the Cornell Medical School has described as performing the Indian rope trick for they seem to be able to function without any visible means of support. (Reader, 1969, 312) These people who sometimes come to the attention of public and private agencies are in very poor physical health, exist in dire poverty, have no family or friends—in fact, seem to be totally lacking in resources. Yet they seem to be able to remain cheerful and can cope with life—in short, they possess an abundance of the elusive factor of emotional resource which somehow enables them to integrate their lives. Dr. Reader said it was a source of amazement to some medical students that such people could even survive. Just as the Indian *fakir* seems to defy the laws of gravity, so these deprived persons seem to defy all the rules and generalizations of social workers and sociologists about the basic resources needed to maintain an integrated life, for somehow they are able to cope.

This schematic presentation obviously leaves out the variations in resource level which must be considered in analyzing the diverse kinds of families. The easiest resource to measure in an objective sense is money; however, the way in which a given set of financial resources is perceived and utilized by older people varies considerably. Streib and Schneider summarized the situation in their longitudinal study of 2000 retirees: "Thus a given amount of income might be considered plentiful by one retiree while the same amount would represent dire poverty to another. The amount of income an individual receives may not be as important as whether he thinks it is 'enough'." (Streib and Schneider, 1971, 82)

Profiles of Families in Trouble

There is another aspect of families in stress situations which requires some analysis, namely, the way in which families respond to difficulties which confront them. This complicated subject is the central focus of a book, *Families in Trouble*, by the sociologist, Earl L. Koos. (Koos, 1946)

In 1946, Earl L. Koos published an imaginative study, based on his field work with lower class families in New York City. He lived and worked closely for two years with 62 families who resided in one tenement block north of the Cornell Medical Center. Although Koos did not specifically focus his attention on gerontological phenomena, there are several aspects of his study which are very pertinent to understanding older families. In the course of his work, Koos made a judgment of what he called the "level of organization" of the families.

He emphasized that he tried to utilize an internal standard used by the families themselves; that is, he did not set down criteria of what was normative for families in American society. The organization or adequacy of the family were considered in terms of the following: "(1) There must be a consciousness of an acceptance by each member of his and of the complementary roles in the family; (2) family members must have a willingness to accept the common good of the family over their own good; (3) the family must provide satisfactions with the family unit; (4) the family must have a sense of direction and be moving in keeping with this, to however small a degree." (Koos, 1946, 33) Koos classified his families into three rough categories according to these organizational criteria with about half the families classified as "average" in their adequacy and about equal proportions of his sample above or below average.

The 109 troubles which these low income families faced comprise a familiar catalogue of difficulties; about a third were financial and about a third of the troubles resulted from illness. (Koos, 1946, 63) There were some problems which resulted from pregnancies (a source of difficulty which most gerontologists do not have to be concerned about very often). Educational problems, alcohol, sexual incompatibilities, and family conflicts were other sources of difficulty.

One aspect of Koos' study which is pertinent to this analysis is the graphic means by which Koos depicted the way in which families coped with their troubles, (Koos, 1946)[3] (See Diagram 1.)

On Profile A the normal interaction and operation of the family is shown roughly by the line a–b in the diagram. The descent into difficulty is depicted by the line b–c and the recovery period is represented by the angle of recovery e. The plateau of recovery is depicted by the line d–f.

The families can be divided into four profile types, according to their response to problems. (Koos, 1946) Profile A represents those families which, after the trouble, returned to the same level of organization they had attained before the onset of the difficulty. Profile B was a kind observed in only one case in which the family attained a higher level of family cohesiveness after the trouble than they had experienced before the trouble. Profile C is the kind observed in about 60 percent of the troubles. In this profile the families never recovered fully after the trouble. Finally about 20 percent of the families exhibited profile D in which the families experienced what Koos called "incomplete recovery" in that a second or third trouble eroded the family's level of organization so that it suffered additional assaults from which it was not able to recoup its earlier level of integration.

How does the work of Koos shed light upon the study of older families? First, it should be reiterated that many of the troubles of these lower class families originated in health and financial matters.

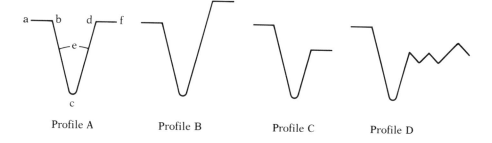

Diagram 1 Family Recovery Profiles

This is a familiar story to those who study or assist families in the later part of the life cycle. Secondly, it should be noted that many of the families had erratic recovery patterns. These profiles are the kind which can be observed in many older families, because the later years are often characterized by a continuing series of troubles: economic, health, and social. Important role losses result from the death or incapacity of friends and relatives. Declining health is the situation for many persons. And financial difficulties resulting from sharp cuts in income upon retirement and the persistent, glacial-like erosion caused by inflation increase economic insecurity and make life a period of trial and tribulation for many. Thirdly, the way in which families cope with difficulties in later life are like the families in Koos' study in that the recovery profile can be best understood as a process and not as an event. Families do not miraculously find ways to deal with their difficulties. They encounter troubles because of their environmental pressures and also because of the resources which they can marshal and which have been a part of the family's capital for some time.

Finally, the way in which families recover from crises is related to their previous level of organization. The previous level of family integration is a key to explaining the recovery period. The families that had profile A, in which they recovered to their previous level, were those who were "average" or "above-average" in the pre-trouble period, and the families who had profiles C and D were often those whose pre-trouble organizational level was "below average," although a substantial proportion of "average" families also exhibited profile C.

The significance of the pre-trouble organizational level is very important in older families. It will be recalled that one dimension of the family's organizational level was the willingness to accept the common good of the family over the personal wishes of individuals. Therefore it would be rather unlikely that a family which has been pulling in

Older Families and Their Troubles

several different directions for 30 or 40 years will suddenly become integrated and accept a goal of the common good in later life. Adversity does bring friends, neighbors, and kin together, but momentary help at a point of trouble and sustained working for the common good is something quite different.

Another finding reported by Koos which is pertinent to older families is that the average number of friendships is correlated with the type of adequacy or integration of the family. The families with higher levels of adequacy also had a greater than average number of friendships. What is also of significance and is congruent with the idea of shared functions is that the "better than average" families had almost twice as many memberships in organizations as did families of "below average" level of integration.

Forms of Intervention and Older Families

To this point the analysis has centered on trying to clarify what is the nature of the family in relation to trouble and stress situations and to specify family types and the resources whose absence tends to create problems. The trajectories of the crisis process have also been described. In the following sections the discussion will focus on the forms of intervention and the way in which resources are employed in meeting troubles. The analysis of the intervention process illustrates how the theory of shared functions works out in practice. The articulation of family is very intricate and thus the following discussion will only highlight a few aspects as they pertain to older families.

The forms of intervention can be classified into three broad categories: (1) help and intervention by family and kin; (2) quasi-family or pseudo-family forms of intervention; (3) institutional or bureaucratic forms of intervention.[4] These categories are not mutually exclusive, but there is utility in considering them separately. The principal criterion employed to distinguish the three forms of intervention is the nature of the relationship between the person offering help and the recipient. Does the intervention agent have an ascribed kin relationship to the recipient? Or does he assume a pseudo-family role in the relationship? Or is the intervention agent acting as a bureaucrat?

The kinds of resources which the three forms of intervention may offer can encompass all of the four resources referred to earlier in the paper, namely, (1) health and medical, (2) emotional and psychological, (3) economic and financial, (4) social or interactional. For example, kinsmen may render nursing care; they may give financial help; and they may also be a source of social interaction and emotional support. Similarly, a government agency or several agencies can and do intervene and offer help which involves one or more and sometimes all of the four resources.

Family Help and Intervention

There is a great deal of popular writing and public discussion about the inadequacy and breakdown of the American family and its failure to meet the needs of older people in an industrialized society. An examination of documented studies presents a picture that is not as bleak or as dysfunctional as some persons assert. (Adams, 1968; Sussman, 1965)

For example, many Americans were moved by the studies made by Ralph Nader's investigators who reported the sad plight of many old people who seemed to be abandoned and forgotten in nursing homes, and perhaps the more so because the investigators were young females. But it would be inaccurate for Americans to hold a stereotyped picture that many older Americans are abandoned by their children. It will be recalled that eight percent of persons over 65 have never married. (Riley et al., 1968) Not all married persons have surviving children for of the non-institutional population over 65 about 25 percent do not have any living children. (Stehouwer, 1965)

What do research studies show concerning interaction of older families and their adult children? One almost universal finding from family studies in western society is summarized in the phrase offered by Rosenmayr and Kockeis, "intimacy at a distance." (Rosenmayr and Kockeis, 1963) Again and again in surveys, case studies, and from clinical observations one learns that old people wish to have continuous meaningful contact with their children and other kin, but they do not wish to reside in the same household. This is what is meant by "intimacy at a distance."

The form in which intimacy at a distance manifests itself has been clearly demonstrated in numerous studies which show that the great majority of older Americans who have children live within one-half hour driving distance of at least one child. Moreover, they see one another quite frequently. In the nationwide study conducted by Ethel Shanas and her associates 65 percent of the elderly in the sample had seen at least one child in the 24 hour period prior to the interview.[5] (Shanas et al., 1968)

George Rosenberg found in his recently published book about Philadelphians that 90 percent of his respondents had at least one primary or secondary relative living outside their household in metropolitan Philadelphia. (Rosenberg, 1970) And over 80 percent received a visit from at least one such relative in the seven days preceding the interview.

Older Families and Their Troubles

One aspect of the kin network interaction patterns of older persons is the well documented observation that there are mutual help patterns present in many older families. (Sussman, 1965) In the Cornell Study of Retirement, for example, it was found that more help in the form of baby sitting, home repairs, and help during illness flowed from the older generation to the adult child than vice versa. (Streib, 1958)

Another aspect of parent-child relations in old age which is rarely brought to public attention is the way in which *some* older parents exploit and tyrannize their adult children. An example is a case study known to the author. Mr. Jones, father of five children, is 82 and comfortably situated financially. As a businessman, he was accustomed to giving orders. When his wife died five years ago, he demanded that his 45-year-old bachelor son give up his job and move in to take care of him (he is in a wheel chair). This seemed a reasonable solution to all the children as Buddy did not like his job anyway. Thus he became Dad's nurse, being given an allowance of $50 a week, a new car, and free board and room. Now, five years later the arrangement is still continuing. Dad is completely satisfied and refuses to consider any other arrangement. *But what about Buddy?* When his father does finally die, what chance will he have to get a job again? To some old people this may sound like an ideal arrangement for Mr. Jones, but the cost to Buddy must be considered also.[6]

The crucial variable in this case is that the older person has enough money to buy this life style. A combination of an authoritarian personality and sufficient money enables him to enforce his wishes. Also, it must be emphasized that this example reveals as much about Buddy's personality as Dad's. Gerontological studies have tended to overlook the rights and needs of the adult children and have seemed to blame them if they do not work out an arrangement that keeps the aged parent happy and comfortable. There has not been enough attention to the needs of the adult children when a "crisis" extends for ten or fifteen years. But as medical advances extend life, there will be more and more persons living for several years when they are not necessarily "happy." And no amount of care and sensitive arrangements by a loving and concerned family can really solve this problem. (Goldfarb, 1965)

Quasi-Family Involvement

A further illustration of how the theory of shared functions operates in regard to older families is shown by the development of quasi- or pseudo-family types of intervention. Some of these programs may be supported by private or governmental agencies or organizations, but the nature of the relationship between the persons involved—usually older and younger—is that of a quasi-family relationship.[7] The persons act toward one another and assume the role of family members during the period of social contact. But they are not genuine family members. The name of one of the best-known of these programs indicates the quasi-family nature—Foster Grandparents. (Nash, 1968)[8] This program employs persons 60 and older to work in close association, on a one-to-one basis, with children in orphanages, schools for mentally retarded persons, and other institutional settings. There are other volunteer programs, such as SERVE, which are similar in their operation. (Sainer and Zander, 1969) The important aspect to stress here is the dual benefits through the creation of a warm family kind of relationship between the older persons and the children and young people they serve.[9] The program gives the older person a role in the community as a quasi-family member and at the same time the child receives the kind of love and attention that is essential for development.

There is a number of other programs which have been initiated in the last few years in which younger persons—usually teen-agers—take on a quasi-family role in relation to the older person.[10] Some of these have been started by Girl Scout troops. One program in New York State is operated in connection with a state training school for girls. In this instance the girls from the training school visit as "granddaughters" the residents of a nursing home who become "grandparents" to the girls. These programs, like those in which the initiative was taken by older persons, seem to have a very positive and enriching benefit for all who take part.

There is also a number of programs in some states which are operated in connection with the discharge of patients from mental hospitals. While these programs do not have a specific concern for the elderly, they often help older persons. (Cowne, 1970) In these programs a person may become a quasi-relative for the former patient so he can make a more satisfactory adjustment upon his return to his home community.[11]

Bureaucratic Intervention and Help

The theory of shared functions involves the notion that both primary groups and bureaucratic organizations are important for achieving a variety of tasks in American society. There are thousands of bureaucratic groups which are concerned with the health and welfare of older families in the United States. It would be a formidable task to even list the many public and private bureaucracies which offer services to older Americans. The Social Security Administration is the one bureaucracy which contacts the most older persons; the Veterans Administration, the Social and Rehabilitation Service, and the numerous health and welfare agencies which are in contact with thousands of older persons at the local, state, and national levels of government also offer a wide variety of services. In addition, the bureaucracies affiliated with educational, religious, health, and private charitable organizations provide hundreds of programs. It is clear why the problem of referral and coordination of bureaucratic services is a major need of older persons which must receive more attention in the near future.

In this section of the paper it is proposed to focus upon the ways in which the mass media of communication, particularly television and radio, may play a greater role in coordinating the work of bureaucracies by serving as information and referral agencies, and also by assuming a new role of offering emotional and interactional resources to older persons.

Why should the mass media be singled out as possible means of increasing the social resources and particularly the emotional health of older people? It is because these powerful omnipresent communications media of modern society already permeate the residential units of almost all Americans. A variety of statistical information points to the high degree of participation of persons over 65 years of age in the use of television and radio. For example, in a typical 24 hour day in which an older person spends approximately nine hours in sleep and six to seven in obligated time (eating meals, housekeeping, personal care) the next largest segment of time is devoted to leisure. Of this 6.5 hours of leisure, 2.8 is devoted to television. (Riley et al., 1968)[12]

Another way to obtain a picture of the leisure activities of older people is by a survey of 5000 OASI beneficiaries in four urban areas. In this survey it was found that 70 percent of the 5000 persons had watched TV a median number of three hours on the day preceding the survey. (Riley et al., 1968) In terms of the total number of hours involved, this activity engaged more time than any other leisure activity reported. No other leisure activity was reported by such a large percentage of older persons.

The attitude of many gerontologists is to deplore the fact that housebound older people spend so much time with the mass media. The author thinks that more attention should be given instead to making the media a positive mechanism for enriching their lives.

From many surveys that were conducted the last few months preceding the Second White House Conference on Aging, it was found that one of the prime needs of older citizens is the provision of transportation so they can attend meetings, religious services, go visiting, etc. Indeed it is important to develop cheap public transportation for old and young in this society. Given the fact, however, that local, state, and national legislative bodies are reluctant and even recalcitrant to take steps to deal with the complex problems in urban transportation, an auxiliary approach can be the more imaginative use of mass media—particularly local stations—as a means of informing and involving older people in programs and activities which are specifically geared to their needs and stage of the life cycle.

What kinds of programs might be developed which would offer a meaningful and realistic fare for America's older families? [13] These are suggestions based on limited present-day knowledge of the older population and which may be modified with increasing knowledge of the wishes of older viewers and a more precise understanding of the impact of various kinds of programs and services transmitted by television. For example, the content of more programs could be devoted to health and nutrition of the aged; the problems of inflation as it relates to social security, medical insurance, taxation—local, state, and national. There is a great range of programs which could be specifically geared to older ethnic, regional, and language audiences. Hobby shows and displays of arts and crafts could be offered. Reminiscing—what Dr. Robert Butler has called the "life review" could be more widely presented and also "meet the traveler" and historical programs. These are a few things which an amateur suggests. If the vast talents of the mass media were utilized, many other kinds of subjects could be discovered and developed into attractive programs. Local programs which involve the concept of a "Help Column," now found in many newspapers, might be used on television. Closely related to this kind of program would be some kind of ombudsman program which would mediate grievances of the elderly. There should be more attempts to involve the viewer into the local programs. In many places a large percentage of the aged have telephones so they could call in and easily participate in various kinds of programs.

It is essential to stress the nature of the electronic communication media in American society in their broadest social context—in their structure, their control, and their operations. In the minds of most people, the mass media are viewed only as an entertainment device and the main emphasis is upon programming to maximize the audience of viewers and listeners. It is necessary to broaden our expectation of what television can provide.

At the time when licenses for stations come up for review by the Federal Communications Commission, the owners of stations and the commission engage in a public minuet showing how they operate "in the public interest." However, this is sometimes a charade which masks completely the true operation of the electronic media in their singular neglect of the needs and interests of America's 20 million older persons. Local stations may point with pride to occasional interviews with the director of the local Senior Citizens Center or an occasional conversation with a prominent retiree or older person. Less frequently the networks may produce a documentary that bemoans the plight of one segment of America's older population. The impact of such programs in the short run is probably beneficial by focusing public attention for an instant on a severe, neglected social problem. However, the sustained concern and attention by the electronic media to the needs and interests of approximately ten percent of the population is minimal and niggardly.

Perhaps the primary reason for the studied neglect of America's older viewing families is the obvious fact that television and radio are primarily geared to selling goods and gadgets which America's older population either cannot afford or do not want. This tremendous concern with the huckstering of products to the maximum number of the youthful audience is a misuse of the airwaves which belong to all Americans, including its 20 million senior citizens. The very fact that older people do not have the money to purchase the products does not mean that their needs should be neglected. Older people are less mobile and thus cannot have the social contacts enjoyed by other segments of the population. This makes it even more imperative that relevant and useful materials are offered them—not merely to entertain them but to inform, to educate, and to give them some feeling of importance, worth, and dignity. The mass media can be their lifeline to the outside world and its more imaginative use can serve to inform them, inspire them, raise their spirits, and perhaps develop more feeling of community with other older persons. It can also direct them to the available bureaucratic services which are already provided but which, too often, they do not know about.

Summary

Both the analyst and the practitioner who is concerned with older families must be cognizant of the diversity of older families and their varying access to four major resources; physical health, emotional health, economic resources, and social resources. The accessibility and management of these resources may involve family members, kinsmen, and outsiders and for this reason the theory of shared functions is a useful analytical tool.

Generally speaking, older families are resourceful in coping with troubles. Available evidence indicates that younger family members also provide a great deal of help and assistance for older families. The picture of abandonment and neglect is not as bleak as is sometimes portrayed. However, a realistic assessment requires an understanding of the complexity of the troubles and their long-term nature and that individuals and family groups can only deal with *some* of the problems. For those who have no immediate kin or whose family members are too far away to help, the possibility for raising the level of family integration can be increased by quasi-family members. There are a number of exciting programs of this kind exemplified by Foster Grandparents, Foster Grandchildren, SERVE, and other kinds of quasi-family projects which are being developed in many communities. The present programs could be greatly expanded for they are still very limited in the number of persons who are involved, and their financial support is minimal.

Other developments which might contribute new psychic and social resources to older families involve better utilization of bureaucratic structures. One of the most challenging possibilities is to find new ways for the mass media of communication, particularly television and radio, to enrich the lives of older people who have less mobility and decreased social contacts than formerly. It can also inform them of the services available from the many agencies and organizations already designed to serve them.

Part of the neglect of ten percent of America's population, its older citizens, is due to the fact that commercial television is oriented to maximizing the sales of youth-oriented products and services. Older populations are neglected. There is little doubt but that the commercial networks and their affiliated stations should be made aware of their responsibilities to serve older families. The great amount of time and talent which is devoted to promoting products to young buyers can be rechanneled to serving older persons. Governmental bodies share some of the responsibility for the continued wasteland nature of television as it relates to older Americans.

There are also increasing opportunities—presently untapped— for educational television and for cable television to be more sensitive to the listening and viewing needs of older Americans. More attention should be given to using technology to serve *all* citizens—not just the youth. There is little doubt that many older people are in trouble and their burdens can be eased and their lives enriched—psychologically and socially—if the imagination, resources, and skills of the society are shifted to helping more older families.

There is now greater understanding that care of older families in trouble is not merely a private family burden. Other persons—nonfamily, quasi-family members, can visit and help on a volunteer basis as pseudo-family members. Finally, there must be greater recognition and utilization of the many services of bureaucratic organizations by older families if the United States is to become a more humane industrialized society.

References

Adams, Bert N. *Kinship in an Urban Setting*. Chicago: Markham, 1968.

Aging, Washington, D.C.: Administration on Aging, Department of Health, Education and Welfare.

Bell, Daniel. Notes on the Post-Industrial Society. *The Public Interest*, 1967, No. 7, 102–118.

Blenkner, Margaret. Social Work and Family Relationships in Later Life with Some Thoughts on Filial Maturity. In Ethel Shanas and Gordon F. Streib (Eds.) *Social Structure and the Family: Generational Relations*. Englewood Cliffs, N.J.: Prentice-Hall, 1965, 46–59.

Byron, Evelyn S. A Friendly Visiting Program. Case Study No. 13. Washington, D.C.: Special Staff on Aging, Department of Health, Education and Welfare, 1961.

Cowne, Leslie J. Approaches to the Mental Health Manpower Problem: A Review of the Literature. *Mental Hygiene*, 1969, 53, 176–187.

Cowne, Leslie J. Case Studies of Volunteer Programs in Mental Health. *Mental Hygiene*, 1970, 54, 337–346.

Cumming, Elaine. *Systems of Social Regulation*. New York: Atherton, 1968.

Goldfarb, Alvin I. Psychodynamics and the Three-Generation Family. In Ethel Shanas and Gordon F. Streib (Eds.) *Social Structure and the Family: Generational Relations*. Englewood Cliffs, N.J.: Prentice-Hall, 1965, 10–45.

Gurin, Gerald, et al. *Americans View Their Mental Health: A Nationwide Interview Study*. New York: Basic Books, 1960.

Hill, Reuben, et al. *Families Under Stress*. New York: Harper, 1949.

Koos, Earl L. *Families in Trouble*. New York: King's Crown Press, 1946.

Litwak, Eugene. Extended Kin Relations in an Industrial Society. In Ethel Shanas and Gordon F. Streib (Eds.) *Social Structure and The Family: Generational Relations*. Englewood Cliffs, N.J.: Prentice-Hall, 1965, 290–323.

Litwak, Eugene and Henry J. Meyer. A Balance Theory of Coordination Between Bureaucratic Organizations and Community Primary Groups. *Administrative Science Quarterly*, 1966, 11, 31–58.

Litwak, Eugene and Josefina Figueira. Technological Innovation and Theoretical Functions of Primary Groups and Bureaucratic Structures. *American Journal of Sociology*, 1968, 73, 468–481.

Litwak, Eugene and Ivan Szelenyi. Primary Group Structures and Their Functions: Kin, Neighbors, and Friends. *American Sociological Review*, 1969, 34, 465–481.

Mogey, John. Family and Communities in Urban-Industrial Societies. In Harold T. Christensen (Ed.) *Handbook of Marriage and The Family*. Chicago: Rand McNally, 1964, 501–529.

Nash, Bernard E. Foster Grandparents in Child-Care Settings. *Public Welfare*, 1968, 26, 272–280.

Reader, George. Group Discussion. Seminar: Geriatrics and the Medical School Curriculum. *Journal of the American Geriatrics Society*, 1969, 17, 312.

Riley, Matilda W., et al. *Aging in American Sociey*. New York: Russell Sage Foundation, 1968.

Rosenberg, George S. *The Worker Grows Old.* San Francisco: Jossey-Bass, 1970.

Rosenmayr, Leopold and Eva Kockeis. Propositions for a Sociological Theory of Aging and the Family. *International Social Science Journal,* 1963, 15, 410–426.

Rosow, Irving. Intergenerational Relationships: Problems and Proposals. In Ethel Shanas and Gordon F. Streib (Eds.) *Social Structure and The Family: Generational Relations.* Englewood Cliffs, N.J.: Prentice-Hall, 1965, 341–378.

Sainer, Janet and Mary Zander. Guidelines for Conducting a Viable Volunteer Program for Older Persons. Paper presented at the Eighth International Gerontological Congress, Washington, D.C., August 1969 (mimeographed).

Shanas, Ethel, et al. *Old People in Three Industrialized Societies.* London: Routledge and Kegan Paul, 1968.

Special Committee on Aging, United States Senate. *Developments in Aging—1970.* Washington: U.S. Government Printing Office, 1971.

Stehouwer, Jan. Relations Between Generations and the Three-Generation Household in Denmark. In Ethel Shanas and Gordon F. Streib (Eds.) *Social Structure and The Family: Generational Relations.* Englewood Cliffs, N.J.: Prentice-Hall, 1965, 142–162.

Streib, Gordon F. Morale of the Retired. *Social Problems,* 1956, 3, 270–276.

Streib, Gordon F. Family Patterns in Retirement. *Journal of Social Issues,* 1958, 14, 46–60.

Streib, Gordon F. and Clement J. Schneider. *Retirement in American Society,* Ithaca, N.Y.: Cornell University Press, 1971.

Sussman, Marvin B. Relationships of Adult Children with their Parents in the United States. In Ethel Shanas and Gordon F. Streib (Eds.) *Social Structure and The Family: Generational Relations.* Englewood Cliffs, N.J.: Prentice-Hall, 1965, 62–92.

Wray, Robert P. Projects in Gerontology. Appendix 3. In Rosamonde R. Boyd and Charles G. Oakes (Eds.) *Foundations of Practical Gerontology.* Columbia, S.C.: University of South Carolina Press, 1969, 255–261.

What's Ahead for Television. *Newsweek,* May 31, 1971, 72–79.

[1]The theory of coordination of groups has been developed by Litwak and Meyer (1966). Other writers have also been concerned with the subject. For example, John Mogey (1964) reviewed the literature and provided a valuable discussion. From a different perspective Elaine Cumming (1968) discussed systems of social regulation in one city, Syracuse, New York. Rosow has criticized Litwak's early work on the articulation of functions between family and bureaucracy. (Rosow, 1965)

[2]Bernice Neugarten made a distinction between the "needy aged" (a minority) and the "typical aged." See: *Aging,* No. 127, May 1965, 6.

[3]The utility of Koos' profiles is shown by the research of Hill and his associates. They studied the adjustment of families which were separated by the father's absence due to war service and they developed a large number of profiles to describe the 116 Iowa families. See: Hill *et al.,* 1949, 74–99.

[4]A fourth form of intervention is that initiated by the person himself. Psychotherapy and counseling with the individual person is, of course, an important kind of intervention.

[5]It should be noted that visiting and assistance patterns tell very little about the emotional or affective dimensions of the interaction. See, for example, Adams, 1968, for a discussion of the subjective aspects of kin interaction and the significance of filial obligation.

[6]A side issue to be mentioned in the kinship patterns is that research has shown that daughters give much more attention and support to their parents than do sons. Hence, the burden of care in crisis situations in most instances falls to the daughter in families with children of both sexes. (Blenkner, 1965, 51)

[7]For a list of a variety of research and community action projects, see Wray, 1969.

[8]For a descriptive account of the Foster Grandparent program see *Aging*, No. 130, August 1965; No. 136, February 1966; No. 137, March 1966; No. 139, May 1966; No. 141, July 1966; No. 142, August 1966; No. 144, October 1966; No. 163, May 1968; Nos. 180–181, October–November 1969.

[9]See *Aging*, No. 165, July 1968 and No. 170, December 1968.

[10]For examples of these kinds of programs see: *Aging*, No. 134, December 1965; No. 145, November 1966; No. 156, October 1967; No. 162, April 1968; No. 195, January 1971. There is also a number of programs which involve home visitors who help with shopping and transportation, act as interpreters, etc. See: *Aging*, No. 125, March 1965; No. 144, October 1966; No. 146, December 1966; No. 164, June 1968. For a more detailed account of one program, see: Byron, 1961. Other examples of pseudo-family kinds of intervention are foster homes for the aged (*Aging*, No. 126, April 1965) and meals-on-wheels. (*Aging*, No. 127, May 1965)

[11]In one program in California a "family agent" acts as a knowledgeable friend who cuts through red tape, gets in touch with agencies, etc. See: Cowne, 1969.

[12]It is important to point out that these figures were reported by Riley and Foner and their associates in their monumental study, *Aging and Society*, published in 1968. This thorough and carefully documented handbook of facts concerning the aged had to rely on surveys conducted in 1957 and 1958. These figures are an underestimation of the present utilization of television-radio by America's older families. A nation-wide survey of 1500 viewers recently conducted for *Newsweek* by the Gallup Organization reported the average household watches TV about six hours per day. (*Newsweek*, 1971, 73–74)

[13]Some years ago a series of 20 educational TV programs sponsored by the State University of New York was developed. The series was called "Living for the Sixties," and topics such as diet, exercise, social security benefits, etc., were included. The series was shown by Station WPSX of University Park, Pennsylvania and a few other educational TV stations. See *Aging*, No. 143, September 1966. For a description of a local radio program for older persons produced by a retired person see: *Aging*, Nos. 176–177, June–July, 1969.

Speculations on Innovations to Conventional Marriage in Old Age

Ruth Shonle Cavan

Research and discussion on innovations to satisfy the drive for self-actualization and reaching one's potential are focused on young adults. Similar needs of the old have been neglected. It is the thesis of this paper that old people have personal needs very similar to those of the young and that some of the innovations now being tried out by young people may be equally applicable to the old.

Some of the Crucial Needs, Desires, and Interests of the Old

We will assume that the physical needs of housing, food, and medical care are reasonably well supplied. My interest is in certain personal and emotional needs: sexual drive, dependence on younger kin, peer relationships, and inclusion in a family.

Interest in and capacity for sex continue after retirement. It was formerly considered that sex was unseemly for the old or that the drive died out entirely. Women, in particular, were thought to be sexless. However, studies by Gebhart (1971) supported by Masters and Johnson (1966), and others, indicate that interest and activity in sex continue past middle age but with decrease in urgency and frequency. Gebhart's study (1971) of 632 white women who were separated, divorced, or widowed shows that three-fourths of young divorced women had nonmarital coitus; at age 56–60, 43% were having coitus. Among widows, 42% of those in their early 20s had sexual contacts and 24% of those aged 56–60. Although there is a marked decline, it seems reasonable to assume that coitus would continue into older ages. Whether these were chance contacts or cohabitation is not shown.

Other studies show a desire for close contacts with younger kin, usually with adult offspring (Troll, 1971). The tie to grandchildren and siblings is less strong. When there are no biological kin, fictive kin may be found. The care given by institutions, pensions, and Medicare eases the trauma of old age but does not supply the feeling of emotional security and right to a dependent relationship that most old people (perhaps all people) need. However, neither old people nor adult

From *The Gerontologist*, Vol. 13, No. 4, Winter 1973. Reprinted by permission of the Gerontological Society and the author.

offspring crave joint residence, although they often wish to be near enough for visiting and mutual exchange of services.

The above need is complicated by a movement that will increasingly reduce the number of available offspring. This is the Zero Population Growth movement and the still newer National Organization for Non-Parents, whose slogan is None is Fun. The movement toward fewer children per family began long before the trend was dignified by a name and organization to support it. Old people who were involved in the early stages of these movements now find themselves with one or two children, whereas a larger number could more readily meet the financial and dependency needs of their parents.

The relation of the old to adult sons and daughters stretches over a generation gap. Old people need peers, whose experiences cover a historical period prior to the birth of adult children, such as World War I, the Great Depression, and industrialization (Shanas, 1971; Trela & Simmons, 1971). The peer relationship and the old-parent-adult-child relationship are not interchangeable. They supply different needs; they involve different areas of experience and they need not conflict.

Another need, not explicitly stated but derived from the above, is for a family relationship in a family with the main positions held by an elderly peer group.

To summarize, the unmet personal needs of the old include intimacy and sexual needs; desire for a dependency relationship with younger kin; for a peer group; and for family life with peers.

Do the Innovations Now Found among Young Adults Have Possibilities for Satisfying These Needs If Applied to the Old?

The innovations to be considered are nonmarital cohabitation, homosexual or lesbian companionships, group marriage, communes, and comarital contacts. All are attempts to adapt conventional marriage to modern social conditions or to enrich marriage. They are not alternatives to marriage as is often claimed. In fact, they protect monogamous marriage by providing a way for the deprived or discontented to find another type of intimacy that may be combined, if desired, with monogamous marriage.

The definition of these new developments of inter-sex relationships as supplemental to monogamous marriage and protective of it may make them more acceptable to old people, reared in a time when all except heterosexual monogamous marriage was regarded as sinful as well as illegal, than if they are defined as alternatives to legal monogamous marriage.

Research on innovations and discussion of their ethics has begun on young people but seem not to have reached older segments of the population. Therefore it must be emphasized that the remainder of this paper is purely speculative.

As stated above, one need of old people is for an intimate relationship (including sex for at least a minority) with someone of approximately the same age and of the opposite sex. Why not marriage? Why not ignore the prejudice that marriage of two old people is unseemly? The excess of old women cannot be absorbed through monogamous marriage. Polygyny has been suggested. Our culture is strongly opposed to plural marriage; in fact plural marriage is a criminal offense. To be effective, dignified, and satisfying, plural marriage would have to be legal, practiced openly, and approved by at least a strong reference group, if not the whole of society. It seems doubtful whether a change of this sort is likely to occur in the near future. It is worth remembering, however, that during the period when the Mormons practiced polygyny, a problem of excess women was thus solved with approval of the Church and a minimum difficulty among the plural wives. The polygyny of the Mormons was never legal, but was supported and controlled by the Church. It was abandoned only when the Church decreed that it should be, because of legal and social harassment.

Even when the sexes are balanced, financial objections to marriage may loom large. Some pensions are more adequate for two single people than for a married couple. Or offspring may oppose the marriage, fearing that some of their inheritance may be diverted to a new spouse. Some old people, no one knows how many, have begun pair cohabitation without marriage. Among the young, nonmarital cohabitation has gradually been accepted. Why not also for the old? Why not remove cohabitation for the old from the subrosa, even deviant, category and give it public approval? Cohabitation has advantages for the unmarried old: reinstatement of husband and wife roles, a home, a peer companion, and, if desired, sex relations. Thus many needs can be met in this new relationship without financial complications or lasting commitments.

Another solution for unmarried women is close companionship and sharing of a home by two or a small group of women. Many women, long before old age, have formed such households, which supply peer group companionship and also fulfill dependency needs especially in time of financial or physical stress. However, many sensitive women fear the accusation of lesbianism, even when the relationship is entirely platonic.

Women, even men, may be especially sensitive at this time when male homosexuals and lesbians are engaged in a strong movement to unite under the generic title of Gay Liberation Front. They push for social recognition as normal people and changes in laws that now, in every state except Illinois, make the practice of homosexuality and lesbianism a crime. If these two aspects can be reconciled and the automatic labeling of close one-sex friendships as homosexuals or lesbians removed, close companionships of old people—women especially—might increase and solve a serious problem.

Another innovation that has possibilities for the old is group marriage, defined as three or more persons in a committed relationship in which each feels married to all the others. They form a cooperative communal group. The relationship is very new and illegal; there are as yet few guidelines and there is no place for jealousy. In addition to providing for a variety of sexual contacts, the small groups fulfill the needs for a family group and peer companionship.

Group marriage may also be found in some communes, in which a somewhat larger group shares a total community life. In some communes marital status is strictly observed. In others, members may disregard marital ties and move freely from one partner to another of like mind. In both group marriage and some communes there is a place for the single person who seeks close companionship and sex and is willing to accept these on a shared basis. Most of the new communes are composed of young people. However, the idea has appealed to some old people and from time to time brief news items report old age communes.

Comarital relationships or mate-swapping or swinging also seems adaptable to the old. Some intimate relationships become stale with time but give enough satisfaction that the couple does not wish to dissolve them. Comarital relationships tend to be practices in small groups or clubs of couples that meet for social activities, followed by trading of spouses for sexual purposes, sometimes of an exotic nature (Denfield & Gordon, 1970). The swinging club is protective of marriage: it meets privately, conceals its activities from children, neighbors, and the police, and frowns upon any tendency of members to consistently pair off with the same person and thus threaten their marriage. At present it is an activity of middle-class, middle-aged adults. It seems to have possibilities for older people who wish to add variety and sparkle to their marriage. The relationship is too fragmentary to fulfill the need for peer group dependency.

What of the need for a mutual dependency relationship between the old and younger kin? If there are no younger kin or the contact has been lost, how can this need be met? From a practical approach to material needs, by social work agencies and institutional homes. For a personal relationship and sharing of personal concern and affection the answer is not simple. Fictive younger kin is one answer. The adult children of some close friend or the adoptive grandparent concept may fulfill the need.

Conclusions

Except as some of the innovations have existed in the past as scattered individual exploits, often carried on secretly, they are new. Most of them are illegal, often labeled immoral, and usually discussed in textbooks as deviancies. At present there is some movement toward a more tolerant public opinion.

Opinion polls show that approval of the innovations is chiefly on the part of the young, then by middle-aged people, and by only a few of the old. Disapproval by their own age group will no doubt impede the adoption of any of the innovations by more than a small number of the old. Approval may become more widely acceptable by the fact that the innovations do not advocate the destruction of legal monogamous marriage.

The innovations are still in a state of flux and adaptable to the needs of different groups. At present some of them emphasize sexual freedom—perhaps because they are being developed by young adults. Since most of them also include social or group living or activities, they should be readily adaptable to the interests of older groups searching for group living without the same emphasis on sex, but with permissiveness toward sex where desired.

References

Denfield, D., & Gordon, M. Mate swapping: the family that swings together clings together. *Journal of Sex Research*, 1970, 7, 85–99.

Gebhart, P. Postmarital coitus among widows and divorcees. In P. Bohannan (Ed.) *Divorce and after*. Garden City, N.Y.: Doubleday, 1971.

Masters, W. H. & Johnson, V. E. *Human sexual response*. Boston: Little, Brown, 1966.

Shanas, E. Sociology of aging and the aged. *Sociological Quarterly*, 1971, 12, 150–170.

Trela, J. E., & Simmons, L. W. Health and other factors affecting membership and attrition in a senior center. *Journal of Gerontology*, 1971, 26, 46–51.

Troll, L. E. The family of later life: A decade review. *Journal of Marriage & the Family*, 1971, 33, 263–290.

Economics 5

The selections in this chapter raise some major questions about economics and point out some of the intricate interrelationships among the various social institutions, such as between the political system and the family. They also deal with demographic facts that undergird many policy decisions facing industrial nations. In a broad sense, the major issues dealt with in this chapter are the social arrangements by which income and leisure are allocated throughout the individual's life cycle.

As James H. Schulz notes in "The Economic Impact of an Aging Population," reduced fertility and mortality rates have resulted in aging and aged populations. A nation is classified as having an aged population when 8 percent or more of the total population is over the age of sixty-four. The number of nations falling into this category has been increasing. Schulz poses two major questions about the results of an aging population upon systems: What effect does an aging population have on the ability and willingness of a working population to provide an adequate income for past working generations, for itself, and for future working generations? and How can the income be financed, both within and between generations? These issues are not only economic but are political and ideological as well. The solutions to both short-term and long-term economic problems have broad implications for generations now alive and for their descendants.

Population projections are rarely perfect, and many policy decisions must be based on tenuous predictions. Yet there is a close relationship between increased proportions of older people in industrialized societies and broad-scale public social welfare programs providing for older people. *Social security* is a general term for major programs geared toward some form of income maintenance for older people in the United States and in other industrial societies. In the United States a variety of programs are provided by the Social Security Act: retirement pensions, Medicare, survivor's benefits, and since January 1974, Supplemental Security Income. Currently the U.S. Social Security program is being debated. Questions are raised about its adequacy, its financial base, and its administration. Schulz deals with some of these questions and in the process presents some of the opposing viewpoints on our pension plans. He notes both Friedman's and Samuelson's views on social security and in addition discusses aspects of private pension programs. It is clear that for the majority of Americans, to be old means to be poor or at least to have an income markedly reduced from what one had when employed.

The significance of age as the basis for allocating positions is one of the fundamental questions concerning many gerontologists. The legality of using chronological age as the basis of compulsory retirement is of particular concern. As Erdman Palmore points out in "Compulsory Versus Flexible Retirement: Issues and Facts," mandatory retirement at a specific chronological age is an example of age discrimination. In addition, many people suggest that in our society work has a central meaning to people, and the separation of an individual, through retirement, from his or her job is a matter of great social significance.

Increasing evidence indicates that most people take retirement in stride, but a sizable portion of our population, including many gerontologists, believe that retirement is "bad" and that compulsory retirement is "doubly bad." Palmore discusses the pros and cons of compulsory and flexible retirement and comes down firmly on the side of flexible retirement.

It is clear from Palmore's article and from other sources that chronological age is a poor predictor of most functions. The fact that an individual is sixty-five is far less important in explaining behavior than is sex, social class, or marital status. The question is, what can be used as an accurate measurement of a person's abilities, particularly with reference to work, and what, if anything, can serve as universalistic criteria for moving people into and out of the society's system of jobs? The use of functional age is a preferable criterion, but it also has limitations. A major problem is that there are many functions, a number of which are hard to measure.

Postponement of entry into the market place until the middle or late twenties and institutional arrangements for exit in the early to mid-sixties thus becomes society's way of providing a number of new individuals with employment opportunities in a society with a surplus of labor. However, if demographic predictions are accurate, and if the costs of supporting large numbers of nonemployed adults becomes too great for the system to handle, people might retire at an older age. We can further expect that opposition to flexible retirement policies would dissipate and support of compulsory ones would decrease. As with the application of any universalistic criteria, however, there would continue to be people who want to work and cannot and people who do not want to work but must.

Palmore notes that approximately half of male wage and salary workers may be affected by current compulsory retirement regulations. Over the years the number of compulsory retirement programs in the United States has increased, raising questions about the legality of chronologically determined retirement. In addition to the age discrimination issue, the impact on the individual compulsorily retired concerns many. Others have discussed the hazards of a flexible retirement system. Do we know enough about the decision-making processes that would be involved in selecting who shall be retired and who maintained in jobs? A compulsory retirement system is universalistic, whereas a flexible one is subject to highly particularistic decision making. Regardless of which system is chosen—compulsory or flexible—a core of people will always be "caught between the grids" and dissatisfied. This is not to imply that it makes no difference what we do and what system we have; rather, we suggest that each system has some limitations.

The Economic Impact of an Aging Population

James H. Schulz

When persons speak about the aging of a population, they are generally describing a situation where the proportion of aged persons in the population is increasing. Such a definition is not completely unambiguous, however, since it neglects all other age structure shifts occurring—for example, as a result of changes in the relative proportion of the very young. But the numerous physical, social, and economic problems occurring among the older part of the population raise the question as to what impact demographic changes in the age structure of the population will have on these problems and their solutions.

Investigation has shown that

in the greater part of the world, the age structure [since the earliest recorded censuses] has undergone little change. This is particularly true of the economically under-developed countries, or rather, of all countries with a high fertility . . . The reduction of mortality, as it has occurred historically, has had little effect on the age structure (UN Dept. of Economics & Social Affairs, 1956).

The reduction of fertility, however, in the more developed countries has had a considerable impact.

From *The Gerontologist*, Vol. 13, Nos. 1–4, Spring 1973. Reprinted by permission of the Gerontological Society and the author.

This phenomenon of a population aging is relatively recent and restricted to a small but growing group of countries. Using the classification scheme developed by Rosset (1964), we can classify nations with 8% or more of their population over the age of 64 as having aged populations. Currently, there are over 20 countries meeting this criteria—about half of them with percentages greater than 12%.

As a result of past demographic history, the age patterns of these aged populations tend to have the shape of a barrel rather than a pyramid—as a result of the fact that there are relatively more middle-aged than young persons in the population. This middle-age bulge will grow older and result in increased aging of these nations, being relatively unaffected in the short run by changes in mortality or fertility levels.

In the long run, on the other hand, when the survivors of the present young generations reach old age, a decline in the numbers of the aged can be expected. Whether this decline in numbers will be accompanied by a reduction in the proportion of the aged depends, of course, on the fertility and mortality rates in the intervening period (UN Dept. of Economics & Social Affairs, 1956).

As an example of these developments, Figure 1 shows for the United States the projected ratio of the over 65 population to the 20 to 64 population. Reporting to the 1971 Advisory Council on Social Security (1971), a panel of American actuaries and economists stated:

Given benefit formulas, it is clear that the major problem for social security for the next 75 years will be demographic. In that period, the pattern of births during the past 60 years will produce major shifts in the ratio between the retired population and the gainfully employed. If births continue at the 1965-1970 level or stay in a range 10 percent above or below that level, the retired/active ratio will rise moderately for about 20 years, then decline somewhat more for a period of equal length of time and then rise steeply for still another 20 years. No change in either fertility or mortality of the magnitude experienced in the United States over periods of equal length in this century would reverse the direction of the retired/active ratio. . .

The Economic Problem Stated

When discussing the prospect that there will be a significant rise in the proportion of aged persons in various countries and that there will be rising welfare expenditures accompanying such a development—it is not uncommon for people to become concerned about the increased competition which they anticipate arising among differing age groups as they strive for larger shares of the nation's output. Today, around the world, social security systems—typically covering old-age, sur-

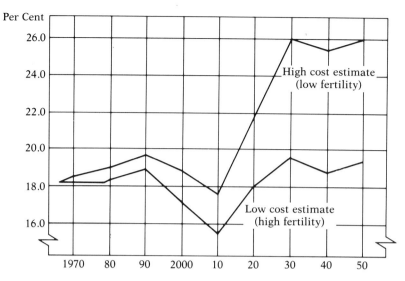

Figure 1   Source: United States Population Projections for OASDI Cost Estimates, Actuarial Study #62, 1966, p. 23. Reproduced in Reports of the 1971 Advisory Council on Social Security. Communication from the Secretary of Health, Education, & Welfare, 92nd Congress, 1st session. Washington: GPO, 1971, p. 94.

vivors, disability and health insurance—are the principal institutional mechanisms used to provide economic security to the retired aged. Such systems are viewed as devices for equitably (in greater or less degree) transferring income (hence output claims) to the aged from those persons in the active working population.

Thus, social security improvements often head the list of demands by the aged segment of the population, while being relatively unimportant to younger workers. But regardless of whether the mechanism for retirement income provision is social security, public assistance, private insurance, private charity, and/or self-help through the use of personal savings—the fundamental economic fact remains that the part of national output consumed in any particular year by the retired aged is produced by the working population. Institutional or cultural device(s) must be put into operation, therefore, to permit and facilitate some of the fruits of labor of the nonretired population to be consumed by those not working—both the very young and the retired aged.

Of course, old people are not the only population group claiming through public programs a share of the available goods and services. Education of the young, manpower programs, support for veterans, expanded preventive and treatment medical service for all ages, general poverty programs, and other general welfare programs in a sense compete with one another for shares of the gross national product.

The Economic Impact of an Aging Population

And to this competition might be added the competing claims of such non-welfare programs as environmental protection, housing and urban development, and transportation—all of which, for example, have become so important as to now justify separate and powerful agencies in the United States government.

It is these (and other) alternative uses of our output that cause people to talk about the competition between the young and the old (U.S. Senate Special Committee on Aging, 1970). Given the prospects for rising retirement income expectations in the future and a rising proportion of aged—together with rising perceived needs of other age groups—it is often suggested that a country will never be able to develop income transfer programs for the aged which will be adequate. The substance of the problem or question at issue, however, should be stated differently. The major economic issue is not whether—in the face of other problems such as general poverty, urban blight, and increased demand for education—a nation can have new and better economic support for the aged. Rather the issue is better posed as to whether the people of the nation want a higher standard of living in their retirement years at the expense of a lower standard during the active working years. If they do, they can take the necessary individual or group action to accomplish this goal (except for the poor whose margin of living leaves little or no room for such choices).

While the economic status of the aged is dependent on the extent to which the society at any particular time is willing to transfer income from workers to the retired, the financing systems of all existing individual or collective private or public mechanisms available to carry out this transfer are intimately bound-up with two fundamental questions:

1.   The earnings-consumption pattern during worklife and the extent to which people are willing and able to postpone consumption until the retirement period.
2.   The retirement age decisions which, together with age of entry, determine the relative size of the working versus nonworking years (taking birth and mortality rates as given).

Thus, to better provide for old age, people must save more during their working years, and/or they must develop institutions which will transfer the income they desire from the population which is working during the period they are retired. Increased saving for retirement means less income in the working years for consumption purposes. Alternatively, the transferring of adequate income in old age, if it is to be done equitably, must be based upon appropriate amounts of payments or tax contributions during the working years to support the then aged.

Failure to base personal and/or national retirement income planning on the essential fact that adequate retirement income must be bought at the expense of consumption during the working years is almost certain to result in the poverty which, for example, characterizes the economic situation of so many of the world's aged today. Attempts to retroactively solve such a poverty situation are likely to create serious problems of intragenerational inequity. Such inequity takes the form of windfall gains in total lifetime consumption by some (for example, the poverty stricken) at the expense of less lifetime consumption for another generation. Typically, taxes are raised on the nonretired population to provide the necessary income.

There is a growing debate in the United States (Projector, 1969) as to the intragenerational equity of both current private and public pension systems. For example, the Nobel prize-winning economist Paul Samuelson argues that because of population growth and continued economic growth, windfall gains will continue for future generations:

The beauty about social insurance is that it is actuarially unsound. Everyone who reaches retirement age is given benefit privileges that far exceed anything he has paid in. And exceed his payments by more than 10 times as much (or five times, counting in employer payments)! (Samuelson, 1967)

In contrast to the Samuelson view is one held by a number of economists including the noted American economist, Friedman (1971):

[Social security] combines a highly regressive tax with largely indiscriminate benefits and, on the average, probably redistributes income from lower to higher income persons . . .

What . . . working people are now doing is paying taxes to finance payments to persons who are not working. The individual worker is in no sense building protection for himself and his family—as a person who contributes to a private vested pension system is building his own protection. Persons who are now receiving payments are receiving much more than the actuarial value of the taxes that were paid on their behalf. Young persons who are now paying social security taxes are being promised much less than the actuarial value that the taxes paid on their behalf could buy in private plans.

And with regard to private pensions, I have previously written the following:

Scholars in the pension field are familiar with the controversy over emphasis upon individual equity versus social adequacy. Private insurance is supposed to be based on the individual equity concept. . . . What, in fact, has happened [in the United States] is that although social security now saves many old people from poverty who paid relatively little into the system, its benefits in no way achieve social adequacy. Private pensions, therefore, have tried to supplement the social adequacy function of social security by past service credits. Unfortunately, the result has been to reduce the individual equity of such plans (Schulz, 1970).

The problem of intragenerational equity arises not only as a result of paying benefits to people who have a relatively few years of participation in the pay-in part of the system. It is created also by the numerous and frequent changes in pension formulas, benefit levels, benefit calculation procedures, and numerous other aspects of the pension system—changes which occur so frequently in almost all countries. All these changes make it difficult to analyze the relationship between the taxes paid and the benefits received by the current generation of retired people and make it almost impossible to make accurate predictions about future generations. Yet given the large number of social security systems in the world today whose benefits are fundamentally related to contributions (taxes) based upon earnings, it is mandatory that serious consideration and study be given to both intragenerational and also intergenerational equity matters. With regard to intragenerational equity, a considerable body of literature has been developed and testifies to the complexity of the subject (Atkinson, 1970; Brittain, 1967; Campbell, 1969; Chen, 1967; Goldin, 1971; Samuelson, 1958). Much work remains to be done.

Thus, to summarize, the economic impact of an aging population should be looked at in relation to two major questions:

1. What effect does the aging of a population have on the ability and willingness of that population to provide for themselves (and prior and succeeding generations) adequate income (and health, disability, and survivorship) protection in retirement?

2. As a population and its pension systems react and adjust to the changing demographic structure in response to question 1—how should the burden or costs of retirement income be allocated among groups within a particular generation and among various generations?

As noted earlier, there is a strong tendency for public discussion and political debate to fail to deal explicitly with these two questions. Instead, at any point in time there is usually an emphasis on the rights and needs of the current group of older people. Their poverty or relatively poor economic status, their large numbers, their prior social contribution to child rearing, and their contribution as former workers to the economic growth and rising productivity of the nation are all typically cited to justify political decisions which would give the current aged a greater share in national output. But to cite these factors adds little specific information to deal with the basic questions raised above.

Let us look now at some of the key factors connected with adequate retirement income and intragenerational equity. First is the demographic factor. Are nations aging and how rapidly?

Demographic Structure

A look at the United States experience illustrates current demographic developments. The U.S. Bureau of the Census makes four different projections which differ in their assumptions for fertility. The series E estimate (reported below) reflects the fact that

it has become increasingly apparent that a low or moderately low level of fertility could occur in a period of relative peace and economic prosperity and not be characterized by delays in childbearing which would result in a high average age at childbearing (U.S. Bureau of the Census, 1971).

The latest population projections of the Census forecast a rising proportion of persons age 65 or older in the total population—rising from 10% in 1970 to 13% in the year 2020. If one looks at the proportion of persons age 60 or older, the proportion increases from 17% in 1970 to 19% in 2020.

In Western Europe there was a well-known drop in the birthrate from 1875 to 1935 which, at the time, created great concern; this trend reversed itself in the late 1930s, and birthrates went up (even during World War II) throughout the 1940s and 1950s. After 1965, however, the trend resumed its downward trend (Sauvy, 1970). There is currently a great deal of speculation among demographers:

. . . experts today are divided into two camps. Some believe that the rise in the birth rate is due to accidental circumstances that will affect only one generation . . . and will soon resume its normal [downward] curve. Others hold the dip in the birthrate from 1875 to 1935 to be an episode, a decline which has passed its low point. The crude birthrate, they believe, will settle at 14–18 per 1,000—not a serious cause for concern.

Data published by the United Nations (1971) show that there are two countries (Austria and the German Democratic Republic) with 15–16% of the population over age 64, five countries (Belgium, France, Norway, Sweden, and England/Wales) with 13%, and seven countries (Denmark, the Federal Republic of Germany, Greece, Italy, the Netherlands, Switzerland, and the USA) with 10–12%.

Benefit Levels

The level of living which older people desire or expect when they retire is a key variable in determining the magnitude of the economic task faced by the working population in supporting the nonworking population. As stated above, a decision to increase living standards in retirement must be bought by a decrease in someone's consumption potential before retirement. Furthermore, equity dictates that there be some relationship between the gains achieved by the retired population and their sacrifices in terms of less consumption when they were young.

Historically, the great bulk of older people in most countries have enjoyed very low living standards—often sharply reduced from their pre-retirement years. It seems clear that this situation resulted not so much from an explicit decision of these people to live in poverty. Rather it resulted from (a) frequent national economic fluctuations with recurring depressions and inflations, (b) individual difficulties in retirement preparation arising from (a) and from the generally low levels of income available during the working years, and (c) the lack of national retirement planning.

With the development of collective means of retirement security through pension systems, the economic situation of the retired has changed significantly. But still it is generally agreed that in almost all countries improvements must be made in pension systems. Thus, it is that the direction and magnitude of these improvements will influence and be influenced by the aging of a nation's population. Specification of any level of retirement income *adequacy* can be translated into its cost on the working population. As the population ages, this cost per worker will rise.

There is no generally accepted definition of what is an adequate pension. This is a very subjective question which many have argued should be ultimately decided by the individual. Increasingly, however, discussion of this question has centered around what proportion of preretirement income is needed and desired during retirement to prevent a sharp drop in living standards. A significant number of social security systems in developed countries now use mechanisms which not only relate pension benefits to prior earnings but seek to guarantee through these benefits a relatively high level of earnings replacement at retirement. Public pension reforms, for example, in Austria, Belgium, France, Italy, Sweden, and West Germany have resulted in systems embodying the principle of high earnings replacement to provide living standard maintenance. *The trend seems to be toward developing public and private pension systems which will permit the retired population to at least maintain a level of living which approximates that which they enjoyed during their working years.* If this trend continues, it means that income transfers to the aged will rise very sharply in the future.

Given prospects for an aging of the population coinciding with this rise in retirement income expectation, there seems a clear need for long-run planning to distribute these rising costs equitably over succeeding generations. But more importantly, there is a need to rethink the allocation of leisure over the life-span since the relative number of workers versus retired persons is determined not only by birth and death rates but also by the age at which people retire.

The Age of Retirement

When a nation establishes by law that a person may receive a full retirement pension at a certain age, the government, in effect, is promulgating a national age of expected or normal retirement. Existing statistics clearly indicate the strong influence of this legislated pension age on the actual age of retirement by persons in the population. In a 1964 survey (David, 1965), for example,

more than one-third of the responding nations stated that the average exact age of initial receipt of pension was either the same as or within one year of normal pensionable age. . . . When there were differences between pensionable and actual retirement age the latter was higher, but for schemes having 65 as the pensionable age the variation was generally small (Kreps, 1968).

Thus, for example, in the USA the participation rate for males over age 64 has dropped from 57% in 1920 to 26% in 1970.

Economic growth—resulting from technological innovation, rising levels of education, the growth of capital, etc.—has permitted living standards in the industrialized countries to increase while, at the same time, workers generally have had to work less to help produce the rising output of goods and services. Thus, as workers' lifetime earnings have increased, hours worked per week or the number of days worked have fallen; the length of vacations has increased; and the period of retirement has generally lengthened.

It is usually assumed that continued economic growth in the future will presumably make it possible to reduce work effort still further while continuing to raise living standards (Kreps, 1971). This means that hours worked per week could continue to fall, and vacations could be lengthened. The question arises, however, as to whether the normal age of retirement should also be reduced and workers allowed to retire earlier. All workers, whether young or old, should seriously consider when and how they want to take the leisure available to them throughout their lifetime. A fundamental problem, however, is how to operationalize this question so that workers can make meaningful choices.

In 1971 the question was posed to delegates in every state who were attending conferences preparatory to the 1971 White House Conference on Aging:

Given that the normal age of retirement in the United States is currently around age 65, should current pressures to lower the *normal* retirement age below 65 be discouraged or encouraged? [emphasis added]

Although this question and the background paper discussion which accompanied it were designed to pose the question of the lifetime mix of income and leisure, the delegates misinterpreted or were unable to grapple with the *normal retirement age* question. Instead, the recommendations of both state conferences and the national conference focused on the problem of *forced retirement:*

Where practical, chronological age should not be a sole criterion for retirement. A flexible policy should be adopted based upon personal desires and needs of an individual, and upon physical and/or mental capacity of the individual.

While there is general recognition and research evidence that people would like to stop working at different ages (Barfield & Morgan, 1969), little has been accomplished toward achieving the goal of flexible retirement (OECD, 1970; Schulz, 1971). Instead, there seem to be mounting pressures for early and mandatory retirement and, most importantly, for social security and private pension full pension eligibility at earlier ages. The motivations for these pressures are not entirely clear and no doubt vary from one country to another, but two factors stand out: the political popularity among middle-aged persons of reducing the social security eligibility age and the economic popularity among businesses, unions, and younger workers of early retirement in order to deal with declining job opportunities due to stagnating industries or high rates of aggregate unemployment.

Recent events in a few countries illustrate the situation. In Sweden a 1969 private pension agreement was reached between the Swedish Employers' Confederation and the salaried employees' union to provide private pensions at age 65 equal to public old-age pensions to be paid at 67 (to be reduced when the public pensions came into effect). This agreement was quickly followed by a similar agreement last year between employers and blue-collar workers. In the Federal Republic of Germany one of the major pension debates is currently over whether to increase pension levels or increase the level of pensions paid before the normal retirement age of 65; current sentiment—according to observers—appears to favor earlier payment. In 1971 French trade unions called for two major pension changes—an increase of 40–55% in old-age pensions under the regime general and a lowering of the retirement age from 65 to 60 for all workers (Weise, 1972); the Government, guided by the recommendations of the Commission on Social Benefits for the Sixth Plan, proposed legislation (subsequently passed) to significantly raise benefits but rejected the proposal to lower the normal retirement age. In the United States, a number of universities laboring under the general education cost squeeze which pervades all higher education have announced early retirement policies as a means of keeping an age-balanced teaching staff.

Many experts argue against reducing the normal retirement age and recommend that countries consider encouraging work beyond age 65 by adopting or expanding financial incentives and flexible retirement rules. It is argued that a concentration of leisure time at the end of the life cycle should be avoided in order to help minimize the financial, social, and psychological problems currently associated with the retirement period.

To reduce the normal retirement age results in a very large increase in the magnitude of the funds required to provide for each person's retirement. This arises not only as a result of the increased transfers required from the working population but also because of the smaller total national output resulting from the reduced size of the labor force—assuming a full employment economy and that the people retiring are employable.

Current practice in most nations is to allow retirement 3 to 5 years before the normal retirement age with reduced pension benefits. While the advantage of this procedure is that it provides some flexibility and a measure of individual choice, such early retirement provisions also tend to encourage institutionalization of the *early* retirement eligibility age as the *normal* age for retirement. At least this seems to have been the experience in the United States where more than half the workers now retire early. Within 4 years of the 1961 amendment to the U.S. Social Security Act, which made men eligible for reduced old age benefits at age 62, one-third of the private pension plans studied by the U.S. Bureau of Labor Statistics reduced the normal retirement age—in most cases from age 65 to 62. In addition, many U.S. corporations now offer early retirement financial incentives, mainly in the form of supplemental benefits over and above the regular pension; this supplemental benefit continues until social security benefits begin or until the worker is eligible for his full social security benefit at the normal retirement age of 65.

As aging in a population occurs, one way to reduce the cost problems arising from a sharply rising retirement population is by discouraging movement out of the work force. This can be done, for example, by instituting one or more of the following policy measures:

1. Liberalizing (but not necessarily eliminating) "retirement test" provisions associated with social security;
2. Exempting workers over the normal retirement age from social security taxes;
3. Removing tax exemption privileges for employer private pension contributions to finance "early retirement" pension incentives;
4. Outlawing or liberalizing mandatory retirement age rules;
5. Making the work experience and work environment more enjoyable to the worker;
6. Developing "flexible retirement" job opportunities.

This list is certainly not exhaustive but, hopefully, shows the range of policy avenues available. Of course, the experience in almost all countries indicates that change in this policy area to help reduce retirement costs is not very likely. Reviewing recent trends, Fisher (1970) concluded:

France, the Federal Republic of Germany, Israel, the United Kingdom and Japan, when facing imbalances between the increase in pension outgo and income [due to the demographic situation], were compelled to seek ways of increasing the income. Only in rare cases could expenditures be reduced by such means as increasing the retirement age (e.g., Argentina).

Concluding Observations

What are the implications of the above discussion and the trends as they seem to be developing? A number of implications seem to be indicated:

1. In trying to predict how soon and how great will be the economic burden of aging populations in various nations, we are faced with the difficulty that the key variables—fertility, pension levels, and the age of retirement—are in a state of flux and essentially unpredictable. This means that long-range planning becomes very difficult. However, at the same time, all these variables are subject to influence by national policy, and, therefore, the magnitude of future problems are subject to control—should a nation desire to do so.
2. The increasing transfer costs of an aging population—together with rising social costs associated with urbanization and the

economic production of a technologically-oriented society—will make it increasingly difficult in the future to raise living standards during the working years in the highly developed nations of the world. In the United States, for example, the problems associated with or arising out of economic growth are creating a need for public expenditures which probably cannot be paid for out of the additional output of surplus of the economic growth itself (Schultze, 1972). Add onto this the increased retirement needs of an aging population, and it is difficult to foresee how living standards in the middle years can continue to grow at past rates.

3. The trend of a lengthening retirement period resulting from medical advances and, more importantly, from retiring at an earlier age needs to be watched closely. Serious thought should be given to reevaluating or, in many cases, establishing a national policy in this area. Perhaps the time has come when discussion of flexible retirement and job redesign can move from the academic and international organizational arena to a meaningful dialogue including governments, labor organizations, and corporations.

4. As the aging of a population develops, there will be a need for a greater awareness of the intra- and inter-generational equity considerations arising out of developing pension systems. As the national cost of aged income maintenance rises, greater attention to equity issues will be necessary in order (a) to maintain public confidence in and support for the systems and (b) to use with maximum effectiveness the retirement funds available.

References

Advisory Council on Social Security, *Reports of the 1971 Advisory Council.* Communication from the Secretary of HEW, 92nd Congress, 1st session. Washington: GPO, 1971.

Atkinson, A. B. National superannuation: Redistribution and value for money. *Bulletin of the Oxford University of Economics & Statistics,* 1970, *32,* 171–85.

Barfield, R., & Morgan, J. *Early retirement: The decision and the experience.* Ann Arbor: Braun-Brumfield, 1969.

Brittain, J. A. The real rate of interest on lifetime contributions toward retirement under Social Security. In U.S. Joint Economic Committee, *Old Age Income Assurance,* Part III. 90th Congress, 1st session. Washington: GPO, Dec., 1967.

Campbell, C. D. Social insurance in the United States: A program in search of an explanation. *Journal of Law & Economics,* 1969, *12,* 249–65.

Chen, Y. P. Inflation and productivity in tax-benefit analysis for Social Security. In U.S. Joint Economic Committee, *Old Age Income Assurance,* Part III. 90th Congress, 1st session. Washington: GPO, Dec., 1967.

David, A. M. Problems of retirement age and related conditions for the receipt of old-age benefits. Report IX of the 15th General Assembly. *Bulletin of the International Social Security Association*, Feb.-April, 1965, *18*, 97–109.

Fisher, P. Developments and trends in Social Security throughout the world, 1967–1969. Address delivered at the XVII General Assembly, International Social Security Association. Cologne: Sept., 1970.

Friedman, M. *Social Security: Universal or selective?* In Rational Debate Seminar. Washington: American Enterprise Institute, 1971.

Goldin, K. D. Social insurance finance. *Revista di Diritto Finanziario e Scienza delle Finanze*, 1971, *30*, 355–79.

Kreps, J. *Lifetime allocation of work and income.* Durham, NC: Duke University Press, 1971.

Kreps, J. *Lifetime allocation of work and leisure.* Research Report No. 22, Office of Research and Statistics, Social Security Administration. Washington: GPO, 1968.

OECD. *Flexibility of retirement age.* Paris: OECD, 1970.

Projector, D. S. Should the payroll tax finance higher benefits under OASDI? A review of the issues. *Journal of Human Resources*, 1969, 4, 61–75.

Rosset, E. *Aging process of population.* New York: Macmillan, 1964.

Samuelson, P. Social Security. *Newsweek*, Feb. 13, 1967, p. 8.

Samuelson, P. An exact consumption-loan model of interest with or without the social contrivance of money. *Journal of Political Economy*, 1958, *66*, 467–482.

Sauvy, A. The "old world" grows older. *Interplay*, 1970, 3, 26–28.

Schulz, J. *Retirement—background and issues.* Prepared for the 1971 White House Conference on Aging. Washington: GPO, 1971.

Schulz, J. Statement in U.S. Senate Special Committee on Aging. *Economics of aging: Toward a full share in abundance.* Part 10A—Pension Aspects. Washington: GPO, 1970.

Schultze, C. L. *Setting national priorities—the 1972 budget.* Washington: Brookings, 1972.

United Nations. *Demographic yearbook 1970.* New York: UN, 1971.

United Nations Dept. of Economics & Social Affairs. *The aging of populations and its economic and social implications.* Population Studies No. 26. New York: UN, 1956.

U.S. Bureau of the Census. *Current Population Reports*, Series P-25, No. 470. Washington: GPO, 1971.

U.S. Senate Special Committee on Aging. *The stake of today's workers in retirement security.* 91st Congress, 2nd session. Washington: GPO, April, 1970.

Weise, R. W. Higher old-age pensions in France. *Social Security Bulletin*, May, 1972, *35*, 30–32.

Compulsory Versus Flexible Retirement: Issues and Facts

Erdman Palmore

The local, state, and national conferences involved in the 1971 White House Conference on Aging have increased concern with one of the most controversial issues in gerontology: that of compulsory retirement at a fixed age versus flexible retirement based on ability. Debate on this perennial issue also seems to increase as compulsory retirement policies affect more and more workers who are still able to work and as the national costs of maintaining incomes and health care for the retired steadily escalate. Some argue that compulsory retirement is a clear case of discrimination against an age category and should be banned along with other forms of age, sex, and race discrimination in employment (Gould, 1968).

Various arguments and theories supporting one side or the other have appeared in scattered reports and articles (Busse & Kreps, 1964; Havighurst, 1969; Hyden, 1966, Kreps, 1961; Koyl, 1970; Lambert, 1964; Mathiasen, 1953; Palmore, 1969a). This article attempts to summarize these arguments and present the relevant facts as a basis for future private and public policy.

We will first present the facts on the extent of compulsory retirement, then discuss the theories and facts supporting flexible retirement, and third, discuss those supporting compulsory retirement. Finally, we will present three proposals for encouraging flexible retirement policies.

Extent of Compulsory Retirement

The practice of compulsory retirement apparently became widespread only in this century and grew along with the swift industrialization and growth of large corporations in the early 1900s (Mathiasen, 1953). A series of national surveys conducted by the Social Security Administration and others show that compulsory retirement policies affect a large and growing proportion of older workers. A comparison of the reasons for retirement given in the 1951 and the 1963 Social Security surveys of the aged indicate that the proportions of male beneficiaries who retired because of compulsory retirement provisions doubled during those 12 years (11% in 1951 and 21% in 1963 for wage and salary workers retired within the preceding 5

From *The Gerontologist*, Vol. 12, No. 4, Winter 1972. Reprinted by permission of the Gerontological Society and the author.

years [Palmore 1967]). In their 1969 Survey of Newly Entitled Beneficiaries, the Social Security Administration found that 52% of the
nonworking beneficiaries, who had been wage or salary workers and
who became entitled at age 65, had retired because of compulsory
retirement (Reno, 1971) (those who retired before they reached 65,
about 2/3 of the new beneficiaries, usually gave poor health or job
discontinued as the main reason, rather than compulsory retirement).
A national survey of retirement policies found that 73% of companies
with pension plans (which includes most large companies) had compulsory retirement at a fixed age for some or all workers (Slavick &
McConnell, 1963). The majority of these had compulsory retirement
at age 65. The 1966 SSA survey of retirement systems in state and local governments found that 79% had compulsory or automatic retirement at a fixed age (Waldman, 1968). This is an increase from the less
than one-half of the systems in 1944.

Thus, it appears that compulsory retirement policies may affect
about half of the male wage and salary workers retiring at age 65 and
will affect more in the future if recent trends continue.

The Case for Flexible Retirement

1. Compulsory retirement is by definition discrimination against an
age category, contrary to the principle of equal employment opportunity. Federal law now prohibits discrimination in employment based
on race, sex, or age for persons under 65. It is ironic that the present
law against age discrimination in employment is limited to persons
under 65, because persons over 65 are the ones who are most likely to
be discriminated against by such policies as compulsory retirement.
It seems possible that restricting this law to persons under 65 could be
considered unconstitutional in the sense that it does not provide equal
protection of the law to all persons.

Supporters of compulsory retirement might argue that such
discrimination is as legal and justifiable as child labor laws and policies which restrict the employment of children. However, there seems
to be a valid difference in that child labor restrictions are designed
primarily for the protection of children while compulsory retirement
policies are usually justified on grounds other than those of protecting
older persons.

2. Age, as the sole criteria for compulsory retirement, is not an
accurate indicator of ability because of the wide variation in the abilities of aged persons. Twenty years ago the National Conference on
Retirement of Older Workers concluded that

Both science and experience indicate that the aging process and its effects
show such wide variance among individuals as to destroy the logic of age as

the sole factor in determining whether a person should retire or continue to work (Mathiasen, 1953).

Recently the Gerontological Society's Committee on Research and Development Goals in Social Gerontology echoed this conclusion by stating

age limitations for employment are both socially and economically wasteful, since chronological age is rarely a reliable index of potential performance (Havighurst, 1969).

All the available evidence agrees that despite the declining abilities of some aged, most workers could continue to work effectively beyond age 65 (Riley & Foner, 1968).

3. Flexible retirement would better utilize the skills, experience, and productive potentials of older persons and thus increase our national output. If the millions of persons now forced to retire were allowed to be gainfully employed, the national output of goods and services could increase by billions of dollars. In a previous review (Palmore, 1969a) we concluded,

Many gerontologists have pointed out that because of the aged's extensive experience and practice, many have developed high levels of skills, emotional stability, wise judgment, and altruism. They agree that these abilities can and should be channeled into constructive roles.

4. Flexible retirement policies would increase the income of the aged and reduce the transfer payments necessary for income maintenance. Since the average income of retired persons is about one-half that of aged persons who continue to work (Bixby, 1970), it follows that flexible retirement policies might double the average incomes of those who were forced to retire but are willing and able to work. Similarly, over twice as large a proportion of retired aged persons have incomes below the poverty level as do aged persons who continue to work. Thus the millions of aged persons with poverty incomes might be substantially reduced by flexible retirement, which would increase their employment opportunities. This in turn would substantially reduce the amount of old age assistance and other welfare payments currently given to the aged with inadequate incomes. Similarly, Social Security payments could be reduced substantially because of the provision which reduces retirement benefits for earnings of over $1,680 per year. Considering the fact that over 20 billion dollars a year are paid by Social Security to retired workers and their dependents, it is easy to see that several billion dollars could be saved

from income maintenance programs if only a minority of the aged could avoid forced retirement.

5. Flexible retirement, in providing more employment, would improve life satisfaction and longevity of the aged. Most evidence indicates that retirement does tend to decrease life satisfaction. A recent review concluded:

> Overall satisfaction with life is greater among older persons who are still working than among those who have retired. This pattern seems to arise in part (but only in part) because the kinds of people who remain in the labor force are very different from those who retire (tending to be healthier, better adjusted, more advantaged on the whole). Yet quite apart from such factors as health or socioeconomic status, the pattern of lower satisfaction among the retired persists. (Riley & Foner, 1968).

Streib (1956) found that even for persons with similar levels of health and socioeconomic status, morale still tends to be comparatively higher among the employed. Thompson (1960) found that decreases in satisfaction over 2-year period were somewhat greater among older persons who retired than among those who continued to work; and decreases in satisfaction were substantially greater among reluctant retirees. The Duke Longitudinal Study (Palmore, 1968) found that reductions in economic activities including retirement were closely associated with reduction in life satisfaction. Dr. Thomas Green (1970), of Syracuse University's Educational Policy Research Center, has concluded,

> Surely there is nothing more damaging to the human spirit than the knowledge—or belief—that one's capacities are unused, unwanted . . .

There is less evidence supporting the idea that retirement has negative effects on health and longevity. Most of the association of poor health and greater mortality with retirement is probably due to the fact that people in poor health and with shortened life expectancies are the ones who tend to retire (Martin, Doran, 1966; Riley, 1968). However, we found that work satisfaction was one of the strongest predictors of longevity in our longitudinal study of normal aged (Palmore, 1969b). It may be that lack of work satisfaction, which can occur among the employed as well as among the retired, is the factor which reduces longevity.

6. Flexible retirement reduces the resentment and animosity caused by compulsory retirement. Apparently, many workers bitterly resent being thrown on the trash dump while they are still capable of working. Flexible retirement policies, by allowing such workers to continue work, eliminate this problem.

The Case for Compulsory Retirement

1. Compulsory retirement is simple and easy to administer. Flexible retirement would require complicated tests which would be difficult to administer fairly and difficult to explain and justify to the worker. This may be the main reason for the popularity of compulsory retirement among administrators. Proponents of flexible retirement agree that it would be somewhat more difficult to administer, but many with experience in the administration of flexible retirement plans assert that the complications have been exaggerated and that adequate tests of retirement based on ability are "not the monsters they were made out to be" (Mathiasen, 1953). Various groups have been working on improving techniques for measuring functional ability as a basis for retirement practices (Koyl, 1970).

In fact, most organizations have implicit or explicit standards, more or less based on ability and merit, which they use to decide who should be hired, fired, transferred, or promoted among workers under 65. Flexible retirement policies can use these same standards, or somewhat more exacting standards, to decide who should be retained and who retired among workers over 65.

2. Compulsory retirement prevents caprice and discrimination against individual workers. Proponents of flexible retirement also grant this point, but point out that prevention of individual discrimination is bought at the price of wholesale discrimination against an entire age category. They argue that the net number of workers willing and able to work who are forced to retire would be much less under policies of flexible retirement.

3. Compulsory retirement provides predictability. Both employer and employee know well in advance that the employee must retire on a fixed date. Thus, both can plan ahead better. On the other hand, some predictability can be built into flexible retirement by requiring workers and management to give a certain amount of advance notice to the other party of any intended retirement.

4. Compulsory retirement forces management to provide retirement benefits at a determined age. Most compulsory retirement plans are accompanied by retirement pension systems (Slavick & McConnell, 1963). On the other hand pension systems are often combined with flexible retirement policies with no great difficulty (Mathiasen, 1953).

5. Compulsory retirement reduces unemployment by reducing the number of workers competing for limited jobs. This is especially important in declining or automating industries or plants with an over supply of workers. On the other hand, it could be pointed out that compulsory retirement tends to increase unemployment among older workers by forcing them to leave one job at which they are experi-

enced and seek another job in a new area in which they may be disadvantaged. Using compulsory retirement to reduce unemployment
is analogous to firing all women or all blacks in order to reduce the
number of workers competing for jobs. A better solution to the unemployment problem is for the government to stimulate the economy
or to create additional jobs by being the "employer of the last resort."
In a previous analysis we concluded,

> The idea that society can provide only a limited number of jobs and that
> therefore it cannot provide enough jobs for aged workers is no longer accepted
> by most modern economists. Society could create a useful role for every adult
> if it were willing to devote the necessary attention and resources to this end.
> Certainly there would be major economic and political problems involved.
> But there is an unlimited amount of goods and services needed and desired in
> our American society (Palmore, 1969a).

If a smaller work force is really desired, this could be accomplished by shorter work weeks, longer vacations, delayed entry
into the labor market by more education, etc. (Kreps, 1969).

6. Compulsory retirement prevents seniority and tenure provisions from blocking the hiring and promotion of younger workers.
This is certainly true when seniority and tenure provisions are used to
retain workers who have become less efficient and productive. A solution to this problem under flexible retirement would be to eliminate
seniority and tenure provisions at a fixed age and require the older
workers to compete periodically for their jobs on the basis of ability
rather than seniority.

7. Compulsory retirement forces retirement in only a few cases
because most workers 65 and over want to retire or are incapable of
work. This claim is probably not true as shown by the surveys cited
earlier.

It is true that 69% of men over 65 not at work say they are not well
enough to work and another 16% say they are not interested in work,
but many of these responses may be rationalizations for inability to
find suitable employment (Palmore 1967; Sheppard, 1969). The only
way to accurately determine how many older workers are forced to
retire, but willing and able to work, is to eliminate compulsory retirement and count how many take advantage of the opportunity to
continue working.

8. Compulsory retirement saves face for the older worker no
longer capable of performing adequately. The older worker does not
have to be told and does not have to admit that he is no longer capable
of working but can blame his retirement on the compulsory retirement policy. Such a face-saving device undoubtedly has important
value for many workers, but the number of such workers should be

balanced against the perhaps equal number of capable workers forced to retire by compulsory retirement and the resulting frustration, loss of status, reduction of income and of national productivity.

9. Most workers 65 years old have impaired health or only a few years of health left. The facts do not support this argument. Life expectancy for a 65-year-old person is now about 15 years, and the majority of aged do not appear to have disabling impairments. Only 37% of persons 65 and over report any limitation in their major activity (National Center for Health Statistics, 1971).

Seventy percent of the Social Security male beneficiaries retiring at age 65 because of compulsory retirement report no work limitation (Reno, 1971). Furthermore, despite compulsory retirement and other discrimination against the aged, about one-third of men over 65 continue to do some work (Bogan, 1969). Thus, it appears probable that the majority of workers age 65 can expect a substantial number of years in which they will be capable of productive employment.

10. Most older workers are inferior and cannot perform most jobs as well as younger workers. This appears to be another of the stereotypes about the aged which has little or no basis in fact. A recent review of the evidence concluded,

Studies under actual working conditions show older workers performing as well as younger workers, if not better, on most, but not all, measures. Thus, those men and women who remain in the labor force during their latter years are not making generally inferior contributions, despite their frequently poor performance under laboratory conditions (Riley & Foner, 1968).

11. Compulsory retirement does little harm because most workers who are forced to retire could get other jobs if they wanted to. Again the evidence is contrary to this theory. When workers 65 and over lose their jobs, they have much more difficulty in getting another one than younger men. The proportions of older workers in the long-term unemployed categories are about twice as high compared to workers age 20–35 (Riley & Foner, 1968). Educational differences do not explain these differences in long-term unemployment (Sheppard, 1969). More than one-half of all private employees in states without age-discrimination legislation in 1965 admitted age limits in hiring practices and many more probably informally discriminate against older workers (Wirtz, 1965).

12. Most workers forced to retire have adequate retirement income. Again the facts appear to be to the contrary. We do not know exactly what percentage of those forced to retire are in poverty, but 30% of all retired couples and 64% of the retired non-married persons have incomes below the official poverty level (Bixby, 1970). And it is precisely those forced to retire early who have incomes substantially lower than those who retire early voluntarily (Reno, 1971).

Compulsory versus Flexible Retirement

Proposals for Increasing Flexible Retirement

As may be obvious from the preceding review, I favor flexible retirement policies primarily because I conclude compulsory retirement is unfair to the capable older worker, psychologically and socially damaging, and economically wasteful. The remaining question then is how to bring about more flexible retirement policies.

The most extreme proposal would be to outlaw all compulsory retirement by removing the age limitation in the present law against age discrimination in employment. The main objection to such a proposal is that at present it would be politically difficult if not impossible to pass such a law and that even if it could be passed it would be extremely difficult to enforce effectively. A counter-argument would be that the difficulty of enforcement should not prevent passage of a just law. We have many excellent laws which are difficult to enforce, such as laws against murder, robbery, and racial discrimination. Another serious objection is that while compulsory retirement may usually be unjust, in some situations it may be less unjust than a system with no retirement criteria or with completely arbitrary decisions as to who must retire.

A more moderate proposal would be to provide tax incentive for flexible retirement policies. A reduction in the amount of Social Security tax paid by the employer with flexible retirement policies could be economically justified by the savings in Social Security benefits that would result from continued employment of workers not forced to retire.

The most modest proposal would be to encourage some kind of compromise between complete compulsory retirement and flexible retirement based on ability alone. Brown (1950) of Princeton University proposed such a compromise plan over 20 years ago. Under this plan a definite age would be set at which all employees recognize that the promise of continued employment ends. At this time all seniority rights and further accumulation of pension credit ends. Then retired employees can be recalled to work as temporary employees, subject to the needs of management.

In this way, selected individuals can be recalled for specific needs on the basis of changing demands for personnel and the physical, mental, and personality adjustment of the particular worker to advancing age.

Such plans are in fact already operating smoothly in many businesses and institutions.

In conclusion, I hope that this article may clarify the issues and facts involved and may become a basis for reducing the millions of cases of compulsory retirement and the resulting social and economic waste of our older citizens' talents and skills.

References

Bixby, L. Income of people aged 65 and older. *Social Security Bulletin*, 1970, *33*, 4, 3–34.

Bogan, R. Work experience of the population. *Monthly Labor Review*, 1969, *92*, 44–50.

Brown, J. The role of industry in relation to the older worker. In *The aged and society*. New York: Industrial Relations Research Assn., 1950.

Busse, E., & Kreps, J. Criteria for retirement: a re-examination. *Gerontologist*, 1964, *4*, Pt. I, 117–119.

Gould, D. Let's ban retirement. *New Statesman*, 1968, *75*, 411.

Green, T. Panel examines new technology. *New York Times*, Jan. 30, 1970.

Havighurst, R. J. (Ed.). Research and development goals in social gerontology. *Gerontologist*, 1969, *9*, Part II.

Hyden, S. *Flexible retirement age.* Paris: Organization for Economic Cooperation & Development, 1966.

Koyl, L. A technique for measuring functional criteria in placement and retirement practices. In H. Sheppard (Ed.), *Towards an industrial gerontology.* Cambridge, Mass.: Schenkman, 1970.

Kreps, J. Case study of variables in retirement policy. *Monthly Labor Review*, 1961, *84*, 587–91.

Kreps, J. Economics of retirement. In E. Busse & E. Pfeiffer (Eds.), *Behavior and adaptation in late life.* Boston: Little, Brown, & Co., 1969.

Lambert, E. Reflections on a policy for retirement. *International Labor Review*, 1964, *90*, 365–75.

Martin, J., & Doran, A. Evidence concerning the relationship between health and retirement. *Sociological Review*, 1966, *14*, 329–343.

Mathiasen, G. (Ed.), *Criteria for retirement.* New York: G. P. Putnam's Sons, 1953.

National Center for Health Statistics. Current estimates from the Health Interview Survey—1969. *Vital & Health Statistics*, Ser. 10. No. 63, 1971.

Palmore, E. Retirement patterns. In L. Epstein & J. Murray, *The aged population of the United States.* Washington: Government Printing Office, 1967.

Palmore, E. The effects of aging on activities and attitudes. *Gerontologist*, 1968, *8*, 259–263.

Palmore, E. Sociological aspects of aging. In E. Busse and E. Pfeiffer (Eds.), *Behavior and adaptation in late life.* Durham: Duke University Press, 1969. (a)

Palmore, E. Predicting longevity. *Gerontologist*, 1969, *9*, 247–250. (b)

Reno, V. Why men stop working at or before age 65: Findings from the Survey of New Beneficiaries. *Social Security Bulletin*, 1971, *34*, 6, 3–17.

Riley, M., & A. Foner, *Aging and Society*, Vol. II. New York: Russell Sage Foundation, 1968.

Sheppard, H. Aging and manpower development. In M. Riley & A. Foner, *Aging and Society*, Vol. II. New York: Russell Sage Foundation, 1969.

Slavick, F., & McConnell, J. Flexible versus compulsory retirement policies. *Monthly Labor Review*, 1963, *86*, 279–81.

Streib, G. Morale of the retired. *Social Problems*, 1956, *3*, 270–276.

Thompson, W., Streib, G., & Kosa, J. The effect of retirement on personal adjustment. *Journal of Gerontology*, 1960, *15*, 165–169.

Waldman, S. *Retirement systems for employees of state and local governments,* 1968. Washington: Government Printing Office, 1968.

Wirtz, W. *The older American worker.* Washington: Government Printing Office, 1965.

Politics

6

The relationship between politics and age focuses on three topics: the political *participation* of older people, the political *power* of older people, and finally, older people as the *object* of government programs and politics. Politics can be approached from the viewpoint of either the individual or the social system or both. The individual approach deals with such questions as: How does an individual's political behavior differ or change over the course of the life cycle? How are people socialized politically? Is there an internal consistency in political attitudes and values over time or at any given point in time? Does the degree of consistency change as a function of age? These are only a few of the possible questions that could be raised about the aging individual and politics.

The viewpoint of the social system leads to questions such as: How does an individual's place in an age cohort influence his or her political behavior and beliefs? What are the political consequences of having experienced specific historical events? How salient is chronological age, compared with such other factors as social class, in influencing political beliefs and behavior? Related to this question is the perennial issue of whether the aged constitute a significant voting bloc in the same sense that blacks, Jews, or other social categories are considered to be a voting bloc. Is age-related legislation supported primarily by older people, the families of older people, or both? What kinds of groups function as lobbyists or advocates for older people, and even more importantly, why?

We have selected three articles to illustrate different approaches to the topic of politics, government, and aging. The first, by Leonard D. Cain, Jr., is concerned with legal definitions based on chronological age. Ours is a time-bound and time-oriented society.

In "The Growing Importance of Legal Age in Determining the Status of the Elderly," Cain raises a series of issues concerning the use of chronological age in establishing legal old age and the results of its use. He asks important questions about the relationships between legal age and gerontological theory, between theory and policy, and between chronological and functional age. If we do not use chronological age as the basis for allocating positions and roles, as a means of

173

providing legal protection, or as the basis of discriminatory practices, what other universal and rational bases can be used? Cain suggests that practitioners and theorists in many professions, including gerontologists, can be important in developing nonchronological criteria. Cain also points out that the realities of politics, economics, and historical events have been far more important than information or "constitutional consistency" in establishing age-related laws.

Cain's selection raises important questions about the use of chronological age to protect older people on the one hand and yet deprive them on the other, and about whether knowledge of chronological age is a useful indicator of an individual's functional capacities.

The selection by Anne Foner, "Age Stratification and Age Conflict in Political Life," draws upon a perspective that views age as the basis of an age stratification system similar to any other stratification system. (See the selection in Chapter 1 by Matilda W. Riley.) Age is seen as a major factor influencing individual behavior, just as social class is. Most models are of some heuristic value and certainly the age stratification model is no exception. It sensitizes observers to aspects of age-related behavior that they might otherwise overlook. In addition, it takes into consideration existing research findings and strategies and draws upon a historical perspective in building its case.

Foner builds upon Riley's framework by providing the empirical data necessary to examine changes in political attitudes over time. In the process of drawing her conclusions, Foner calls attention to the problems of separating age, time of measurement, and other aspects of social change. The reader may want to return to K. Warner Schaie's article in Chapter 2 to reexamine some of these particular issues from the psychological perspective. It is interesting that the same research concerns cut across disciplines.

Foner concludes that opposing forces both emphasize and reduce intergenerational political conflict. The balance seems to depend on the specific issue. She also lists several factors that reduce the importance of age strata and suggests some hypotheses concerning the nature of intergenerational relationships.

In "Interest-Group Liberalism and the Politics of Aging," Robert H. Binstock focuses on the national scene, examining the state unit of government in relation to the national picture. A political scientist, he examines the organizations that are involved in the politics of aging, electoral politics, and the situation of the needy aged. He takes the position that older people do not form a bloc of voters as such. For the most part, he says, political identifications are reinforced by age, not caused by them. In other words, political identifications gain strength over time. He also discusses the differences between older people who are poor and those who are not. The higher the socioeconomic class of the person, he finds, the less likely he or she is to define himself or herself as old. Certainly this reinforces the observation made earlier that the older population is heterogeneous. And these vast differences among the older population prevent the development of an older voting bloc.

The analog for a voting bloc of older persons was the Townsend Movement of the 1930s. Yet, Binstock points out, the circumstances at that time were different from recent and current events, thus making the recurrence of a major political organization of older people unlikely. Instead, a number of organizations—consisting either of older people themselves or of others—play an advocacy role on behalf of older people. He classifies these organizations into two broad types: those concerned with direct income transfer politics and programs and those which he terms middleman policies and programs.

Binstock calls attention to economic aspects of aging and distinguishes between the "Old Welfare" and "New Welfare." The economic conditions of the disadvantaged elderly are less likely to be improved as the result of political activities of a coalition of old people than as the result of a coalition of the disadvantaged from all social categories in the population. Yet realistically, the poor have little power—politically, economically, or otherwise. He also points out that the older voter does not have a direct impact upon policies and programs; rather, policies are developed through organized groups.

Binstock interprets the political events following the passage of the Older Americans Act. If past events shape future occurrences, then certainly an understanding of the development of policies and procedures is essential. The information may also provide a better understanding of the social organization of gerontologists and of the field of gerontology.

The selections in this chapter approach the politics of aging from two disciplinary viewpoints, that of the sociologist and that of the political scientist. They vary in the emphasis on age as a determinant of behavior. Both touch upon related research findings; each tends to draw upon historical events. In Binstock's article particularly the close interrelationships between the politics and economics of aging can be seen. Both disciplines raise questions about intergenerational relationships and the competing priorities of different social categories.

The Growing Importance
of Legal Age in Determining
the Status of the Elderly

Leonard D. Cain, Jr.

Laws which distinguish between the status of the "infant" and the "adult" can be traced from antiquity. For example, Blackstone (Ehrlich, 1959), writing in the eighteenth century about long standing laws in England, noted:

> The parent may lawfully correct his child, being under age, in a reasonable manner . . . The consent or concurrence of the parent to the marriage of his child under age, was also directed by our ancient law . . . The legal power of a father over the persons of his children ceases at the age of twenty-one: for they are enfranchised by arriving at years of discretion, or that point which the law has established when the empire of the father, or other guardian, gives place to the empire of reason.

Currently in the United States a vast array of laws, built mostly upon the foundation firmly laid before the time of Blackstone, continues to distinguish the minor from the adult.

Some Historical Roots of a Separate
Legal Status for the Elderly

In sharp contrast, laws which distinguish between the status of the "adult" and the "elderly" are of quite recent origin. Blackstone made no significant reference whatever to a distinctive old age status.

Otto von Bismarck, Chancellor of Germany a century ago, is sometimes credited with introducing into Western social policy laws which provide for a separate legal status for the elderly. As early as 1850, before Bismarck had risen to power, there had been proposed in the Frankfort parliament (Dawson, 1890):

a tax upon all employers of labour for the benefit of workpeople who had through advancing age or other causes become less efficient, and for the establishment and maintenance of homes for the aged and worn-out labourers.

The adoption of such a program had to wait until the leadership of Bismarck. In 1881 he presented this goal to the Reichstag (Dawson, 1890):

From *The Gerontologist*, Vol. 14, No. 2, April 1974. Reprinted by permission of the Gerontological Society and the author.

The end I have in view is to relieve the parishes of a large part of their poor-law charges by the establishment of an institution, having State support and extending to the entire Empire, for the maintenance of old and incapacitated people . . .

In 1889 the Old Age Insurance Law was adopted by the Reichstag. A worker became eligible for an annuity upon reaching 71 years of age or being rendered permanently incapacitated; a qualification was that to be eligible the worker must have contributed to the retirement fund for 30 years or, in the case of incapacity, for at least 5 years.

It was another two decades before proposals comparable to those of Bismarck began to appear in American political discourse. Chapman and Talmadge (1970) trace the history of health care proposals for the elderly back to 1912. However, in 1908 the Socialist Party included this plank (Porter & Johnson, 1956):

[We support] the improvement of the industrial condition of the workers . . . by abolishing official charity and substituting in its place compulsory insurance against unemployment, illness, accident, invalidism, old age and death.

In 1912 the Progressive Party proclaimed:

[We support] the protection of home life against the hazards of . . . old age through the adoption of a system of social insurance . . .

By 1916 the Democratic Party had included an "old age" plank, albeit a narrow one:

[We support] an equitable retirement law providing for the retirement of superannuated and disabled employees of the civil service . . .

The Prohibition Party in 1916 had a broader plank:

We declare for the enactment of an equitable retirement law for disabled and superannuated employees . . .

In 1928 the Republican Party platform acknowledged a separate status for the elderly:

Steps have already been taken by the Republican Congress to make the [civil] service more attractive as to wages and retirement privileges . . .

But it was not until the 1930s that "old age" was discovered by the two major parties. The Democratic platform of 1932, however, gave little hint of the Social Security Act shortly to come. It read, simply, "We advocate unemployment and old-age insurance under state laws." The Republican Party was silent on the issue that year. In 1936 the Democrats boasted:

We have built foundations for the security of those who are faced with the hazards of unemployment and old age . . . On the foundation of the Social Security Act we are determined to erect a structure of economic security for all our people . . .

The Republicans in 1936 countered:

Society has an obligation to promote the security of the people, by affording some measure of protection against involuntary unemployment and dependency in old age. The New Deal policies, while purporting to provide social security, have, in fact, endangered it.

The adoption of the Social Security Act in 1935 heralded the emergence of a distinctive legal status for the elderly. Tibbitts (1961) has observed:

Aging has forced its way into the field of political action with increasing intensity [since the early 1930s]. Government activity on behalf of older people has expanded enormously. . . .

Aging entered the modern field of political action during the twenties when socially concerned individuals and organizations became aware of the increasing detachment of old people from the family and from employment and assured sources of income; and when it became apparent that some of the basic needs of a majority of the rapidly growing number of older people could no longer be met by themselves or through established institutions such as the family, religious organizations, and charitable agencies, the first broad scale political action thus came on behalf of, rather than by, older people.

The Use of "Chronological" Age

Efforts during the last four decades to isolate old age as a separate legal status have typically built upon "chronological" rather than "functional" criteria. In a report on gerontological development in the fifteen years following World War II (Cain, 1959), some complications resulting from use of chronological age to determine status were identified:

[There] is the task of establishing legal bases for determining old age which are consonant with the attributes of the ageing as well as the resources and values of the society. There are complications and unanticipated consequences . . . , however . . . [P]aradoxically, as the legal terminus for adulthood has been established and as 'old age' has become a statistical category, studies which confirm vast variations in rate or maturation and in retention of skills, in ability to learn and adapt in later years, and in retention of stamina in old age have been reported. Thus, as chronological age has increasingly become a determinant for assignment to the old age status, researchers confirm the inadequacy of chronological age as an appropriate method for determining old age.

A wide variety of legislative acts and administrative decisions during the 1960s, and extending into the 1970s, has cast this paradox in ever bolder relief.

Although the use of chronological age to determine elibigility for various welfare and health support services, or for retirement from the work force, is widely known, there is a burgeoning of statutes and policies and debates related thereto, which relate chronological old age to a shift of status. For example, a hotly debated topic of recent years has been property tax exemptions for the elderly. Chen (1967) poses the dilemma:

[T]he case for property tax concessions to the aged appears tenuous [in economic terms]. Taxpaying ability of the aged . . . may be exaggerated, however. An important part of their net worth consists of home ownership. . . . Ownership of homes by the aged enhances their economic position on the one hand but subjects them to property taxes on the other. This . . . poses a problem only when there is insufficient income out of which to pay taxes.

Other examples include: eligibility for long term FHA loans for housing; Fair Employment Practices protection from age 40 to age 65, but not beyond; reduced fares for the local bus or theater; reduced fees to play golf or enroll in college; free hunting and fishing licenses.

A recent announcement printed on Dept. of Health, Education, & Welfare (1972) letterhead suggests that the onset of "legal" old age may occur well before the age of 60:

The National Institutes of Health offers Research Career Development Awards to foster the development of young scientists with outstanding research potential for careers of independent research in the sciences related to health.

. . . Candidates must be less than 40 years of age on the day the application is received . . . .

In response to my inquiry asking for the constitutional, legislative, and administrative authorization for restricting eligibility to this award to those under 40 years of age, the Deputy Chief of the Career Development Review Branch responded, on December 1, 1972:

> In order to provide the nation with outstanding biomedical research scientists, after careful study and evaluation of experiences in other programs, the N.I.H. in 1961 instituted the Research Career Development Award for the young scientist . . . The senior scientists naturally competed more effectively than the junior scientists because of their experience, training, and research capacity. Thus a way had to be found to aid the young developing scientist. Examination has shown that a young scientist, making use of the support mechanisms available to him, is pretty well launched on his career by age 40 . . . Another factor considered was the cost benefit to the nation in supporting a young scientist in his prime years of research productivity, innovation, and creativity, as opposed to supporting senior people, leaders in the field with fully developed careers, who generally had other sources of stable support . . .

The constitutional and legislative bases for denying equal access to public funds for those over 40 remain unanswered.

With the recognition of the pervasiveness of chronological age in the determination of the status of the elderly in American society, a number of challenges and invitations to gerontologists immediately present themselves. Some of these tasks are rather conventional: gerontologists need to be about the task of historical research to determine the circumstances in which chronological age and age spans have been adopted by legislators and administrators and confirmed by judicial authorities to distinguish between adulthood and old age; and they surely need to keep close inventory on the plethora of laws and rules which grant or deny privileges because of achievement of a specified older age.

Two somewhat more complicated tasks also emerge. One task is to understand more fully the link, if any, between gerontological research discoveries and subsequent legislation related to aging. The second task is to monitor the impact of laws which define and modify the status of the elderly, regardless of whether they are built on gerontological theory, as a means not only of examining the actual changes in the conditions of the elderly but also of checking on the soundness of gerontological theories.

Although anthropological field reports occasionally make reference to chronological age in reviewing the status of the elderly, it appears that in most societies until fairly recent times the acknowledged onset of old age was associated with evidence of declining physical ability or with certain societal role needs—the need for tribal elders, for example—rather than with the attainment by a given individual of a specified chronological age. With the emergence of the complex, industrialized society, especially its need for rationalizing the flow of membership in the labor force and for centralizing the planning for and control over welfare services to the elderly, resort to chronological age to distinguish the old person from the adult has increased. Improvements in census data collecting and in making demographic projections have made important contributions to the rationalizing of policies in employment, retirement, and welfare. Improvements in the recording of dates of births and deaths made it possible to determine eligibility of individuals for various services.

The Political Process in Selecting a Specific Age

How is a particular age chosen as a demarcation between the adult and the elderly? Wilbur Cohen (1957), a key figure in the development of the original Social Security legislation in the mid-1930s, provides an illuminating answer:

> The simple fact is that at no time in 1934 did the staff or members of the Committee on Economic Security deem feasible any other age than 65 as the eligible age for the receipt of old age insurance benefits. There is, therefore, very little material available to analyze the economic, social, gerontological, or other reasons for the selection of this particular age . . . The Committee made no detailed studies of alternative ages or of any proposals for voluntary retirement or of any flexible retirement program in relation to the disability of an individual.

Dr. Cohen sought to explain the reasons age 65 was chosen:

> It was understood that a reduction in the age below 65 would substantially increase costs and, therefore, might impair the possibility of . . . acceptance of the plan by Congress. A higher retirement age, of say 68 or 70, was never considered because of the belief that public and congressional opposition would develop against such a provision in view of the widespread unemployment that existed.

The process of drafting and passing legislation on behalf of the elderly, of developing administrative rules, and of implementing programs, is poorly understood. Economic costs, political expediency, social conditions at a particular historical time, factors which may be extraneous to the actual status needs of the elderly, have typically prevailed in determining the emerging legal status of the elderly. Not only have theories and data resulting from gerontological research been overlooked in much of the legislation, but constitutional consistency has been bypassed as well. Ten Broek (1965), in focusing on legislation at the state level, has illustrated the latter point vividly:

The reason for the differences as to responsibility of relatives between county aid and aid to the mentally irresponsible, on the one hand, and the aged, blind, and disabled programs on the other, is practical and political rather than doctrinal and constitutional. The aged and blind, and recently the disabled, have been able to organize and bring concerted pressure to bear upon the legislature. The mentally irresponsible and . . . recipients of indigent aid have not found this possible. . . . Where the forces moving the political branches of government are absent, and where evenhanded justice and principles of equal treatment imperatively call for fulfillment, the court intervened to apply and enforce the Constitution.

Binstock (1972), in a review of politics of aging, has provided a rather different emphasis. He observed that, although numerically and organizationally the aged in America appear to have access to political power equal to that of other groupings of citizens, little headway has been made in providing for basic needs of the disadvantaged elderly. The goals of the several large political organizations which promote governmentally supported programs to aid the elderly do not include, according to Binstock, pressure to achieve redress of the miserable condition of the severely disadvantaged aged. One possible solution

lies in the development of a social identity that would bind together a new, forceful coalition [among the severely disadvantaged within several traditionally defined groups] able to seriously disrupt the political, economic, and social order of American society.

Marmor (1973) has developed a detailed analysis of the political process through which the United States Congress adopted a health insurance program for the elderly (Medicare) in 1965.

Personal reflections of the kind presented by Cohen, reviews of organizational efforts and strategies of the kind developed by Binstock, and policy analysis of the depth advanced by Marmor, are needed if the emerging legal status of the elderly is to be understood. Likewise, there is a need to catalog and classify the mass of statutes and administrative rules which incorporate an older chronological age as a status determinant. For now a hasty review of some recent Federal legislation must suffice.

Recent Legislation

Recently, the Special Committee on Aging of the United States Senate (1972) published a brief report, "Action on Aging Legislation in 92D Congress." In its 11 pages there are at least 15 explicit references to older chronological ages or age spans:

Widows and dependent widowers aged 65 or older would be entitled to 100 percent of their deceased spouses' Social Security benefits instead of only 82½ percent as under present law. (H.R. 1)

[The] earnings in and after the month in which a person attains 72 would not be included, as under present law, in determining total earnings for the year. (H.R. 1)

Social Security benefits would be increased by 1 percent for each year from age 65 to 72 that a person delays retirement. After age 72, a person can receive his full Social Security benefits, regardless of the amount of his earnings. (H.R. 1)

Men (as under present law for women) would take into account earnings up to age 62 in computing their benefits, instead of age 65. (H.R. 1)

Nearly 1.7 million disabled Social Security beneficiaries under age 65 would be entitled to Medicare coverage . . . (H.R. 1)

A $100 million funding level would be authorized to provide community service employment opportunities for approximately 40,000 low-income persons 55 and older . . . Priority attention would be given to the employment of persons 60 and over. However, the Secretary of Labor would provide by regulations for the employment of indiviuals aged 55 to 59 [in special circumstances]. (H.R. 15657)

[The Middle-Aged and Older Workers Training Act] would establish a midcareer development services program . . . to authorize training, counseling, and special supportive services for unemployed and underemployed persons 45 and older. (H.R. 15657)

[The new Nutrition Act for the Elderly] will provide 250,000 nutritious meals a day to persons 60 and over [and to their spouses, regardless of age]. (H.R. 16654)

[The] participation of persons 45 and older in the public employment programs would, to the extent practicable, be consistent with their proportion of total unemployment in the United States. (Public Law 92-54)

[The Nutrition Program for the Elderly is] a national hot meals program for persons 60 and over . . . (Public Law 92-258)

[A] new golden age passport . . . would exempt persons 62 and over from any admission fees at Federally operated outdoor areas [and would entitle holders] to a 50 percent reduction in daily recreation user fees. (Public Law 92-347)

The report also includes a statement by Senator Church, the Committee Chairman, which points toward two proposals which would modify the resort to fixed age in law: (1) the proposal to abolish rules which require compulsory retirement at a specified age; and (2) the proposal to establish eligibility of minority group members to receive Social Security and related benefits at an earlier chronological age than whites, because minorities have fewer years of life expectancy than whites.

What do these new laws mean? Through legislative enactment altered statuses have been defined for at least some older people upon reaching age 45, or 55, or 60, or 65, as well as each additional year after 65 up to age 72. Indeed, members of American society have become accustomed to "age status asynchronization" (Cain, 1964) for the shift from childhood to adulthood. A youth may become eligible to drive a car at one age, purchase liquor at another, vote at still another. Now, it appears, laws are producing asynchronization in the shift from adulthood to old age. Amazingly, gerontologists have asked very few questions about the rationale for the use of several chronological ages, or about the consequences for the rights and well-being of older persons.

Legal Age and Gerontological Theory

More specifically, how do these laws interrelate with gerontological theory? In recent years several efforts to promote social and psychological theorizing have been advanced. Atchley (1972) has identified six of these so-called theories: (1) *disengagement theory*, which proposes that the number of interpersonal relationships declines with onset of old age and that those relationships which remain are altered; (2) *activity theory*, which associates successful aging with retention of middle-age behavior, and includes the notion that if some roles are relinquished others need to be added; (3) *continuity theory*, which asserts continuity in habits, preferences, and associations beyond middle age into old age, although replacement of lost roles is not essential; (4) *subculture theory*, which builds upon observations that older people are forced to turn to each other for support, which in turn produces a group consciousness, or subculture, (5) *minority group theory*, which supports the notion that discrimination against the elderly has produced a minority group status for them which is comparable to that suffered by certain racial groups; and (6) *the identity crisis theory*, which emphasizes difficulties of the aged in adapting to involuntary changes in their social position.

The relationship between any of these theories and recently enacted laws is not clear. It would appear, however, that programs which emphasize "outreach," or which plan to deliver services to residences in which the elderly reside, give credence to "disengagement" theory, but apparently seek, at times, to promote behaviors which would exemplify "activity" theory. Surely the privilege to enter Federal parks without paying the customary fee reflects "activity" theory. Those programs which seek to bring older people together in group processes may be inadvertently promoting the development of a "sub-culture." Gerontologists have an opportunity, possibly the mandate, to monitor their own theories, as laws which embody one or more theories of aging are translated into programs.

Traditionally the proper role for the theorist has been to stay in quest of the best theory. Recently, social scientists have been increasingly recruited as consultants to policy makers, although it is not clear that theories of these consultants have regularly been taken seriously by the policy makers. With an apparently closer link between theory and policy, the situation changes. There is prospect that one theory of aging may become dominant in law. If, for example, the elderly are forced to behave as though they are disengaging so that they can obtain certain services, the society through legislation may promote disengagement, and thus the theory could become a self-fulfilling prophecy.

The paradox mentioned earlier becomes increasingly complicated. On the one hand, use of chronological age to provide various subsidies and protections for the elderly continues; on the other hand, there is an expanding effort to abolish chronological age as a basis for restriction of opportunity, especially in regard to compulsory retirement laws. The irony is that some of those who are exploring removal of compulsory retirement regulations are at the same time strong advocates for increased protections and privileges based on chronological age.

The White House Conference on Aging

The resolutions from the recent White House Conference on Aging (1971) provide other cases in point. The report of the "Employment and Retirement" section, for example, includes these statements:

Our long established goal in employment and retirement policy is to create a climate of free choice between continuing in employment as long as one wishes and is able, or retiring on adequate income with opportunities for meaningful activities.

Chronological age should not be the sole criterion for retirement. At the same time, the "Retirement Roles and Activities" section submitted the following resolution:

In order to encourage further activity on the part of older Americans, it is recommended that the work means test be modified so as to allow unlimited earnings without the reduction of Social Security benefits.

Thus, if both these resolutions became law, chronological age would apparently be abolished as the sole criterion for determining time of retirement, but would be established as the sole criterion for determining time of eligibility to draw full Social Security benefits.

The paradox is illustrated further by citing additional Conference recommendations:

Public expenditures for education for older persons must be increased and directly related to the proportion of older persons within the population. ("Education" section)

... the U.S.A. must guarantee to all its older people health care as a basic right ... ("Physical and Mental Health" section)

Since older persons have special needs, we recommend that public programs specifically designed for the elderly should receive categorical support ... ("Retirement Roles and Activities" section)

Reduced or no fare transit for elderly people. ... the elderly [should] be allowed to travel at half fares or less on a space available basis on all modes of public transportation. ("Transportation" section)

The legal stage has been set for an older person to earn full income, maintain double deduction on income tax for self and spouse, receive full and tax exempt Social Security payments, travel free on public conveyances, have access to complete and apparently free medical care, enter federal parks and other facilities free, and so on. There may shortly be political repercussions; and surely the courts may begin to apply the "equal protection" and "equity" arguments in new ways, especially if young workers and taxpayers threaten to revolt. A comparable revolt and court response are already incipient in the area of civil rights.

The White House Conference section on "Legal Aid and the Urban Aged" recommended:

... special security measures should be included in all housing occupied exclusively or largely by the elderly ...

The criminal justice system should give special assistance to elderly persons who are victims of crime or are witnesses in criminal cases. ... Elderly witnesses may need to be provided with transportation. ... Trials may have to be conducted more promptly to relieve the burden on the elderly from repeated and protracted court appearances.

The elderly should be provided free, competent attorneys in all proceedings relating to civil commitment, conservatorships, and other proceedings brought to restrict their freedom or other legal rights.

Some Unresolved Issues

Conclusions drawn from gerontological research about the status of the elderly are in process of being responded to by law. However, there are at least three major unresolved issues related to legislative responses which incorporate chronological age into statutes: (1) the issue which results from the fact that chronological age does not effectively reflect the actual ability or need of every older individual; (2) the issue which emanates from efforts to remove age restraints on work at the same time that there are efforts to increase benefits based solely on the achievement of a specified age; and (3) the issue which results from the practices of building laws, case by case, statute by statute, with the result that a jungle of age status asynchronization has been produced.

There are peculiar complications of law resulting from the opposite situation, that is, the absence of chronological age specifications to guide decisions to withdraw privileges of status in old age. If an employee is not under the constraints of compulsory retirement rules, under what conditions can an employer rightfully dismiss an older worker who is believed to be declining in work capacity? Under what conditions can a manager of a public housing project for the elderly complete eviction proceedings against a tenant who becomes less and less capable of maintaining himself or herself on a day-by-day basis? Under what conditions can authorization to drive a vehicle be revoked? Apart from the role of psychiatrists and some others in declaring older people incompetent to manage their own affairs, there are few guidelines in our society to remove rights on the basis of old age (Alexander, 1973), except those related to general rules based on chronological age (United States Senate, 1970, 1971). Herein lie emergent roles for physicians, psychologists, attorneys, administrators, and gerontologists to develop criteria other than chronological age to remove privileges and extend protection to those who display symptoms associated with becoming old.

Much of the legislation which provides distinctive status to the elderly is built on the premises that the elderly as a class are poor and in addition have obstacles which prevent their achieving parity with those younger. Compulsory retirement, reduced energy, discrimination in employment, inflation, contribute to this condition. Therefore, law goes beyond "equal protection" to "equity." But there may be complications when special effort is made to serve the elderly poor. Let me cite an example.

Those past age 65 who have assets of no more than $7,500 and monthly income of no more than $350 are eligible for admission to federally supported housing for the elderly. An additional effort to serve the poorer of the poor is found in the provision that no more than 25% of a tenant's income may be collected as rent in a housing project. Since the housing needs of the poorest of the poor have provided the emotional incentive for publicly subsidized housing, it would seem that these poor would be granted top priority in occupying such housing. Yet, inasmuch as housing administrators have budgets to balance, there are circumstances in which it is virtually necessary to shun an older person who has very limited income, although he or she may have been on a waiting list for a long period, in favor of a tenant who can pay near the maximum collectable.

This peculiar denial of public housing to the poorest among the poor elderly may be traced to a circular, "Housing a Cross-Section of Low-Income Families in Low-Rent Public Housing" (HM746512), June 2, 1971, issued by U.S. Dept. of Housing and Urban Development, Housing Management:

Each Local Authority having a graded rent system, if it has not already done so, is urged to immediately establish ranges of specified rents and to make admissions to its projects from among eligible applicants at such rents or within such ranges of rent as may be necessary to achieve, maintain, or improve the solvency of its operation and to insure, insofar as is possible, serving a representative cross-section of the low-income families in its locality.

More recently, the Area Director, Region X, H.U.D., in an undated (Fall, 1972?) memorandum, "Housing a Cross Section of Low Income Families," sent to "All Local Housing Authorities (in Management)," has implemented the June 2, 1971, recommendations:

Establish rent ranges of specified rents and make admissions to projects from among eligible applicants within such ranges as may be necessary to achieve, maintain, or improve the solvency of the operation: . . .
[I]n selecting eligible applicants to fill vacancies the [Housing] Authority will make selections from the following rent ranges so that, in so far as possible, the projects will be occupied by an equal number of families from each range.

Monthly Gross Rent Ranges

Range I	Range II	Range III	Range IV	Range V
$0–$15	$16–$30	$31–$45	$46–$60	Over $60

Prospects for a Gerontology of Legal Age

Gerontologists have neglected the study of problems surrounding legal age. Frequently, the "Legal Problems" section of the quarterly bibliographical service, "Current Publications," published in *Journal of Gerontology*, has no entry at all. However, contributions such as Bernstein's (1969) "Aging and the Law," Kraus' (1971) "The Legal Problems of the Elderly Poor," and the recent special issue on the elderly of the *Clearinghouse Review* (1972) strongly indicate that gerontologists can no longer overlook the issue.
    Bernstein begins his perceptive essay by declaring:

The law must accommodate to profound changes in age distribution that have occurred since the turn of the century and will continue at least until its close.

He then suggests that:

> Lawyers as architects of the law—in legislatures, administrative agencies, and universities—must try to design new legal arrangements, possibly whole institutions, to ease the burdens of aging and to maximize the opportunities of the elderly . . .

Bernstein, on occasion, proposes that laws be used actively as weapons to enhance the status of the elderly. For example, he indicates that the promotion of the three-generation household could be accomplished by such legal innovations as providing a public assistance "bonus" to families who have grandparents who live in the same household with a son or daughter and grandchildren, by redesigning public housing so that a second kitchen and entrance could provide an older person semiprivacy even as the grandparent lives with children and grandchildren, or by altering zoning laws to accommodate more joint households. The question, "Is it proper to promote the three-generation household in today's world?," remains unanswered.

Kraus is an even stronger advocate for the elderly than Bernstein. He charges:

> The candid policy of many attorneys is to take advantage of court delay and elderly plaintiffs by postponing trials as long as possible knowing that the pressure for settlement intensifies in proportion to the plaintiff's age, health, and resultant diminishing likelihood of remaining alive to enjoy his financial recovery.

The solution proposed by Kraus is to have all jurisdictions provide a means whereby both elderly plaintiffs and defendants can request and receive trial preference.

The aforementioned issue of the *Clearinghouse Review* almost compels gerontologists to become more alert to the legal status of the elderly. There are articles on such facilities as the National Senior Citizens Law Center and programs such as the California Rural Legal Assistance program for the elderly; there is a review of the Age Discrimination Employment Act of 1967; and there are reports on legal services attorneys, on nursing home occupants, on challenges to relative responsibility laws, and on homeownership problems for the elderly.

The resolution of most of the issues raised in this paper is not yet close at hand. There are many surprises for those who delve into the history of legal age, and the related jurisprudence. The invitation to catalog and classify laws pertaining to the elderly probably has many hidden facets. Most efforts to evaluate the effectiveness of service programs have been ineffective to date. The encouragement to be more cognizant of the growing interrelationship between public policy and social theory has ramifications far beyond gerontology and old age status.

Apart from expanding the analysis of legal age statutes already enacted, among the greatest challenges facing gerontologists during the next few years is to contribute to the establishment of criteria other than chronological age in promotion of equity for the aged. Developing means of employing biological, psychological, and social categories for legal status differentiation is an awesome task.

References

Alexander, G. J., & Lewin, T. H. D. *The aged and the need for surrogate management.* Syracuse: Syracuse Univ. Press, 1973.

Atchley, R. C. *The social forces in later life: An introduction to social gerontology.* Belmont, Ca: Wadsworth, 1972.

Bernstein, M. C. Aging and the Law. In M. W. Riley, J. W. Riley, Jr., & M. E. Johnson (Eds.), *Aging and society: Vol. 11, Aging and the professions.* New York: Russell Sage Foundation, 1969.

Binstock, R. H. Interest-group liberalism and the politics of aging. *Gerontologist,* 1972, *12,* 266–280.

Cain, L. D. The sociology of ageing: A trend report and annotated bibliography. *Current Sociology,* 1959, *8,* 57–133.

Cain, L. D. Life course and social structure. In R. E. L. Faris (Ed.), *Handbook of modern sociology.* Chicago: Rand-McNally, 1964.

Chapman, C. B., & Talmadge, J. H. Historical and political background of federal health care legislation. *Law & Contemporary Problems,* 1970, *35,* 334–347.

Chen, Y. P. Property-Tax Concessions to the Aged. In R. W. Lindholm (Ed.), *Property taxation: USA.* Madison: Univ. of Wisconsin Press, 1967.

Clearinghouse Review, 1972, *6,* 189–308. Articles include: Johnson, E. R., National Senior Citizens Law Center, 189–191; Marlin, D. H., & Brown, R. N., The elderly poor: An overview of the legal services attorney's responsibility, 192–195; Freed, M. G., & Dowell, E., The age discrimination in employment act of 1966, 196–202; Health Law Project, Univ. of Pennsylvania Law School, Legal problems inherent in organizing nursing home occupants, 203–211; Coppleman, P. D., & Hiestand, F. J., Legal challenges to relative responsibility in old age security programs: Establishing the right to grow old with dignity, 212–220; Collins, W. R., & Flanagan, J. M., The Senior Citizens Project of California Rural Legal Assistance: An action arm of the National Senior Citizens Law Center, 220–221; Wallin, P. L., Homeownership problems of the elderly, 227–232.

Cohen, W. J. *Retirement policies under Social Security* (a publication of the Inst. of Industrial Relations, Univ. of California). Berkeley & Los Angeles: Univ. of California Press, 1957.

Dawson, W. H. *Bismarck and State Socialism: An exposition of the social and economic legislation of Germany since 1870.* London: Swan Sonnenschein, 1890.

Dept. of Health, Education, & Welfare. Undated and unsigned announcement of award opportunities (received in the mail in Nov., 1972) under the letterhead of: Dept. of Health, Education, & Welfare, PHS, NIH.

Ehrlich, J. W. *Ehrlich's Blackstone.* San Carlos, CA: Nourse, 1959.

Kraus, J. The legal problems of the elderly poor. *New York Law Journal,* 1971, 165, 1 ff.

Marmor, T. R. *The politics of Medicare.* Chicago: Aldine, 1973.

Porter, K. H., & Johnson, D. B. (Eds.). *National party platforms: 1840–1956.* Urbana: Univ. of Illinois Press, 1956.

Ten Broek, J. California's dual system of family law: Its origin, development, and present status. *Stanford Law Review,* 1965, *17,* 614–682.

Tibbitts, C. Politics of aging: Pressure for change. In W. Donahue & C. Tibbitts (Eds.), *The politics of age: Proceedings of the Univ. of Michigan 14th Annual Conference on Aging, 1961.* Ann Arbor: Div. of Gerontology, Univ. of Michigan, 1962.

U.S. Senate, Special Committee on Aging. *Legal problems affecting older Americans: A working paper.* Washington: USGPO, Aug., 1970.

U.S. Senate, Special Committee on Aging. *Legal problems affecting older Americans: Hearing before the Special Committee on Aging, U.S. Senate, 91st Congress, Second Session, St. Louis, Aug., 1971.* Washington: USGPO, 1971 (especially the testimony of G. C. Alexander, 10–15).

U.S. Senate, Special Committee on Aging. Action on aging legislation in 92d Congress. Washington: USGPO, Oct., 1972.

White House Conference on Aging, 1971. *A report to the delegates from the Conference Sections and Special Concerns Sections* (distributed to Conference delegates in Washington, Dec. 2, 1971).

Age Stratification and Age Conflict in Political Life

Anne Foner

The political rebellion of youth in the 1960's and early 1970's has generated a great outpouring of commentary and analysis. Although this outpouring has heightened awareness of age as an important influence on social life, there has been as yet relatively little systematic attention to age in its own right as a source of social inequalities, values, group loyalties, and societal conflict. This paper focuses on

From the *American Sociological Review,* Vol. 39, No. 2, April 1974. Reprinted by permission of the American Sociological Association and the author.

this last point, going beyond the recent youth protests to explore age generally as a basis of political cleavage in modern society.

A few writers have sought through historical and comparative analysis to broaden our perspective on contemporary youth movements. For example, it has been noted that youth movements emerge periodically, tending to develop around such broad social issues as peace and the rights of oppressed or deprived groups (see, for example, Altbach and Peterson, 1972; Feuer, 1969; Laqueur, 1969; Lipset, 1971). Apart from the reputed idealism of youth, however, there is no general agreement about the conditions giving rise to youth protests. In fact, Lipset (1971:743–4) seems to interpret youth movements not primarily as an expression of age conflict, but rather as unrestrained action to realize the ideals to which young people have been socialized. Conversely, Laqueur (1969:33–41) detects in youth revolts a rejection of ideas received from the older generation. He also remarks, without explaining his assertion, that these rebellions prosper only against a background of rising affluence. Thus a number of questions have been raised about the general phenomenon of age as a basis of political dissension, questions that invite further analysis.

It is the thesis of this paper that such analysis can be brought into focus from the perspective of age stratification. The emerging theory of age stratification, outlined by Riley, Johnson, and Foner (1972) treats age as a centrally important characteristic—like class, sex, or ethnicity—influencing individual behavior and societal structure. In particular, this paper addresses a few broad issues: First, what is the potential for age conflict in political life? What are the age-related roots in the social structure of such conflict? Second, if there is a high potential for age cleavage, why do sharp political struggles between young and old erupt only sporadically? Third, what conditions are likely to foster political conflicts along age lines?

Age Stratification and Sources of Age-Related Conflict

Several concepts and assumptions are germane to understanding age as a base of stratification and those age-related processes which may lead to clashes between age strata.

Some Elements in the Theory of Age Stratification The theory of age stratification (Riley, Johnson, and Foner, 1972: Chap. 1 especially) assumes that age "locates"[1] individuals or groups of people in the social structure. Age strata are viewed as layers which cut across the whole society, just as class strata do, but which order people and roles by age rather than economic position. Thus each age stratum is composed of people similar in age or life stage, who tend to share capacities, abilities, and motivations related to age. Age is also a criterion for entering or leaving roles, and for the different rewards and obligations associated with these roles. In short, age is a basis of "structured social inequality."[2] Of particular relevance for political conflict, age strata are unequal in access to positions of political power. In most societies, young adults are less likely to be political leaders than middle-aged and older adults. Moreover, younger and older people often differ markedly in their political attitudes and ideologies (Riley and Foner, 1968: Chap. 19).

The age-related differences in behavior and orientations at any given period are linked to two independent processes: (1) aging, as the individual changes psychologically and physiologically over the life course from birth to death, passes through role sequences, and acquires experience in these roles; and (2) cohort flow, as one cohort (generation) succeeds another, each having lived through a different historical period. In political terms, aging differentiates age strata insofar as people may become more conservative as they age, or may gain greater access to political power. And differing cohort experiences can distinguish age strata because each cohort starts its political career in a different social climate or experiences unique events which have a lasting impact on its members' political views (Mannheim, 1952; Cain, 1964; Ryder, 1965).

These dynamics of aging and of cohort succession can lead to sharply polarized age strata, though such an outcome is clearly not ineluctable. Much depends on the direction and strength of changes with age, and on the particular impact of new cohorts entering the polity. For, while the two processes of aging and cohort succession are analytically independent of one another, in any given period their joint operation influences the similarities or differences between age strata.

The Impact of Aging and Cohort Succession—An Illustration An empirical example,[3] drawn from a fuller analysis by Agnello (1973), illustrates how aging and cohort succession are each involved in age-related changes in political attitudes over a sixteen-year span. As Table 1 shows, repeated national surveys reveal a marked decline (from 80% in 1952 to 49% in 1968) in overall agreement with the statement, "Voting is the only way that people like me can have any say about how the government runs things." These figures suggest not only a general decline in an exclusive reliance on electoral politics, but a change in the relations among age strata. In 1952 there were only minimal cross-section age differences; but by 1968 the differences between the youngest and the oldest strata had become pronounced.

Let us consider how aging and cohort succession may have contributed to these changing patterns in the above attitudes toward voting. (Table 1 alone, based like most cohort tables only on the two independent variables of age and date, does not permit one to disentangle the "effects" of these two processes from many other aspects of social change (see, for example, Riley, 1973).[4] Such a table does, nevertheless, provide invaluable clues to the two processes as these are intertwined with complex historical trends.) First, with respect to aging, the rows in Table 1 show how, within each cohort, there is a change over the life course toward less agreement with the statement. Thus aging is not necessarily associated with inflexibility of attitude, although the decreasing acceptance in the earlier cohorts (born before 1924–1931) lags behind the sixteen-year trend in the total electorate.[5] Second, with respect to cohort succession, (seen in the diagonals of Table 1), the differences among cohorts are even more noticeable than the life-course differences as each more recent (younger) cohort is less likely to agree with the statement (especially at the start of the political career, age twenty-one to twenty-eight). Combining both processes, one might imagine a situation in which life-course and cohort differences offset each other exactly, resulting in the persistence to 1968 of the similarity among all age strata observed in 1952. In fact, however, the life-course changes, though tending to counteract, are not strong enough to offset the differences in cohort succession. Such findings indicate that both aging and cohort succession are implicated here in the societal trend.

Aging, Cohort Succession, and the Political Context   In this one illustration, then, one could attribute the gap between young and old in good part to the influx of new cohorts with decidedly less traditional

Table 1   Percentage Agreeing with the Statement, "Voting is the only way that people like me can have any say about how the government runs things."

Year of Birth	Election Year (age in parentheses)		
	1952	1960	1968
1940–1947			37% (21–28)
1932–1939		69% (21–28)	41% (29–36)
1924–1931	79% (21–28)	69% (29–36)	44% (37–44)
1916–1923	74% (29–36)	67% (37–44)	49% (45–52)
1908–1915	81% (37–44)	74% (45–52)	56% (53–60)
1900–1907	82% (45–52)	74% (53–60)	62% (61+)
1892–1899	84% (53–60)	78% (61+)	
Before 1892	80% (61+)		
Difference between oldest and youngest strata	+1	+9	+25
Total electorate	80%	72%	49%
Total sample	1,899	1,954	1,557

Source: Adapted from Thomas Agnello, 1973:257. Data for his analysis, originally compiled by the Michigan Survey Research Center, are drawn from comparable cross-section probability samples of the United States.

Politics

orientations than older cohorts. But on other political questions, age strata may align quite differently. Life-course change does not always lag behind the general societal trend (see, for example, Evan, 1965). And new cohorts are sometimes less liberal than earlier ones, as is hinted in various cross-section data that show, for example, post-revolutionary Cuban workers, aged twenty-one to twenty-seven, as less favorable to the revolution than the (now older) rebel generation of Castro (Zeitlin, 1967:227); or young Southern whites (under twenty-five) as less liberal on racial issues than their slightly older counterparts (Sheatsley, 1966:226).

As data are forthcoming, and more detailed theories aid the analysis of many specific issues and of the people's general political stance, it should become possible to specify the political cir-cumstances in which aging and cohort succession work jointly to sharpen or minimize age differences in political attitudes and behav-iors. There are some fragmentary clues already about political changes accompanying the process of aging. Contrary to widespread assumptions about growing rigidity with age, certain studies, like the Agnello example in Table 1, indicate that people do change political attitudes as they grow older, often becoming more liberal. Data on various specific issues—for example, attitudes toward trade unions, United States participation in a world organization, or equal pay for equal work for men and women—show that changes with age tend to be in the same direction as the general trend in the society (Evan, 1965, adapted by Riley, Johnson, and Foner, 1972:133–7). Such clues suggest that people, as they age, can respond to a changing political climate.

An intriguing hypothesis is suggested by one set of questions that contrasts specific attitudes with overall political stance (Evan, 1965, adapted by Riley, Johnson, and Foner, 1972:133–7). While on several specific issues the changes with age follow the societal trend (some-times conservative, sometimes liberal), the life-course pattern of a general political orientation was quite different. Thus when people were asked whether they viewed themselves as conservative or liberal in politics, there was a net shift with age toward a more conservative position in every cohort for which there are data, even though in the society as a whole there was no similar trend. This apparently grow-ing inclination to consider oneself conservative in some general sense suggests a wish not to rock the boat. Perhaps, the influx of new, more liberal cohorts prompts the desire of established cohorts to make haste slowly. One can also interpret such responses as commitment to the existing institutions and associated values with which people are familiar and to which they have made an adjustment (Foner, 1972:139; cf. Becker, 1960; Ryder, 1965:858). The finding does not mean that, as they age, people cannot accept piecemeal changes; for the data on specific issues indicate that many do adapt to specific changes they can evaluate in the light of their own experience. In view of the hypothesized commitment to the fundamental social structure, such piecemeal changes are probably accepted because they seem to fit into, rather than threaten, existing social institutions.

In short, whether changes occur with age seems to depend on the issues being debated. If future analysis bears them out, these interpretations suggest that calls for sweeping changes in the society are most likely to provoke sharp age rifts by heightening the general resistance to change among people as they age.

Scattered clues are also at hand to suggest how the political climate affects cohort succession. It is often assumed that young cohorts, in "fresh contact" (Mannheim's phrase) with the political world, whose political ideas are just being formed, will be especially responsive to new political trends (Mannheim, 1952; Heberle, 1951:118–22; Lipset, 1963:279–83; cf. Ryder, 1965:848–51). Agnello's data (see Table 1) give an illustration of this process. In this instance, the new cohorts' lesser acceptance of voting as the only means to political influence would seem to mirror the wave of civil disobedience and protests in which young people participated in the 1960's. It has also been suggested that major events like wars and economic crises not only have a special impact on young cohorts, but that youthful responses tend to influence political views and behavior throughout the life course. One recent analysis, for example, points to the depression years as strongly influencing the political views of the undergraduates of that period. Lipset and Ladd (1972) re-analyze Gallup data to show that the generation in college from 1929–1933 was consistently more liberal in its voting behavior in the elections of 1956, 1964, and 1968 than both older and younger cohorts.[6]

Such examples, though limited, suggest how the political context may affect the direction in which people change (or fail to change) their political views with age, and how it can influence the character of new cohorts. Certain political occurrences appear to impinge on both aging and cohort succession to heighten age disagreements, as, for example, foreign policy crises or sharp economic fluctuations, which may prompt young cohorts to espouse radically new ideas, the very kinds of ideas likely to raise the hackles of the old. Thus, especially in periods of rapid social change, the potential for age cleavage in political life seems far-reaching.

Age Stratification and the Potential for Reducing Age-Related Conflict

Although our society has undergone dramatic changes over the century, it has not always experienced concomitant age-youth struggles

—as the "silent generation" of the 1950's reminds us. Why is it that age differences, seemingly omnipresent beneath the surface of social life (Sorokin, 1969:193), do not regularly erupt in sharp political conflicts?[7] And when these conflicts emerge, why are the issues so often related to peace, morality, or justice? I propose that, just as there are age-related roots in the social structure precipitating age conflict, there are age-related mechanisms for reducing conflict. I shall first suggest how these conflict-reducing mechanisms are likely to operate and then consider how they may relate to the ebb and flow of issues of central political concern in the society. In discussing the possibilities of containing or preventing age conflict, I consider factors which may either minimize age-related political differences or, if such differences do emerge, forestall the outbreak of sharp and bitter struggles. Two features of social life that hold promise for reducing open conflict seem particularly age-related: membership in age-heterogeneous groups and age mobility.[8] These two features can serve to forge ties across age strata or reduce the possibility of enduring solidarity within strata.

Age-Heterogeneous Groups   Multiple group affiliations often serve to reduce conflict in highly differentiated societies, with their many groups and potential bases of conflict. For the individual, membership in several groups may loosen his commitment to the values and goals of a single group; and for the society, conflicts within the various groups can sometimes offset each other. As Edward A. Ross (Coser, 1964:76) noted many years ago:

A society . . . which is ridden by a dozen oppositions along lines running in every direction may actually be in less danger of being torn with violence or falling to pieces than one split just along one line.

Age strata seem particularly subject to cross-cutting allegiances. Unlike class stratification, where it is possible to conceive of members of particular classes having few contacts with people in other classes, members of age strata nearly always belong also, at critical points in their lives, to at least one age-heterogeneous group—the family. What, then, are the mechanisms by which age-heterogeneous memberships reduce political conflict? Under what conditions are these mechanisms most likely to work?

For one thing, members of such age-heterogeneous groups as a church or work organization often have common goals and interests that may override age differences on political matters. On the job, workers of all ages may unite to improve working conditions, especially where individuals of different ages hold similar jobs. In addition, association with people of other ages in primary groups tends to bring about feelings of mutual loyalty and responsibility, and to forge close emotional bonds among all members. Such ties heighten the incentive to avoid political actions that might weaken or sever mutual attachments. Finally, interaction among age-heterogeneous members in these groups enables persons of differing political persuasion to socialize each other. It is no accident that children in the United States so often follow the party identification and voting patterns of their parents, so much so that, reminiscent of the Gilbert and Sullivan lyric, Hyman (1959:74) remarks that individuals may well be born into a political party. While this observation stresses the impact of parental ideas on children, children also teach their parents—or, at least, children, as they become politically aware, reactivate their parents' long-held but possibly latent views (cf. Riley et al., 1969). There was journalistic speculation, for example, that many prominent political figures in the United States were greatly influenced in their anti-Vietnam war positions by their college-age children.[9]

People of different ages in particular social groups are often held together, then, by common interests, shared sentiments, feelings of allegiance to one another, and sometimes, affection. Such ties can transcend political disagreements among age strata and check extreme polarization. And where political cleavage tends to follow the divisions between age strata, these cross-age relationships can minimize the likelihood that cleavage will erupt in open conflict.

But what if these groups themselves are sub-divided by age conflicts? If the issues dividing age strata within these groups are not the bases of political struggles, then intra-group age rifts seem unlikely to become politicized, to spawn political conflict in the larger society. In such circumstances, moreover, struggles in societal sub-systems may serve as a safety-valve by restricting to non-political arenas the expression of resentments and frustrations that might otherwise erupt in the larger society. By contrast, should the issues dividing age strata in the various societal groups coincide with those involved in the age conflicts in the polity, then the age cleavages are likely to reinforce each other.

The Inevitability of Aging   The process of aging also holds promise for reducing age conflict although, like membership in age-heterogeneous groups, its effectiveness is related to current issues. Aging *is* mobility—that special type of mobility of individuals from one age stratum to the next. Unlike mobility between class strata, aging is inevitable and universal. Because of its unique characteristics, aging can serve in special ways to minimize conflict among age strata. Consider the class analogy again. Those in the lower classes who seek membership in a higher class often take on the values and ideas of the class to which they aspire (Merton, 1957:262–80), thereby losing a sense of identification with their class of origin. Is not this outcome more likely when mobility is inevitable? That is, young people, especially those on the threshold of adulthood, are undoubtedly oriented to their future adult roles as worker, spouse, or parent and thus to the roles, with their associated attitudes, of older strata. This process may involve merely becoming more tolerant of the differing views of older people; or it may even involve adopting the viewpoint of more mature people—a type of "anticipatory socialization" or "false consciousness." Older people, on their part, may sympathize with the young because they "have been there" themselves. To the extent that such reciprocal orientations exist, they can weaken the incentive or the capacity to struggle. Young people's acceptance of the norms of older strata can dissipate the feeling of "we-ness" among age peers that is so important an aspect of group solidarity. And sympathetic understanding of each other's views among both old and young breeds mutual accommodation.

But even if the young remain hostile to the views of older people, the inevitability of aging can undermine in other ways their motivation to participate in militant protests. Many youths are unwilling to risk future rewards by engaging in activities that could lead to disciplinary measures, even arrest or expulsion from school or job. Alternatively, young people may be quite willing to accept subordinate status or other deprivations, if they view these as temporary. Indeed, many dissatisfactions with their current status may seem trivial, as long as improvement in the future can be realistically expected.

Certain issues do impel young people to action. Yet, even here, the inevitability of aging may operate—at least as it can hamstring the effectiveness of their struggles. Aging sets limits to the period of youth, which may be nearly ended before political awareness fully develops. Youth movements may have difficulty maintaining continuity of membership and leadership as particular members move on to the next age stratum (cf. Lipset and Altbach, 1967:240). And in the transition to adulthood, people united earlier may lose their sense of common fate, as the concerns of youth lose their relevance, or as their relative impotence is gradually replaced by the power and influence given adults.

Like membership in age-heterogeneous groups, however, aging can sometimes work to kindle militant struggles. This seems particularly likely if an issue—like a war in which the young person must participate—requires prompt resolution. Or, if the individual's future appears to hinge on an immediate outcome. Then the short period of youth that remains to him may heighten his sense of urgency and involve him in struggles seeking instant results. If the issue remains unresolved, the boundaries of age cleavage may merely move forward over the life course. Indeed, in such instances aging may become the instrument for change by disseminating new beliefs across the threshold of an older stratum.

I have proposed, then, that mechanisms which weaken bonds in an age stratum, or those which strengthen ties between age strata, can reduce age conflict. For, if weak solidarity in an age group limits its capacity to confront other age groups, solidarity ties across age lines lessen the motivation to struggle. But whether cross-cutting group affiliations or the inevitability of aging do in fact limit age conflicts in political life appears to depend on the nature of the issues at stake and on the degree to which issues coincide among the many subsystems of society. Let us now consider types of issues that might respond to the conflict-reducing mechanisms I have discussed.

Reduction of Conflict and the Political Context

It is my hypothesis that age-related conflict reducing mechanisms are most likely to be effective when the major issues of political controversy are material rather than ideal, that is, concern the way economic resources are distributed rather than questions of freedom and justice, the rights of all people, or ethical principles.[10] Thus, beyond the youthful idealism noted by poets and philosophers, the propensity of the young to challenge the old—especially around ideal issues—may be deeply rooted in the structure and dynamics of age stratification.

Material Issues and Conflict-reducing Mechanisms   Material issues bring into play class interests involving people of all ages. Many material issues are not clearly age-related. Rather, they are likely to bear upon, and to activate, economic class interests that cut across age lines, thereby reducing the salience of age differences. Where class interests dominate, individuals in a class, whatever their age, will tend to unite in pressing their demands. For example, in a shop or a union, although young and old may differ about how to distribute benefits—present pay increases versus pension increments—they will nevertheless work together to fight a wage freeze or legislation which restricts unions.

Even where such economic issues as taxes or expenditures that favor particular age categories may divide the public along age lines, polarization between age strata is often avoided since the issues also divide along cross cutting class lines. Within a particular class, people belong to age-heterogeneous groups where benefits designed for one age stratum indirectly accrue to people of other ages. Consider the family where public health care for the aged lightens the burden for younger family members, or where government financing of young people's college education reduces the financial obligations of middle-aged parents (cf. Riley, 1971). Or, consider the shop whose younger workers may support legislation providing liberal pensions for older workers to open up jobs for themselves.

The inevitability of aging with its potential for increased financial rewards may also allay young people's discontent with their relatively poor economic status. How great, after all, is the incentive to struggle over economic issues as long as the future holds promise of improvement?

In sum, it appears that membership in age-heterogeneous groups and age mobility can operate to reduce conflict around material issues by superseding age cleavages, or reducing the immediacy of these issues.

Ideal Issues and Conflict-reducing Mechanisms   Ideal issues seem less readily subject to such mechanisms. To be sure, few issues are purely "ideal" or "material." There may well be economic components in issues of war and peace, for example, or ideal components in the unequal distribution of wealth in an affluent society. As pure types, however, the two are distinct; and many specifically ideal issues seem more likely than material issues to drive a wedge between generations.

Ideal or moral issues involving justice or equality for society as a whole do not ordinarily bring into play cross-cutting solidarities. They tend to be broad, general questions touching all major spheres of social life which call forth differences between young and old everywhere. Further, if an age stratum is rebuffed on such an issue, its status and power become issues, reinforcing the basis of age cleavage (cf. Gusfield, 1966:173). Nor is age mobility likely to reduce the dissensions. Self-interested anticipation of improvement at the next stages of their own lives which might otherwise induce young people to postpone struggle, is irrelevant when the struggle is for justice or equality for all. And to the extent that the issues seem urgent, youth's right to be heeded now becomes more crucial than the possibility of higher status in the future. Finally, for youth these may be all or nothing issues requiring sweeping social changes.[11] It is such basic changes that older people see as a threat to their way of life and are especially likely to oppose.

The characteristic immediacy of many ideal issues and the inability or unwillingness of older people to change for them prompt young people (at least important segments of the youth) to resort to militant political methods.[12] Their sense of urgency is in keeping with the strong emotional overtones of ideal issues and the fact that some of these—like war—raise doubts about the very shape of their future or whether there will be a future at all. This impatience of youth is exacerbated by slow paced government agencies, dominated by mature strata unable, even when willing, to make such rapid changes. But older people are often not willing. When youth demand fundamental changes, the resistance of the old is aroused, and the militancy of youth increased.

For such reasons, ideal issues seem less amenable than material issues to processes that might reduce age conflict. It is controversies over such broad issues that seem so threatening to the old, so pressing to the young.

In sum, this paper has emphasized age in its own right as an important base of societal stratification. Because of the dynamic processes leading to an age-stratified society—with different strata often having unequal power and opposing political views—there is a high potential for political conflict along age lines. At the same time there are age-related mechanisms for reducing sharp age struggles. I have hypothesized that these conflict-reducing mechanisms are least effective when ideal issues predominate in political life. The fact that these types of issues are not always paramount in the polity helps explain the sporadic nature of sharp age conflicts. And since it is likely that these issues will be most prominent during periods of affluence, age conflicts may well prosper in the best of times.

References

Agnello, Thomas J. Jr. 1973. "Aging and the sense of political powerlessness." Public Opinion Quarterly 37 (Summer): 251–9.

Altbach, Philip G. and Patti M. Peterson. 1972. "Before Berkeley: historical perspectives on American student activism." Pp. 13–31 in Philip G. Altbach and Robert S. Laufer (eds.), The New Pilgrims: Youth Protest in Transition. New York: David McKay.

Becker, Howard S. 1960. "Notes on the concept of commitment." American Journal of Sociology 66 (July): 32–40.

Berelson, Bernard R., Paul F. Lazarsfeld, and William N. McPhee. (1954), 1966. Voting: A Study of Opinion Formation in a Presidential Campaign. Chicago: University of Chicago Press.

Cain, Leonard D., Jr. 1964. "Life course and social structure." Pp. 272–309 in Robert E. L. Faris (ed.), Handbook of Modern Sociology. Chicago: Rand McNally.

Cohn, Richard. 1972. "Mathematical note." Pp. 85–8 in Riley, Matilda White, Marilyn Johnson, and Anne Foner, Aging and Society. Volume III, A Sociology of Age Stratification. New York: Russell Sage Foundation.

Coser, Lewis A. (1956), 1964. The Functions of Social Conflict. New York: The Free Press.

Crittenden, John. 1962. "Aging and party affiliation." Public Opinion Quarterly 26 (Winter):648–57. 1969–1970. "Reply to Cutler." Public Opinion Quarterly 33 (Winter):589–91.

Cutler, Neal E. 1968. The Alternative Effects of Generation and Aging Upon Political Behavior: A Cohort Analysis of American Attitudes Toward Foreign Policy, 1946–1966. Oak Ridge, Tennessee: Oak Ridge National Laboratory. 1969–1970. "Generation, maturation, and party affiliation: a cohort analysis." Public Opinion Quarterly 33 (Winter):583–8.

Evan, William M. 1965. "Cohort analysis of attitude data." Pp. 117–42 in James M. Beshers (ed.), Computer Methods in the Analysis of Large-Scale Social Systems. Cambridge, Massachusetts: Joint Center for Urban Studies of the M.I.T. and Harvard University.

Feuer, Lewis S. 1969. The Conflict of Generations. New York: Basic Books, Inc.

Foner, Anne. 1972. "The polity." Pp. 115–59 in Riley, Matilda White, Marilyn Johnson, and Anne Foner, Aging and Society. Volume III, A Sociology of Age Stratification. New York: Russell Sage Foundation.

Gerth, H. H., and C. Wright Mills (eds.). 1958. From Max Weber. New York: Oxford University Press.

Glenn, Norval D. and Michael Grimes. 1968. "Aging, voting, and political interest." American Sociological Review 33 (August):563–75.

Glenn, Norval D. and Ted Hefner. 1972. "Further evidence on aging and party identification." Public Opinion Quarterly 36 (Spring):31–47.

Gusfield, Joseph R. 1966. Symbolic Crusade. Urbana, Illinois: University of Illinois Press.

Harris Survey. 1971. Reported in New York Post, January 7.

Heberle, Rudolph. 1951. Social Movements. New York: Appleton-Century-Crofts.

Heller, Celia S. (ed.). 1969. Structured Social Inequality. New York: The Macmillan Company.

Hofstadter, Richard. 1964a. "The pseudo-conservative revolt (1955)." Pp. 75–95 in Daniel Bell (ed.), The Radical Right. New York: Doubleday, Anchor Books. 1971. "Youth and politics." Pp. 743–91 in Robert K. Merton and Robert Nisbet (eds.), Contemporary Social Problems. New York: Doubleday, Anchor Books.

Hyman, Herbert H. 1959. Political Socialization. Glencoe, Illinois: Free Press.

Keniston, Kenneth and Michael Lerner. 1970. "The unholy alliance against the campus." New York Times Magazine (November 8):28–9, 56–86.

Klecka, William R. 1971. "Applying political generations to the study of political behavior: a cohort analysis." Public Opinion Quarterly 35 (Fall):358–73.

Laqueur, Walter. 1969. "Reflections on youth movements." Commentary 47 (June):33–41.

Lipset, Seymour Martin. (1960), 1963. Political Man. New York: Doubleday, Anchor Books. 1971. "Youth and politics." Pp. 743–91 in Robert K. Merton and Robert Nisbet (eds.), Contemporary Social Problems. New York: Harcourt Brace Jovanovich, Inc.

Lipset, Seymour Martin and Philip G. Altbach. 1967. "Student politics and higher education in the United States." Pp. 199–252 in Seymour Martin Lipset (ed.), Student Politics. New York: Basic Books.

Lipset, Seymour Martin and Everett Carll Ladd, Jr. 1972. "The political future of activist generations." Pp. 63–84 in Philip G. Altbach and Robert S. Laufer (eds.), The New Pilgrims: Youth Protest in Transition. New York: David McKay Company.

Mannheim, Karl (1928), 1952. "The problem of generations." Pp. 276–322 in Paul Kecskemeti (ed. and tr.), Essays on the Sociology of Knowledge. London: Routledge and Kegan Paul.

Mason, Karen Oppenheim, William M. Mason, H. H. Winsborough and W. Kenneth Poole. 1973. "Some methodological issues in cohort analysis of archival data." American Sociological Review 38 (April):242–58.

Merton, Robert K. 1957. Social Theory and Social Structure. The Free Press of Glencoe.

Reinhold, Meyer. 1970. "The generation gap in antiquity." Proceedings of the American Philosophical Society 114 (October):347–65.

Riley, Matilda White. 1971. "Social gerontology and the age stratification of society." The Gerontologist 11 (Spring, Part 1):79–87. 1973. "Aging and cohort succession: interpretations and misinterpretations." Public Opinion Quarterly 37 (Spring):35–49.

Riley, Matilda White and Anne Foner. 1968. Aging and Society. Volume I, An Inventory of Research Findings. New York: Russell Sage Foundation.

Riley, Matilda White, Anne Foner, Beth Hess, and Marcia L. Toby. 1969. "Socialization for the middle and later years." Pp. 951–82 in David A. Goslin (ed.), Handbook of Socialization Theory and Research. Chicago: Rand McNally.

Riley, Matilda White and Marilyn E. Johnson. 1971. "Age stratification and the society." Presented at the Annual Meetings of the American Sociological Association, Denver, Colorado.

Riley, Matilda White, Marilyn Johnson, and Anne Foner. 1972. Aging and Society. Volume III, A Sociology of Age Stratification. New York: Russell Sage Foundation.

Ryder, Norman B. 1965. "The cohort as a concept in the study of social change." American Sociological Review 30 (December):843–61.

Sheatsley, Paul B. 1966. "White attitudes toward the Negro." Daedalus (Winter):217–38.

Sorokin, Pitirim. (1947), 1969. Society, Culture, and Personality. New York: Cooper Square Publishers.

Zeitlin, Maurice. 1967. Revolutionary Politics and the Cuban Working Class. Princeton, New Jersey: Princeton University Press.

[1]This term is borrowed from Karl Mannheim (1952), one of the first to formulate certain similarities and differences between age and class.

[2]Heller (1969) uses this term as a title for her reader on social stratification. For a discussion of social inequality based on age, see Riley and Johnson (1971).

[3]Full data for such analyses are not readily available. They must include information about several cohorts at the start of their political careers, when political orientations are first being formed. In addition, comparable data for each cohort for several periods of time after entry into the political system are necessary for disentangling cohort differences from life course differences. A growing number of cohort studies deal with such political topics as party identification, voter turnout, and various political attitudes (for example, Crittenden, 1962; Cutler, 1968; Evan, 1965; Glenn and Grimes, 1968; Glenn and Hefner, 1972; Klecka, 1971). Such studies vary in their approximation of the "optimum" form of cohort analysis, facing many difficulties in achieving comparability of sampling or question wording, in allowing for mortality and migra-

tion, and in the knotty problems of analysis. (For a discussion of such possible pitfalls and a general overview of the problems, assumptions, and principles underlying cohort analysis, see Riley, Johnson, and Foner, 1972:22–90, 583–618, and, especially relevant to analysis of political data, 115–59.)

[4]In the growing literature on this "identification problem" in cohort analysis, see Cohn (1972) and, as one of the special instances for which relevant solutions have been developed, see Mason et al. (1973). Another procedure is exemplified in a further analysis of Table 1, in which Agnello (1973:258) "controls" on education as one factor in social change which, highly correlated with age, might confound the effects of age. (In fact, this control does not change his original finding. And, of substantive interest, is the possibility that the large size of the educated sector of the young cohort might itself serve to stimulate attitude change.)

[5]Methodological issues involved in comparing life course changes in cohorts with changes over time in the total sample are discussed in Riley, Johnson, and Foner (1972:72–3); Cutler (1969–1970); Crittendon (1969–1970); and Glenn and Hefner (1972).

[6]However, the finding does not hold for the earliest period examined, 1948; and the authors note that other survey data do not show comparable behavior for the depression cohort. Further, in 1964 and 1968, each entering (youngest) cohort was even more likely to support the Democrats than the depression cohort (Lipset and Ladd, 1972: 75–8).

[7]Feuer (1969:8) claims, for example, that revolutionary change in modern times has often been unaccompanied by a younger generation in conflict with an older one. See also Lipset and Altbach (1967:240) for comments on cycles in student political action, and Reinhold (1970) for examples of varying patterns of age conflict in antiquity.

[8]Parallel factors, such as cross-pressures and social mobility, have been examined as they affect class polarization in the polity. Discussions of status inconsistency are also pertinent to age (as in Riley, Johnson, and Foner, 1972:413–14).

[9]Such hypothesized effects of membership in age-heterogeneous groups are, of course, likely to be attenuated to the extent that actual contact and interaction between people of different ages is reduced, as in the case of young people living away from home.

[10]The distinction is based on Weber's analysis (Gerth and Mills, 1958:180–94) and its later elaborations by Gusfield (1966:13–24, 172–88) and Hofstadter (1964a:84–5, 88, 1964b:98–100). Cf. Berelson, Lazarsfeld, and McPhee (1966:183–4) and their general discussion relating these types of issues to cleavages in political life (194–214).

[11]In 1970, a period of vigorous student dissent, a survey of college students, for example, found 75% agreeing that "basic changes in the system will be necessary" to improve the quality of life in America (Keniston and Lerner, 1970:56).

[12]Evidence that many young people did not look askance at non-conventional politics at a time when student protests were flourishing is suggested, for example, by late 1970 surveys of eighteen to twenty year olds (both college and non-college) which found that 54% regarded student protests as a healthy sign (Harris Survey, 1971).

Interest-Group Liberalism and the Politics of Aging

Robert H. Binstock

This is a discussion of aged Americans as a case of disadvantaged constituencies in the American political system. The case is instructive because even though the aged's access to political power is at least equal to that of other broad groupings of American citizens, there is little indication that this access provides a means for substantially alleviating the economic and social problems of the severely disadvantaged aged. In this respect the politics of aging adds some dimension to the growing body of political science literature that is critical both of the American political system and of those who have studied it during the past several decades.

Among the many contemporary critiques of American politics and political science, that of Theodore J. Lowi (1969) seems the most cogent for understanding the politics of aging. The case of the aged is very well described and accounted for by Lowi's characterization of American politics. Moreover, the ideas he poses in his search for reform provide an excellent point of departure for considering the ways in which the politics of aging may add to the general understanding of American politics.

Most students of American politics are now acquainted with Lowi's argument. He characterizes the functioning of American politics as "interest-group liberalism." He charges that even as laissez-faire economics was a handmaiden of "big capitalism," pluralist theory has been even more fully the handmaiden of interest-group liberalism, fostering acceptance of the notion that "the public interest" or social justice is brought about through conflicts and accommodation among organized groups, each seeking fulfillment of its own interests. Groups rather than citizens are represented in the formulation of public policy. Government does not use its coercive power to implement specific policies derived from democratic processes in which citizens are represented. Rather, it parcels out to private groups the power to make public policy. If the groups are held accountable at all, it is through procedural rather than substantive accountability. When the legitimacy of government is challenged, our "public men" respond by trying to organize "latent" interests, so that they can sit down with other groups at the bargaining tables where public policy is formulated and implemented. This reduces inconsistencies in the ways in which government relates to the society, but not

From *The Gerontologist*, Vol. 12, No. 2, Part I, Autumn 1972. Reprinted by permission of the Gerontological Society and the author.

in its relations to the citizenry. In short, interest-group liberalism is the implementation of an empty ideology rather than social justice.

To examine the politics of aging in the context of Lowi's characterization, the aged will be identified, for purposes of brevity and clarity, in terms of chronological age: generally, the 20 million persons who are 65 years of age and older (Brotman, 1971a); in a few contexts, some of the additional 9 million who are 60 to 64. Similarly, this discussion will focus on the income situation of the aged as an illustrative frame of reference for the disadvantaged status of the aged in American society.

Despite all the assistance provided to the aged through Social Security, Old Age Assistance, Medicare, private corporate pensions, and other programs, one quarter of the 20 million Americans 65 years of age and older have incomes below the poverty line, a budgetary measure based on "an economy food plan for emergency use" (Brotman, 1971b). If one uses a measure that provides a slightly more tolerable standard of living, the "near-poor poverty threshold" (which adds 25% to the poverty-line measure), one-fourth of the older persons living as families are below the standard, and fully 60% of the aged living alone are below it (Brotman, 1971c). If one employs various measures of adequate income developed by the Bureau of Labor Statistics, the proportion of older persons living as families that is below standard can reach as much as 75% (Sobel, 1971).

The relatively low income position of the aged should suffice, without elaborating other arguments, as a standard in considering the need for improvement of the situation of the aged through politics. (It should be kept in mind, however, that relative income deprivation extends disadvantages to virtually all aspects of contemporary life— such as housing, medical care, nutrition, and transportation—for which purchasing power is needed to compete favorably.)

The first and second sections of this article examine electoral politics and the politics of organized groups as means for redressing the situation of the disadvantaged aged. The examination is largely restricted to national politics. A final section reconsiders prospects for the aged and other groups achieving an adequate measure of social justice through American politics.

Electoral Politics

In searching for means by which the disadvantages of older persons might be ameliorated through national politics, partisans of the aged have tended to focus on two possible sources of strength—the large numbers of aged persons who vote in national elections and organized groups working to advance the interests of the aged. Those few political scientists who have addressed themselves to this issue have tended to agree that votes and organized groups are the possibilities most worth examining, although they have not been as optimistic as the partisans (Campbell, 1971; Carley, 1969; Pinner, Jacobs, and Selznick, 1959; Holtzman, 1963; Sundquist, 1968).

The Case for the Aged Vote Advocates for the aged are fond of citing statistics to portray aged voters as an important and potentially decisive constituency in American electoral politics. But these portrayals rarely seem to have much impact upon the judgment and behavior of politicians experienced in national politics. The reason is that the best case that can be made for the importance of the aged vote is impressive only in the most superficial sense. It rests upon a series of assumptions that are mostly invalid. Moreover, such importance has neither been documented satisfactorily through scholarly work nor demonstrated impressionistically in the experience of politicians and their staffs.

The most impressive, superficial cases frequently used by advocates for the aged are put in terms of the proportion of voters who are old. While the aged are 10% of the nation's population, they are an even larger proportion of the electorate, no matter which of many ways one might wish to construct the proportion. Depending on the statistics chosen, it is possible to make a case that persons 65 years of age and older constitute as much as 16% of the national electorate. In the 1968 presidential election, for instance, they were 15.8% of those eligible to vote (US Bureau of the Census, 1970). Of those actually voting in the 1968 election, they constituted 15.4%. In non-presidential national elections, the aged are typically a slightly higher proportion of those voting than in presidential elections; in 1966, for instance, they constituted 16% of those actually voting (US Bureau of the Census, 1968).

How will the Twenty-Sixth Amendment to the Constitution change this picture? A projection for the 1972 presidential election, based on the 1970 Census distribution of population by age and applying the 1968 election turnout rates for voters 65 and older and voters under 21, suggests that the older group will be 15% of those who vote (US Bureau of the Census, 1970, 1971). In short, even considering the Twenty-Sixth Amendment, one can use gross statistics to support the claim that aged voters have been and will continue to be at least one-seventh of the actual voters in any given election.

It is possible to argue that many of the "near aged" under 65 years of age who share the immediate interests of the aged should be included in an estimate of the size of the aged vote. First, there are persons who have retired before the age of 65 and for all intents and purposes might be said to be subject to the same range of retirement-associated problems as persons over 65. Second there are the younger spouses of retirees, possibly influenced by the outlook of their spouses and by the economic and other experiences brought upon the household by retirement. And third, there are those who are about to retire and who may be sufficiently conscious of retirement problems to respond politically in much the same way as the retiree. No data are available to provide a good estimate of the number of such persons. A ridiculously generous rough estimate could be made by adding in all persons 60 years of age and over as persons who would behave as "aged voters." Applying the 1968 turnout rate for voters 65 and older (since we are assuming, for these purposes, that these younger persons are like their elders), one could project that 20.8% of those voting in 1972 will be 60 years of age and older (US Bureau of the Census, 1970, 1971).

The Weaknesses of the Case   The game of building up the case for the aged vote in these superficial terms can be, and is, played endlessly. It takes a wide variety of forms, including the manipulation of statistics on relations between health or level of education and turnout rate, and likely changes in the health and education levels of older people. Or it can get into such matters as a larger-than-average number of older persons residing in certain key states in the electoral college. There is little point, however, in dwelling on all these possibilities. For as large as one could build the potential aged vote, there are many critical limitations on electoral politics as a source of strength for solving the problems of the disadvantaged aged under present conditions.

One limitation, of course, is the general limitation on elections as means for overcoming disadvantages through our political system. It is one thing for a group to be able to influence the outcome of an election. It is quite another for the outcome to have an important bearing upon the solution of a group's problems. For this to be the case, the victorious party or candidates would have to be distinctively committed to a position that represented a major solution, which was subsequently implemented, and proved to be reasonably effective. It is probably not too much to say that such scenarios are rarely enacted in American politics. Perhaps the most notable modern exception, potentially, was the Johnson-Goldwater race of 1964, in which it might be argued that the candidates were strongly identified as for and against, respectively, major solutions to the problems of the aged. Even for this election, however, no one has produced an analysis to show a shift to Johnson and Democratic Congressional candidates among normally Republican voters that was greater among the aged than among younger segments of the population. Nor would anyone seriously argue that the enactment of Medicare during President Johnson's administration has substantially alleviated the problems of the disadvantaged aged.

While most politicians wish to avoid offending the aged, and many favor proposals to provide incremental benefits to older persons, few are disposed to develop special appeals to the aged among the central issues of their campaigns. They regard the partisan attachments of the aged to be among the most stable within the American electorate, not likely to be shifted substantially by special appeals. This judgment commonly made by politicians is borne out by the studies of Angus Campbell and his associates, who attribute the notable stability of the aged voter to the longer period of time he has had to develop a strong partisan self-image (Campbell, 1971). Despite the influences of cohort socialization, and because of the social, economic, and geographic heterogeneity of the older population, the political attitudes of aged voters, as well as their partisan attachments, are diverse. As Campbell (1971) expresses it:

... because each age cohort includes people who differ profoundly in many important conditions of life it is not likely that any group will be very homogeneous in its attitudes. The evidence which national surveys provide us does in fact demonstrate that attitudinal differences between age groups are far less impressive than those within age groups.

The attitudes of older persons are more cohesive than usual, however, on issues that seem to involve their self-interest as an age group. Survey questions proposing greater tax support for public schools are among the few that typically elicit responses which differ significantly by age. While such issues are customarily posed in local politics through referenda, and rarely set forth sharply in national politics, the greater degree of cohesion in older persons' responses to them does raise a possibility worth some consideration.

If major issues in national electoral politics were recurringly framed in terms of the special interests of the aged, and voters were presented with a clear choice among candidates and/or parties, would older persons be likely to form a cohesive voting bloc that would be able to reequalize the aged? Evidence bearing directly on this question is not extensive. But the evidence that does exist tends to indicate that the prospect of a decisive bloc of aged voters is unlikely.

Various studies suggest that a substantial proportion of older persons, ranging from 40 to 65%, do not even identify themselves as old or aged (Riley & Foner, 1968). Data suggest that most of them are relatively well-off, ranking high in socioeconomic status and health (Riley & Foner, 1968; cf. Kutner, 1956). Apparently these older persons wish to avoid identification as aged because they feel that it would lead others to regard them as old, "different," and perhaps, deviant (Blau, 1956; Barron, 1961). To the extent that they are concerned with problems and grievances that are linked to old age, some fragmentary evidence suggests that they do not perceive these problems as stem-ming from the fact that they are aged (Kastenbaum & Durkee, 1964).

Whether the comparatively disadvantaged older persons, who are most likely to identify as aged, tend to see their income, health, housing, safety, and transportation problems as "aging problems" is unclear. There are no systematic studies bearing directly on this question. Nonetheless, less specialized scholarship in the field of developmental psychology as well as in political science leads to the reasonable inference that even if the disadvantaged aged see their problems as age-related problems, they see them in other contexts as well (Neugarten, 1964, 1968). A full life cycle of socialization, experiences, and attachments—family, schooling, ethnicity, occupation, income, residence, peer and other associations—presents a multitude of sources for group identification and perceptions of special interest. It would not be unreasonable to infer that many of those who identify as aged, and who are responsive to the special interests of the disadvantaged aged, would have stronger competing identifications and interests. Presumably these competing factors would substantially dilute a response to attempts to mobilize a cohesive voting bloc of the disadvantaged aged, based on their special interests.

Given all the limitations on the potential development of a cohesive bloc of "disadvantaged aged voters," it is probably not too much to say that most recruits would be from the pool of the most severely disadvantaged elderly. A generous estimate, say, would be the 5 million or so whose inadequate purchasing power leaves them below the poverty line. One might build a tenuous argument that, given the proper circumstances, a cohesive bloc of up to 5 million voters could "swing" a national election and use that situation to extract major, substantial policy and program concessions to further its self-interest. But even if one accepts such a tenuous argument, cohesive behavior by 5 or even several million aged voters would require much sharper articulation and advocacy of their presumed special interests than takes place at present.

Organized Groups

One possible source for stronger and sharper articulation of the interests of the aged is organizations consisting of older persons or their advocates. The precedents and general character of American politics suggest that organizations, in fact, are the most likely sources of political leverage for the aged, whether through effective articulation of interests leading to the development of a cohesive voting bloc or through other modes of organized political activity.

The major precedent for organizations of the aged in American national politics is the Townsend Movement, which began in California in 1933 (cf. Pinner, Jacobs, & Selznick, 1959). At its peak in 1936, it had members in every state and probably included as many as 1½ million persons, but it quickly died out in the 1940s (Holtzman, 1963). Townsend, a Long Beach physician, proposed the enactment of a tax on all business transactions to finance a $200-a-month pension for every citizen over the age of 60. At one time it was widely suggested that the Movement played a decisive role in the passage of the Social Security Act. Subsequent scholarship indicates, however, that its major impact was probably to accelerate somewhat the timetable for serious consideration of old-age insurance as a national policy (Holtzman, 1963).

The major legacy of the Townsend Movement seems to be that it has brought a specter of "senior power" into gerontologists' discussions of American politics. Because the Movement demonstrated that old age can be the basis for the development of a political organization, it often serves as a frame of reference for evaluating contemporary organizations of the aged (Sheppard, 1962; Tibbitts, 1962). Yet the methods through which the Townsend Movement was developed, and the economic, social, and political circumstances of the Depression Era in which it thrived, distinguish it considerably from contemporary organizations active in national politics related to old age. The current organizations of older persons and of those interested in the aged require assessment in their own terms.

On the present scene there are literally hundreds of organizations that engage in the politics of national policies and programs affecting the aged. In preparing for the White House Conference on Aging of late 1971, the Conference planning staff effectively legitimated the roles of these organizations by inviting over 400 to send representative delegates to the Conference. In a seeming burlesque of Lowi's characterization of American politics as "interest-group liberalism," the Conference staff officially determined that business, labor, and consumers; the professions; religious, fraternal, social, and service organizations; and community action organizations all deserved representation in formulating national policy toward the aging in the 1970s.

The vast majority of these organizations, however, engage in the politics of aging only on an *ad hoc* basis, when an aging-related legislative proposal or other imminent policy issue happens to affect their organized interests in more than a passing way. For example, when US Senator Yarborough several years ago introduced bills for sweeping reform of private corporate pension plans, a variety of banking and insurance trade associations that rarely engage in the politics of aging entered the arena for brief flurries of intensive and effective activity. Alternatively, a milestone event such as the White House

Conference on Aging of 1971 will encourage an organization like the American Psychological Association to form a special Task Force on Aging to assemble a comprehensive agenda of policy recommendations.

Only ten organizations that actively engage in politics at the national level are more or less exclusively preoccupied with issues relating to the aged.[1] For purposes of discussion, they might be conveniently termed "the aging organizations." Three of them are mass membership organizations consisting primarily of aged persons. Four are trade associations. Another is a professional society. Still another is a loose confederation of social welfare agencies. And, activated just within the past 2 years is a coalition of individual professionals attempting to bring special attention to the plight of black older persons.

The membership rolls of the three mass membership organizations total about 5½ million.[2] It is unclear, however, what proportion of the aged population this figure represents. No data are available to indicate how many persons belong to more than one of these organizations, or the extent to which the membership rolls include persons under 65 years of age who may be spouses of retirees or who may have retired in their early 60s or younger.

The National Council of Senior Citizens (NCSC) recruits its membership of about 3 million from the ranks of organized labor. It was developed by organized labor in the early 1960s, with Walter Reuther and the United Auto Workers in the forefront of the organizing effort, for the express purpose of helping achieve the passage of Medicare. It has remained active in national politics related to the aging ever since. In its early years, NCSC received financial support and staff services from the unions. By the late 1960s, it became self-supporting through membership dues. It provides its membership with newsletters and offers them discount drugs and group insurance plans.

The American Association of Retired Persons (AARP) and the National Retired Teachers Association (NRTA) function in national politics as if they were one organization (hereafter referred to as AARP); their combined membership totals 2½ million. Although the two component units formally retain separate identities, they share professional staff and various elements of program. AARP was developed through the late 1950s and early 1960s by an insurance entrepreneur. He began by selling a group insurance plan to the retired teachers organization, which had existed for several decades. Subsequently, he reached out to a wider market through a new vehicle, the AARP. While the teachers organization wished to retain its separate identity, it endorsed and assisted the recruitment efforts of AARP and has maintained a formal working alliance. AARP has recruited its membership through a variety of means: direct mailings, mass-media advertisements, local chapter campaigns, and so on. Like NCSC, it provides its members with group insurance plans, discount drugs, travel packages, newsletters, and magazines. It did not become particularly active in national politics until the latter half of the 1960s.

The third mass membership organization, the National Association of Retired Federal Employees (NARFE), has only about 150,000 members, largely concentrated in the Washington metropolitan area. While it has been in existence for some decades and has taken public stands on proposals affecting Federal retirement benefits, it began to engage actively in national politics only within the last 2 years. It, too, provides its members with newsletters and discount plans.

The larger membership organizations, NCSC and AARP, have active (though informal) ties with the Democratic and Republican parties, respectively. They do not jeopardize their tax-free status with the Internal Revenue Service by endorsing candidates or officially campaigning for them. But, indirectly, especially in the case of NCSC, they become involved in electoral politics. Since the 1964 presidential campaign, NCSC has shared staff services and informally cooperated with a number of *ad hoc* campaign organizations that have worked for the election of Democratic Presidential and Congressional candidates, in particular those endorsed by organized labor. In the last several years, NCSC has helped establish a more permanent political action organization known as Concerned Seniors for Better Government. While AARP began to develop informal partisan links with the advent of the Nixon Administration, its efforts along this line are not as fully developed as those of NCSC. The history of AARP's early development is not at all comparable to NCSC's direct genesis from Democratic politics, and no existing mechanisms like the unions provide AARP with a ready-made unofficial link to partisan activity.

Politicians and activists in the field of aging perceive the two organizations as having somewhat different types of memberships. The stereotypical image of the NCSC member is that of a working-class Democrat in the industrial Northeast. The AARP member is viewed as a white-collar or professional Republican who may come from any part of the country. The organizations themselves tend to vaguely acknowledge these stereotypes in off-the-record conversations (although NCSC strives to promote an image of broader geographical distribution). They make no data available, however, for outsiders who are interested in developing a more precise picture. When attempts are made in public forums to label the organizations with these stereotypes, the leaders counter by vigorously asserting the heterogeneity of their memberships in terms of income, former occupation, geographic distribution, and other characteristics. They do this because when they "speak for" their memberships, they often want to portray themselves as speaking for *all* aged persons. They imply that their memberships are representative samples of at least 20 million older voters, and not merely narrower, self-seeking sub-groups. But the very act of saying what their members want, and implying that this is what all old people want, puts them in the paradoxical situation of speaking as if the interests of their members, as well as the interests of the American aged, were monolithic. This puts a tremendous strain on their credibility as "representatives" of the aged.

Of the four trade associations that are active in national politics and mostly preoccupied with issues related to aging, three are com-prised of affiliate organizations concerned with long-term care facilities for the aged. These are the American Association of Homes for the Aging (about 1,000 affiliates), the American Nursing Home Association (federated through 48 states and 8 regional associations), and the National Council of Health Care Services (consisting of a relatively small number of major commercial enterprises in the long-term care business, such as the nursing-home-chain subsidiary of Holiday Inns). The fourth trade association, the National Association of State Units on Aging (NASUA), consists of the administrators of the government agencies in each state (and also Puerto Rico, the Virgin Islands, Guam, American Samoa, and the Trust Territories) sup-ported by federal grant-in-aid funds under the Older Americans Act of 1965. NASUA's membership also includes the chairmen of the techni-cal, advisory, and supervisory committees, commissions, boards, and councils associated with each of the state grant-in-aid units.

The trade associations invest virtually all of their efforts in na-tional politics in getting more federal funds for their operations and in seeking adjustments in the detailed official conditions under which they ply their trades. Most of this activity takes the form of direct pleading with Congressmen and administrative officials. While some of the affiliates comprising these trade groups have active links with political party organizations, the trade associations themselves do not. They are financially supported through affiliate dues and con-tributions.

The professional association active in policy issues, the Geron-tological Society, has about 2,500 individual members and several affiliates. Its membership includes behavioral and social scientists, biologists, physiologists, physicians, social workers, architects, nurses, and social agency administrators. They are bound together by their specialized interests in aging within their larger professional fields. The organization is supported through membership dues, jour-nal subscription fees, and federal grants and contracts for research and training. While it has existed for 25 years, it has only become active on public policy issues since 1968. The Society states policy positions on a wide variety of issues affecting the aging. It is especially vigorous in seeking earmarked appropriations for research and academic training in aging, through frequent communications with Congressional committee chairmen and their staffs.

The National Council on the Aging (NCOA) claims about 1,400 organizational affiliates, mostly public and private health, social work, and community action agencies. It developed out of a Committee on Aging of the National Social Welfare Assembly that became a separate entity in the late 1950s with the assistance of a grant from the Ford Foundation. Since its inception, NCOA has attempted to play the role of technical consultant to all organizations in the country that have been or might be undertaking programs to solve the problems of older persons. NCOA has performed this role rather well, considering that throughout most of its history it has had to struggle for operating funds. In large measure its survival can be traced to the mid-1960s when it developed working ties with NCSC and organized labor. This alliance (described below) helped secure from OEO and the Department of Labor several grants that enabled it to maintain operations and strengthen its reputation as a technical resource.

The newest of the ten aging organizations active in national politics is the National Caucus on the Black Aged. It has a membership of nearly 150 individual professionals, including many non-blacks. The Caucus has become politically active only within the past 2 years, searching for means to elevate priorities for black older persons within the range of programs that are generally presumed to be of some benefit for aged persons. The Caucus has testified before Congressional Committees, met with federal administrative officials, and participated in aging conferences and committees. To date, it has not developed any firm working alliances with other aging organizations, black organizations, or political parties.

The Political Activities of the "Aging" Organizations As might be inferred from this short description of the aging organizations, their activities in national politics are hardly militant or radical. Their efforts do not reflect a vigorous pursuit of major changes that could bring about substantial amelioration of the problems of the disadvantaged aged. The activities of these organizations are similar to those in many other arenas of interest that have been examined by students of American politics (cf. Truman, 1960, Ziegler, 1964).

In briefly reviewing the contemporary political activities of these organizations, it is worth distinguishing broadly between two types of policies and programs (cf. Derthick, 1970) because the manner in which aging organizations engage with them are rather different. One type can be characterized as *direct income transfer* policies and programs—that is, those designed to place additional purchasing power in the hands of explicitly designated population groups (defined by income and demography), through specific conditions embodied either in legislation or in implemental administrative regulations and guidelines. Among those in this group would be Social Security, Old Age Assistance, veterans' benefits, Federal Civil Service Retirement Benefits, Railroad Retirement Benefits, Rent Supplements, Medicare, and Medicaid. The other type can be termed *middleman* policies and programs, those that fund and empower public and private organizations to develop and operate properties and to carry out services (training and education; research, planning, program development, technical assistance, and coordination; social, health, and recreational services). Among these are the Hill-Burton Act, OEO Community Action Programs, Urban Redevelopment, Model Cities, a variety of volunteer and paid community service or "action" programs, the Older Americans Act, Manpower Training and Development, innumerable programs administered by the National Institutes of Health and the National Institute of Mental Health, and literally hundreds of others.

The terms used to distinguish the two types of policies and programs are not intended to imply that middlemen (such as hospitals, welfare agencies, nursing homes, and so on) have no role in direct income transfer programs. Rather the distinction has to do with the fundamental nature of the two types, a contrast that is expressed in official legislative and administrative details. The official specifications of direct income transfer programs deal with the explicit conditions under which citizens can get certain amounts of additional purchasing power, the precise form in which that power is made available, and the logistics through which the purchasing power is transferred (sometimes through middlemen, and sometimes involving credit for the purchaser and public reimbursement for the vendor). In contrast, the official details of middleman programs are almost exclusively concerned with specifying the processes within which it will be determined which middlemen will be empowered and funded to develop and operate facilities and to carry out services. These latter programs embody assumptions (often unwarranted) that general groups of citizens may eventually benefit from the distribution of power and funds to middlemen. But the precise nature of the benefits and their distribution is largely within the hands of those middlemen who succeed in obtaining control, or a share of control, over program power and funds.

The "Aging" Organizations and Direct Income Transfer Programs
The activity of the aging organizations in relation to direct transfer payment issues during the past decade has been just about what one would expect. The organizations have not developed and put forth strong proposals for major new policies and programs for redistrib-

uting purchasing power to the aged. It would even be difficult to argue that the contemporary aging organizations played a strong role in helping to bring into being the direct income transfer programs that currently benefit the aged. Undoubtedly, NCSC played some part in the passage of Medicare and Medicaid, since it was part of a coalition of organizations lobbying for the enactment of that legislation and, indeed, was initially developed for that purpose. But those who have analyzed the politics of the Medicare legislation do not portray NCSC and other aging groups as having played an important role (Harris, 1966; Sundquist, 1968). The activities of the aging organizations in relation to direct income transfer issues have largely been efforts to obtain incremental adjustments in existing programs.

The mass membership organizations—NCSC, AARP, and NARFE—adopt policy positions and present testimony in income transfer programs favoring increases in the size of benefits; extension of eligibility for benefits to a greater number of persons; extension of the conditions and time periods for which benefits are due; and relaxation or elimination of the conditions that can make one eligible for benefits. Their attention is directed especially toward Social Security and Medicare, programs that are ideologically nurtured by a "social insurance" mythology. Comparatively little attention is given to Old Age Assistance and Medicaid, programs that transfer stigmata as well as purchasing power. And virtually no attention is given to portions of these programs—such as Title IV of the Social Security Act, making federal grant-in-aid funds available to state welfare agencies for social services to the aged—that do not concern direct income transfer.

There is little contrast among the specific positions adopted by the mass membership organizations. No doubt NCSC and AARP, within their own immediate frames of reference, regard it as important if one organization advocates a 12% increase in Social Security benefits and the other comes out for an increase of 15%. But when one observes that, even with all the increases in benefits and extensions of eligibility enacted through the years, at least 25% of the aged are in poverty, a difference between 12 and 15% on any given round of benefit increases can hardly be evaluated as significant.

NCSC and AARP arrive at their policy positions in similar fashion. Each staff develops proposals with a stable of consulting economists. The proposals are presented to a committee "representing" the mass membership. There are no major debates or internal struggles over the proposals; with occasional minor adjustments, they are ratified.

While changes in direct transfer programs and policies of the kinds advocated by the mass membership organizations are often enacted, it would be difficult for anyone to make a precise judgment of the extent to which the organizations' efforts may be responsible. Generally speaking, however, it is safe to say that their influence is far from decisive. When legislation is enacted that corresponds closely to an organization's proposals, the leaders take some credit; but they do not explicitly assert that their efforts played the decisive role. In newsletters and other organizational communications they report on meetings with key Congressmen and the President in which they have registered the organization's position. These are relatively concrete facts and imply some measure of influence in the legislative process. From all indications at present, however, organizational maintenance needs do not seem to require NCSC and AARP leaders to demonstrate that they are responsible for direct income transfer benefits to older persons. For the present the drug, insurance, and travel programs; the newsletters and magazines; leaders' accounts of dramatic meetings with politicians and their constant recitation of problems of the aged; and the sociability of local chapter meetings; seem to provide members with adequate incentive for paying their annual membership dues.

The activities of the aging trade associations in relation to income transfer issues are somewhat different. One of them, NASUA, the association of state grant-in-aid administrators, virtually ignores them. The long-term care associations—AAHA, ANHA, and NCHCS—not surprisingly are especially concerned with the ways in which transfer programs affect their trades—nursing home and old age home operations. They pay almost no attention to Social Security, but concentrate on Medicare, Medicaid, and Old Age Assistance. They favor benefit increases and extensions of eligibility that will enable their enterprises to function more profitably or more smoothly (in the case of nonprofit organizations, especially those associated with AAHA). They are most active in seeking adjustments in the rules that govern their roles as vendors in the income transfer process. Through testimony, position statements, special conferences, and direct meeting with key legislators and administrative officials, they seek changes in such matters as procedures for third-party payments and standards regarding the kinds of institutions in which beneficiaries can be eligible for transfer purchasing power.

NCOA, the confederation of social work, health, and community action agencies, barely participates in issues regarding income transfer programs. It inserts periodic statements into the public record, favoring incremental increases and extensions of transfer benefits. This is sufficient to maintain its credentials as one of the legitimate aging interest groups, so that it can participate vigorously in political activities concerned with middleman policies and programs.

The National Caucus on the Black Aged is just beginning its activity. Predictably, it is formulating proposals for distributing to black older persons a greater proportional share of direct income transfer payments than to nonblack older persons. The main assets for the

Caucus in this effort, to date, are readily available data to show that in almost every measurable respect, black aged persons are about twice as badly off as the rest of the aged population.

The Gerontological Society invests relatively little effort in activities related to income transfer policies and programs. When it is invited to appear at hearings on income transfer issues, it calls on an individual member, perhaps an economist or an expert on nursing homes, to present testimony. And when it develops monographs on matters relating to aging, it does treat issues of income and medical care. But most of the public policy activity of the organization and its leadership is in relation to the middleman programs.

The "Aging" Organizations and "Middleman" Programs In the politics of middleman programs, the active aging organizations to date have been NCSC, NCOA, AARP, NASUA, and the Gerontological Society. Their behavior has many features in common. They seek to create new programs that would provide funds and authority more or less exclusively to aging organizations. They attempt to earmark or otherwise lay claim to an established share for aging organizations within existing programs that are already making funds and authority available to a fairly broad range of middlemen. They search, without much success, for some authoritative administrative mechanism —typically termed "a means of coordination"—through which they can greatly increase their leverage for carving out shares for aging organizations within the hundreds of existing middleman programs.

The proposals of the aging organizations regarding existing middleman programs, as will be illustrated below, rarely present much detail about the specific means through which the problems of the disadvantaged aged might be solved. Vague substantive content is offered, designed to provide a sufficient rationale for including aging organizations among the middlemen that share in a program. The highly specific proposals set forth by the aging organizations deal with two types of matters. First, they suggest rule changes designed to increase the probability of aging organizations winning a share of middleman programs. Second, they set forth detailed proposals for maintaining or increasing the funds authorized for programs in which aging organizations have already established a share. The only essential differences among the aging organizations in all this activity concern which of them should be receiving middleman shares from which sources, and how much each should get.

The entrance of aging organizations into the politics of middleman programs had its genesis in the campaign for the passage of Medicare and its spillover into Democratic electoral politics. As indicated earlier, NCSC was explicitly created by organized labor to provide support for Medicare, and it quickly became an organizing basis for *ad hoc* "senior citizen" groups that campaigned extensively for Lyndon Johnson and Democratic Congressional candidates. In a parallel set of activities, several Committees in Congress were created for essentially the same purposes. Both the standing Subcommittee on Aging of the Senate Committee on Labor and Public Welfare and the Senate Special Committee on Aging were established by Senator Pat McNamara of Michigan and his Democratic colleagues, largely to bolster the campaign for Medicare and to serve as personal vehicles for creating support among electoral constituents (Vineyard, 1971). Since their creation in 1959 and 1961, respectively, these two committees, but particularly the Special Committee, have served as sympathetic forums for aging organizations to agitate for their interests, and as arbiters of which aging organizations have a legitimate "right" to be heard. The Special Committee, though without legislative authority, has also assisted the aging organizations by formulating legislative proposals and nurturing them through the legislative process.

By late 1964, the aging organizations began to agitate actively for participation in middlemen programs. The prospects for passage of Medicare seemed excellent. NCSC, which had accumulated political credits through its campaign efforts, was searching for a new area of activity to sustain its organizational momentum. NCOA was struggling for financial survival. President Johnson's agenda for the Great Society was generating the OEO War on Poverty and a host of other programs that provided funds and authority to middleman organizations. A 1961 White House Conference on Aging, primarily convened to build support for Medicare, had also set forth innumerable rationales, resolutions, and recommendations that provided justifications for reallocating larger shares of all federal programs to the aging. The Conference also asserted that authoritative mechanisms should be established in the federal government, in each state government, and in every community throughout the nation, for redirecting and coordinating policies and programs to make them more responsive to the aged (Binstock, 1971).

In 1965, through the sponsorship of Senator McNamara (and Representative John Fogarty), and with considerable supportive efforts from the members and staff of the Special Committee on Aging, Congress passed the Older Americans Act. This legislation authorized the one set of middleman programs that to date has been established as the more or less exclusive domain of aging organizations. The Act created an Administration on Aging (AoA) within the Department of Health, Education, and Welfare, headed by a Commissioner who is nominated by the President and confirmed by the Senate. Title II of the Act charged the Commissioner with a vague "responsibility" for coordinating all activities of the federal government related to aging, but gave him no power to do so. Titles III, IV, and V established three middleman programs that had a total allocation of $6.5 million in their first year.

Title III of the Act is a two-tiered grant-in-aid program that provides an equal sum to all states, plus an additional sum to each in accordance with a formula based on the number of persons in each state who are 65 years of age and older. A state Unit on Aging (designated by the Governor) receives one annual sum to help meet the costs of "statewide planning, coordination, and administration." It receives in addition a much larger sum for selective distribution in response to grant proposals from organizations within the state for conducting middleman projects such as the operation of senior centers, social services, information and referral agencies, and other so-called community programs. (In fiscal 1971 the total of "pass-on" grant funds distributed among the states was $9 million, and "planning, coordination, and administration" funds totaled $4 million.) In actual fact, few of the state Units have had much to administer or any power to coordinate. They have been functioning primarily as pipelines for distributing the Title III grant funds to organizations within their states. In effect, Title III set up 50 different middleman programs to be bargained over.

Titles IV and V provide for distribution of grant and contract funds from AoA directly to public and private organizations, without involving the states. Title IV funds research and demonstration; Title V supports Training.

The aging organizations that were active in national politics when the Older Americans Act was passed quickly became disenchanted with AoA. Because of the way Title III was structured, and due to a series of strategic decisions by the first Commissioner of AoA, NCSC and NCOA had little opportunity to obtain much authority or funds through the programs. The first Commissioner, William D. Bechill, had no strong and active ties with any of the aging organizations. He had been the official chiefly responsible for aging programs in California, and was supported for the AoA position by state Democrats influential in the national party and by Wilbur Cohen, then Undersecretary of HEW, who had been closely associated with Bechill at the University of Michigan School of Social Work some years before.

One of the big disappointments to the aging organizations was that the new Commissioner did not attempt to open up a wider range of programs for aging interests by trying to exercise his nominal responsibility for coordinating federal activities. Bechill recognized that he had few resources for enlarging AoA's domain by capturing portions of existing middleman programs for use on behalf of aging. Moreover, he sensed that he would get little practical advantage from investing staff time and energy in establishing procedures and channels for coordination, liaison, planning, and other such ephemeral activities. As would any sensible administrator, he viewed his top priority as the expenditure of the program funds that had been allocated to his agency, without scandal, before the end of the fiscal year.

The immediate challenge involved in successful administration of Title III was getting as many states as possible to qualify for their shares of grant-in-aid funds, and to disperse these funds quickly within their states. As the states filed their qualifying state plans with AoA, appropriated matching funds, designated their state agencies and administrators for the program, and began to distribute grants, it was readily apparent that NCSC and NCOA were not going to be important factors in the politics of Title III programs. State programs were in the hands of administrators who were responsive almost exclusively to the incentives and constraints of state politics. When the state agencies distributed Title III funds to organizations in their jurisdictions, NCSC and NCOA were almost completely shut out. The pattern of distribution varied considerably from state to state, depending on the strategic interpretations of state politics implemented by the agency administrators and their hierarchical and political superiors. In virtually no instances, however, did these interpretations give much political weight to NCSC or NCOA.

As Bechill saw this pattern unfolding, it influenced his strategy for the use of Title IV and V, the two programs over which he had some discretionary control. If he had any doubts that state politics rather than the politics of the existing aging organizations would dominate Title III, they were quickly dispelled. In their first year of operation, the state executives formed their own trade association—NASUA— which quickly began to serve as an instrument of solidarity against even minor threats of interference and nuisance from NCSC and NCOA, as well as from the Commissioner himself. NCSC and NCOA did not figure prominently, either, in Bechill's assessment of his prospects for building continuing support in Congress to sustain and enlarge AoA. He was not especially impressed by the capacity of the two organizations to wield influence in Congress. In the light of these developments and judgments, Bechill made little effort to distribute funds from Titles IV and V to NCSC and NCOA.

Two basic strategies were used by the Commissioner for implementing Title IV. First, it was used to make grants to local and state organizations that were politically important to the Title III state executives. Second, it was employed as a resource for direct bargaining between AoA and specific Congressmen or, more indirectly, as a resource to be used by the Secretary of HEW or the President in bargaining with Congress. In one instance, for example, AoA made a substantial Title IV grant to a Peoria long-term care institution when President Johnson was desperately seeking support from Minority Leader Everett Dirksen on major tax legislation. Grants made to implement either of these two basic strategies emphasized demonstrations rather than research (Jackson, 1971). They went mostly for service projects that could be subsequently reported, in testimony before Congress or in administrative documents, in terms of vast numbers of "senior citizens who have been served."

Control of Title V, the training grant program, was substantially delegated to a career civil servant, Clark Tibbitts, who had been professionally active as a "gerontologist" for several decades. Tibbitts had strong ties with selected academic and clinical professionals in the field of aging, though no particular attachment to NCSC and NCOA. In return for his cooperation and occasional substantive consultation about aging, Bechill gave him a relatively free hand in distributing the training money. (However, using a relatively unique provision of the Older Americans Act that left the Commissioner discretion in allocating the final distribution of funds appropriated by Congress jointly for Title IV and V, Bechill usually reserved about two-thirds of the funds for Title IV.) Tibbitts in turn used some of the funds to support special training conferences and institutes for NASUA. He dispersed the rest mostly to practice-oriented programs in universities—social work, recreation, public administration, extension work, and adult education.

NCSC and NCOA had been disappointed at the outset by Bechill's appointment. Their two candidates for Commissioner had been Charles Odell, Older Worker Specialist of the UAW, and James O'Brien, a staff member of both NCSC and the Steelworkers' union. Both had often been featured speakers at NCOA conferences and participants in NCOA strategies. As the pattern of distribution for AoA funds began to emerge with some clarity, NCSC and NCOA became highly critical of all aspects of the AoA operation. Meanwhile, they intensified a campaign they had begun late in 1964 to establish a recognized share for aging organizations from within the general pool of middleman programs administered at the Office of Economic Opportunity (OEO).

As initially formulated, OEO emphasized youth programs. But NCOA and NCSC, with substantial assistance from the Senate Committee on Aging, were successful in getting through Congress a vague amendment to the Economic Opportunity Act that stated: "It is the intention of Congress that whenever possible the special problems of the elderly poor be considered in the development, conduct, and administration of programs under this Act." (P. L. 89-253, section 610). Using this amendment as leverage, the organizations badgered Sargent Shriver into setting up a special OEO task force to consider programs for poor older persons. The task force consisted almost exclusively of persons connected with NCSC, NCOA, and organized labor (including Charles Odell, as chairman). It quickly reported back in

August 1965, shortly after the signing of the Older Americans Act, recommending that a larger share of OEO funds should be provided for aging programs, that Congress should enact earmarked middleman programs for the aging, and that an OEO special director of older persons' programs should be created (OEO Task Force, 1966).

OEO soon responded by awarding several contracts to these organizations (and to the National Farmer's Union, staffed by a task force member who had been the first staff member of NCSC) to operate several "action programs" for the aged and to serve as technical consultants to all community action programs on what they could be or should be doing for the elderly poor. An Assistant Director in OEO for Programs for the Elderly Poor was appointed in 1966, shortly after the position was authorized through another Congressional amendment.

As it became increasingly apparent in 1966 that AoA was not going to be a source of funds to NCSC and NCOA, they extended to the Department of Labor their efforts to carve out a share of middleman funds. Charles Odell left UAW to take a super-grade appointment as the Department's chief specialist on the older worker. In the next several years NCSC and NCOA (joined by AARP in the Spring of 1968 when it first began to turn its attention to middleman politics) obtained a number of Department of Labor contracts and grants to conduct senior service and older worker programs. By the end of the decade, NCSC, AARP, and NCOA were receiving as aging programs from OEO and Labor a total share equivalent to the approximately $10 million being distributed through the state grant program of AoA.

During the same period, the biologists, physicians, sociologists, and psychologists who were members of the Gerontological Society had succeeded in carving out a share for aging at the National Institutes of Health. While essentially shut out of Titles IV and V of AoA, constant discussions with administrators, Congressmen, and Congressional staff enabled them to have established a special program for research and training in Adult Development and Aging within the National Institute of Child Health and Human Development. This program is not legislatively earmarked (although the Public Policy Committee, other officers, and staff of the Gerontological Society are currently hopeful that Congressmen and their staffs will have earmarked funds appropriated). But by 1971 the established annual share (about $10 million) available from NIH to the academic gerontologists, and to the Society itself, exceeded the total distributed under Titles IV and V of AoA.

The aging organizations have also tried their hand at establishing shares of other middleman programs. At various times they have directed attention to the neglect of the aged in Model Cities programs, Community Mental Health programs, research and training in mental health, adult education programs, nutrition, transportation, and many other areas. The organizations have had some minor successes in these areas, but not as financially substantial or stable as those forays described above.

Once a measure of financial balance was established in the distribution of aging shares of middleman programs, administrative and Congressional proposals for new programs led to squabbles among the aging organizations and their allies in the bureaucracy. In 1968, for instance, five different proposals for senior service corps were under active consideration in the White House and in Congress, ranging in estimated cost from about $2 million to $10 million a year. For about 6 months these proposals were the subject of bitter controversy involving AoA, the Older Worker Specialist in Labor, the OEO Assistant Director for Programs for the Elderly Poor, NASUA, NCSC, NCOA, and AARP. But virtually none of the controversy had to do with the content or merits of the program. Almost all of the discussion was concerned, quite literally, with whether such a program should be lodged in Labor or HEW. Needless to say, NCSC and NCOA were quite sure that such a program belonged in Labor; NASUA was certain that the program could only be effective if it were lodged in AoA, HEW. Through some clever maneuvering, Department of Labor officials managed to resolve the issue in their favor. Labor implemented a senior service program, inevitably, by awarding contracts to NCSC, NCOA, and AARP.

Throughout 1970 and 1971, faced with the Nixon Administration's cutbacks in all aging middleman programs, the aging organizations subdued their differences and came to present a somewhat united front. They stopped their open criticisms of one another. They gave at least token, lukewarm support to each other at Congressional hearings and Administrative meetings, even when the specific program being threatened was not one in which they shared. And they were of one voice in criticizing plans for the December, 1971 White House Conference on Aging. The critical issue the organizations faced was whether the White House Conference would generate substantial additional financial resources for middleman programs. If so, another round of conflict and bargaining among the aging organizations was sure to follow.

American Politics and the Case of the Aged

This characterization of the aging organizations and their activities should be sufficient to make it clear that in terms of the objectives these organizations seem to pursue, they have relatively good access to power in American national politics. In the politics of middleman programs, they have been successful in creating a domain of program funds and authority that is available more or less exclusively to aging organizations. And they have successfully laid claim to established shares for aging organizations within domains that make funds and authority available to a fairly wide spectrum of middlemen. No single organization or faction of organizations has succeeded in dominating these activities or in excluding the others. Each of the organized interests has managed to gain access to an adequate source and supply of rewards. While the organizations engage in conflict as they seek to advance their own shares, they have managed to arrive at a fairly stable pattern of reward distribution and accommodation. In the politics of direct income transfer programs, the various types of aging organizations—the mass membership organizations, the trade associations, and others—pursue somewhat divergent objectives suitable to their interests, but all involving incremental adjustments in existing programs. That the organizations' activities are directly responsible for bringing about the changes they seek in direct income transfer programs is doubtful. Nonetheless, adjustments consonant with those sought by the organizations are continuously effected.

But if it can be said that the aging organizations have sufficient access to power to maintain themselves and their interests, it also must be said that the goals articulated and sought by these organizations are not of a kind suitable to redress the economic and social condition of the severely disadvantaged aged. If one uses as a frame of reference the low income situation of the aged poor, presented at the outset of this discussion, adequate amelioration would require direct transfers of income to the aged poor amounting to at least $6 billion annually (The President's Task Force on Older Americans, 1968). To be sure, setting standards such as these may well raise fundamental questions in some minds concerning conflicts between the welfare of one grouping of citizens and "the common welfare." But these are the standards of change needed merely to bring the aged poor to the poverty line—a rather widely accepted measure of one's minimum "fair share" in American society. They are not, however, the kinds of changes actively sought by the aging organizations.

Even as the aging organizations seem reasonably well-situated to pursue their interests through politics, the access of older voters to power through electoral politics is certainly equal to that of other broad groupings of citizens. If there is no cohesive aged vote to "swing" national elections, neither is there any other cohesive bloc that can. Most politicians are reasonably careful to avoid offending the aged, and in their election campaigns generally support incremental raises in Social Security benefits. Year after year the aged voter consistently receives as much attention in electoral politics as any other broadly designated category of voters, perhaps even more.

Interest-Group Liberalism and the Politics of Aging

Nonetheless, the attention given by politicians to the aged voter does little to further the economic situation of the disadvantaged aged. Numerous specific proposals are available to political leaders (in task force reports and campaign "fact books") for redistributing sufficient income to the aged poor. But for numerous reasons discussed above, national politicians see little advantage in developing an appeal to the special interests of the aged poor as central features of their electoral campaigns.

On the basis of the evidence, it would not be unreasonable to make a general judgment that the aged voter and the aging organizations have their "fair share" of access to power in American national politics. The symbolic responses they elicit and material rewards they receive at least equal and may exceed those gained by comparable categories of citizens and organized interests, if not matching those of the very wealthy, party leaders, "big" business, and "big" labor. Yet their seeming political equality does little to redress the economic and social problems of the disadvantaged aged.

Among other things, the case of the aged suggests that a group can attain political equality—as measured by the standards customarily applied to American politics by political scientists during the past several decades—without achieving social and economic justice. To focus on "representation" by elected officials and "representation" through the bargaining of organized groups in assessing the citizen's means of access to power is to set aside ultimate issues of social justice, and to ignore what may be more important avenues to power.

These implications from the case of the aged have become familiar in recent years through a growing literature of empirical studies and critical essays in political science (cf. Green & Levinson, 1970). The relatively sweeping critique propounded by Lowi, for example, summarized at the outset of this article, is borne out in rich detail by the politics of aging. For instance, the two-tiered grant program under Title III of the Older Americans Act, providing a separate bargaining table for middleman organizations in each state, might have been designed by Lowi to caricature his argument. There is little need, however, to rehash the details of the case in relation to Lowi's ideas. More to the point are his proposals for reform, since they serve as a useful frame of reference for drawing further lessons from the case of the aged.

In The End of Liberalism, Lowi (1969) proposes "Juridical Democracy" as the path to reform, laying out a series of steps to establish the rule of law. Central to his platform is revival of the Schecter rule, so that we may have the Supreme Court "declaring invalid and unconstitutional any delegation of power to an administrative agency that is not accompanied by clear standards of implementation." His argument is that strong statutes, clearly stating objectives and the specific means through which they are to be achieved, must be the foundation of any effort to reform the American political system for the realization of social justice. As a model of such a statute, he cites the Social Security Act of 1935 ("Old Welfare"), a product of New Deal liberalism which he regards as substantially over by the late 1930s. He contrasts it with legislation such as the Economic Opportunity Act of 1964 ("New Welfare"), a typical product of the 1960s, the era of interest-group liberalism. (The contrasting characterization of program types approximates, but is not identical to, the distinction made earlier in this discussion between direct income transfer programs and middleman programs.)

Aside from general criticisms that could be (and have been) made of Lowi's proposal for Juridical Democracy, several observations bearing upon it are suggested by the case of the aged. The most obvious criticism is that the model statute of the Old Welfare has not served as a vehicle for achieving social justice for the aged, even with all the specific improvements made in it for more than three decades. To be sure, Lowi suggests that "the real poverty problem of the 1960s could have been dealt with entirely by mere liberalization of welfare." Mere, indeed! Lowi himself accounts for the enactment of Social Security because it was (and is) a conservative instrument of social control that rests largely on the principle of contributory social insurance, which "does not affect the class structure, the sum total of opportunity, or anything else; on the contrary, it tends to maintain existing patterns." How, then, could the Social Security Act be readily "liberalized" to eliminate poverty? Surely the proposed Family Assistance Plan fits Lowi's model of appropriately specific legislation for Juridical Democracy. Yet he would undoubtedly characterize it, too, as an instrument of social and fiscal control (cf. Piven & Cloward, 1971). Under what circumstances, then, could legislation be enacted that would be specific enough to meet the standards of Juridical Democracy, yet sufficiently radical in principle and redistributive in effect to substantially help the disadvantaged?

As an explanation, Lowi offers the following:

Granted, the rule-of-law requirement is likely to make more difficult the framing and passage of some policies. But why should any program be acceptable if the partisans cannot fairly clearly state purpose and means? We ask such justification of children.

But whether partisans can specify purpose and means is hardly the issue. Rather, the issue would seem to be: Would a relatively radical or redistributive purpose, fairly clearly stated with specific means, have many partisans—enough partisans to be enacted as law? Not very likely.

Perhaps one prospect, suggested by the case of the aged and similar cases, lies in the development of a social identity that would bind together a new, forceful, coalition, able to seriously disrupt the political, economic, and social order of American society. This would not be a coalition of the poor aged and the wealthy aged, a coalition of all racial minorities, or a coalition consisting of the general membership of any traditionally defined groupings of citizens. If it were to form, it would consist of severely disadvantaged persons from within each of many traditionally defined groups.

One recurring theme in the case of the aged is the difficulty of establishing a cohesive identity among older persons for political purposes. Those better off among older persons neither identify themselves as aged, nor identify with the problems of the disadvantaged aged. Neither politicians nor the national aging organizations are articulating goals and problems that would mold the severely disadvantaged aged into a cohesive political force. Even if they did, it is doubtful such a force could be very powerful. The influence of the aged poor's vote, even in a bloc, would be insignificant. Their capacity for militant, direct action is virtually nonexistent. Retired persons, especially those with little income, have no leverage for disrupting American society through economic action. They cannot slow down production or strike. And those most likely to identify as the disadvantaged aged—the 25% below the poverty line—are hardly in a position to undertake effective consumer boycotts. Even if they were, what would be a useful and readily identifiable target? It would be difficult to frame a solution for their grievances that would single out the need for response by a single industry or cluster of industries. Moreover, to the extent that one can generalize, aged persons are far less inclined toward disruptive activity than younger persons. Aside from possible physical limitations on their capacity for picketing, rioting, and other forms of social protest, they are attitudinally disposed against such activities (Campbell, 1971), although it should be noted that this disposition may change in future generational cohorts of the aged.

The prospects of the aged poor for substantially improving their situation through politics may lie in the development of identity ties, not between them and other elders, but with persons who are disadvantaged by circumstances similar to their own. Broadly speaking, these might be the persons within a variety of groupings who, like 5 million aged, are poor because they are in some way artificially barred from obtaining income through productivity. They might include those young people who have finished schooling but unable to obtain a job, those members of racial minorities who are barred from employment by racial discrimination, the physically handicapped, and those deficient in skills necessary for employment (cf. Herrnstein, 1971). Because American economics, culture, and politics have so firmly enshrined productivity as a determinant of adequate purchasing power and so many fundamental conditions of life, adults excluded from employment are in many ways rendered deviant.

One cannot predict that the severely disadvantaged are likely to find their common identity as deviants, transcending their more traditional group identities. Nor can one expect that a mass social movement of deviants will drastically transform American politics. It is simply the one possibility of radical change suggested by the case of the aged.

References

Barron, M. L. *The Aging Americans: An introduction to social gerontology and geriatrics.* New York: Thomas Y. Crowell Co., 1961.

Binstock, R. H. Background paper on planning. Washington: White House Conference, 1971.

Blau, Z. S. Changes in status and age identification. *American Sociological Review*, 1956, *21*, 198–203.

Brotman, H. B. The older population revisited: First results of the 1970 census. In *Facts and Figures on Older Americans*, No. 2. Washington: US Dept. of Health, Education, & Welfare, 1971. (a)

Brotman, H. B. Measuring adequacy of income. In *Facts and Figures on Older Americans*, No. 1, Washington: US Dept. of Health, Education, & Welfare, 1971. (b)

Brotman, H. B. Income and poverty in 1970—advance report. In *Facts and Figures on Older Americans*, No. 3. Washington: US Dept. of Health, Education, & Welfare, 1971. (c)

Campbell, A. Politics through the life cycle. *Gerontologist*, 1971, *2*, 112–117.

Carley, M. The politics of age: Interest group or social movement? *Gerontologist*, 1969, *9*, 259–263.

Derthick, M. *The influence of federal grants.* Cambridge, Mass.: Harvard University Press, 1970.

Green, P., & Levinson, S. *Power and community: Dissenting essays in political science.* New York: Random House, 1970.

Harris, R. Annals of legislation. *New Yorker*, July 2, 9, 16, 23, 1966.

Herrnstein, R. I. Q. *Atlantic*, Sept., 1971, 228, 43–64.

Holtzman, A. *The Townsend Movement*. New York: Bookman Associates, 1963.

Jackson, D. G. (Ed.), *SRS research 1971*. Washington: US Dept. of Health, Education, & Welfare, 1971.

Kastenbaum, R., & Durkee, N. Elderly people view old age. In R. Kastenbaum (Ed.), *New thoughts on old age*. New York: Springer Publishing Co., 1964.

Kutner, B., Fanshel, D., Togo, A. M., & Langner, T. S. *Five hundred over sixty. A community survey on aging.* New York: Russell Sage Foundation, 1956.

Lowi, T. J. *The End of Liberalism.* New York: W. W. Norton & Co., 1969.

Neugarten, B. L. *Personality in middle and late life; empirical studies.* New York: Atherton Press, 1964.

Neugarten, B. L. (Ed.), *Middle age and aging: A reader in social psychology.* Chicago: University of Chicago Press, 1968.

Office of Economic Opportunity Task Force on Programs for Older Persons. *Poverty and the older American. In the war on poverty as it affects older Americans.* Washington: US Senate Special Committee on Aging. 1966.

Pinner, F. A., Jacobs, P., & Selznick, P. *Old age and political behavior.* Berkeley: University of California Press, 1959.

Piven, F. F., & Cloward, R. A. *Regulating the poor: The functions of public welfare.* New York: Random House, 1971.

President's Task Force on Older Americans. *Report of the President's task force on older Americans.* Washington: The White House, 1968.

Riley, M. W., & Foner, A. *Aging and Society, Vol. I.* New York: Russell Sage Foundation, 1968.

Sheppard, H. L. Implications of an aging population for political sociology. In W. Donahue & C. Tibbitts (Eds.), *Old age and political behavior.* Ann Arbor: Division of Gerontology, University of Michigan, 1962.

Sobel, I. Background paper on employment. Washington: White House Conference on Aging, 1971.

Sundquist, J. L. For the old, health care. In J. L. Sundquist, *Politics and policy: The Eisenhower, Kennedy, and Johnson years.* Washington: Brookings Institution, 1968.

Tibbitts, C. Politics of aging: Pressure for change. In W. Donahue & C. Tibbitts (Eds.), *Old age and political behavior.* Ann Arbor: Division of Gerontology, University of Michigan, 1962.

Truman, D. B. *The governmental process: Political interests and public opinion.* New York: Alfred Knopf, 1960.

US Bureau of the Census. *Current population reports,* series P-20, No. 172. Washington: US Dept. of Commerce, 1968.

US Bureau of the Census. *Statistical abstract of the United States, 1970.* Washington: US Dept. of Commerce, 1970.

US Bureau of the Census. *1970 census of population advance report.* Washington: US Dept. of Commerce. 1971.

Vineyard, D. The Senate special committee on the aging, Unpublished paper, 1971.

White House Conference on Aging. Background papers. Washington: White House Conference on Aging, 1971.

Ziegler, H. *Interest groups in American society.* Englewood Cliffs, NJ: Prentice-Hall, 1964.

[1]While there are other national organizations that are primarily occupied with matters related to aging, they are not particularly active in politics compared with the ten organizations discussed in this article. These others, for example, would include The National Association of Jewish Homes for the Aged, the Southern Baptists Association of Executives of Homes for the Aging (a denominational, not a regional organization), the American Geriatric Society, and the Townsend Plan National Lobby.

[2]The sources for this and other statements concerning the aging organizations and their activities presented throughout this article are primary ones and too numerous and disparate to cite explicitly in each instance. They consist of dozens of interviews with organizational officials, correspondence, speeches, official organizational documents, testimony in Congressional hearings, and events recorded through direct observation by the author. To build a fully-documented case for many of the assertions and characterizations set forth here would be beyond the scope of this brief article. The author intends to provide full documentations in a book-length monograph that is in process.

Aging and Social Stratification

The papers in this section deal with some of the structural and situational aspects of aging—aspects relating to social stratification. In a book on the Japanese-American, Kitano (1969) expanded upon Gordon's concept of eth-class (ethnic background, social class) by developing that of eth-gen-class (ethnic background, generation, social class).[1] We would add a fourth variable, sex. We believe that in order to understand the behavior of an older person, we need to know whether we are talking about an older man or an older woman in addition to knowing the individual's social class, ethnic background, and, of course, his or her cohort. The five readings in this section therefore deal with the effects of selected aspects of social stratification on aging—specifically sex, ethnicity, and social class.

The ethnic background of older people has become increasingly interesting to scholars in recent years. The CoRaD report in the spring 1971 issue of *The Gerontologist* is devoted to this topic. We have selected two articles from that issue: Joan W. Moore's "Situational Factors Affecting Minority Aging" and Richard A. Kalish's "A Gerontological Look at Ethnicity, Human Capacities, and Individual Adjustment." These two articles introduce this chapter and provide a theoretical and general orientation to social stratification issues as they apply to aging.

Moore points out that much of our information and ideas about aging is based on studies of middle-class, white Americans. Her emphasis is on the interaction of aging and membership in a minority category and the importance of this knowledge to the study of aging. In order to comprehend this topic we must understand five facts: (1) Each minority category has its own history; (2) this special history has been characteristically accompanied by some forms of discrimination; (3) each minority has developed a specific subculture; (4) some form of coping structures have been developed within the various subcultures; and (5) the first four characteristics have been changing rapidly.

Kalish discusses the purposes of research about the impact of ethnicity on aging, the ethical and methodological problems related to such research, and research priorities. Like Moore, Kalish stresses the importance of historical information in understanding people of different ethnic categories. In order to appreciate the effect of ethnicity on the individual, one must know something about the past experiences of those sharing an ethnic identification and the changes the subsociety has experienced through history. Both he and Moore note that our baseline and descriptive data are drawn from Anglo populations. He suggests, however, that some psychological factors may not be affected by ethnicity. Kalish offers some practical suggestions for immediate and future activities and leaves us with an awareness of the tremendous gaps in our knowledge about this topic.

The next two articles, Donald L. Davis's "Growing Old Black" and Floyd M. Wylie's "Attitudes toward Aging and the Aged among Black Americans: Some Historical Perspectives," provide information about one specific ethnic-racial category—the American blacks, the largest minority category of older people in the United States. Davis's article factually describes aging blacks. He provides a historical demographic picture and projects this picture somewhat into the future. His material highlights the drastic contrasts between older blacks and older whites on a number of social indicators.

Davis observes, as others have, that discrimination experienced in the younger years of life carries into present and future aging. This carryover of the past further compounds the vicissitudes of the black's old age. If an older person's income is typically half that of a younger person's, then the older black's income is even less. If living without a spouse is common among older people, it is particularly so among older blacks. The older black male is forced into retirement earlier than his white counterpart, and the older black female remains in the labor force in greater proportions than her white counterpart. Davis says, "Even if every racial barrier were immediately eliminated for the aged black worker, the mass of aged blacks would still face a disastrous economic future."

Wylie deals with another aspect of growing old black—attitudes of black Americans toward aging and toward older black people. Despite the double jeopardy of being old and black in a white society, Wylie points out that within the black society people accept old age and are less likely to deny their old age than are whites. He examines the historical roots of these attitudes, tracing the origins to the African cultures from which American blacks came. Wylie makes the interesting point that the shared experiences of bondage provided a substitute for blood kin relationships. The extension of these relationships to include the larger social category in effect replaced family ties lost when family members were sold into slavery. The shared fate of members in the same ethnic category provides the glue for social cohesion. Values and attitudes toward old people have persisted from a shared past. (Those interested in similar studies about other ethnic categories or societies may want to examine a newly emerging body of writings in the social history of aging. Two such articles are Spector's "Old Age and the Sages" (1973) and Achenbaum's "The Obsolescence of Old Age in America, 1865–1914" (1974).[2])

Any system of social class stratification is essentially a system of structured inequality. We know very little about how this system affects aging; nor do we know much about the social class characteristics of older people. From an objective perspective, we would anticipate that old age is accompanied by downward mobility, in part a consequence of the typical income decrease experienced in old age. At the same time, because a person's social class may be maintained symbolically, the older person may experience conflicting social class placements. He views himself as identified with one social class; by reputation he is seen as a member of another social class; and objectively his level of living is characteristic of still another social class. Because of the tremendous importance of social class on all forms of behavior, our lack of information is surprising. Robert C. Atchley points out that we have little data that integrates various aspects of stratification.

Moreover, we have even less information about the interrelationships of different aspects of stratification. Atchley's article is one of the rare discussions of the consequences of more than one kind of stratification on aging. He deals with both social class and sex stratification. We have demographic descriptions of male-female differences in old age, but he notes that we have little unconfounded data describing sex differences in social and psychological aspects of aging. In research designed to control the confounding of other effects—such as marital status, age, and educational level—with the effect of sex, he examined sex differences in patterns of work and retirement and in other social and psychological behaviors. He found some significant differences between women and men in a variety of dimensions. For example, retired women tend to be lonelier, more sensitive to criticism, more depressed, more anxious, and tend to have less self-esteem than retired men. Not surprisingly, women reported their incomes as less adequate than men's. On the whole, retired middle-class women appeared to have more personal and social problems than retired middle-class men. Equally interesting, Atchley found that middle-class women were committed to the importance of work in their lives, and contrary to stereotypes, women had greater difficulty than men in giving up jobs. Another gerontological myth has bitten the dust—the housewife role does not ease the adjustment to retirement for women.

The first four authors in this section deal with some of the current consequences of the past, with the double jeopardy of being old and a member of a minority category that is discriminated against. They indicate clearly that the difficulties of aging are compounded by membership in a minority category. All of the articles deal also with the need for more and better data about the consequences of social stratification on aging. Atchley deals specifically with the necessity for learning more about how various aspects of stratification interrelate with one another and how they affect and are affected by aging.

[1]Gordon, Milton M., *Assimilation in American Life: The Role of Race, Religion, and National Origin* (New York: Oxford, 1964). Kitano, Harry H., *Japanese Americans* (Englewood Cliffs, N.J.: Prentice-Hall, Inc., 1969).
[2]Spector, Samuel, "Old Age and the Sages," *International Journal of Aging and Human Development*, Vol. 4, No. 3 (1973), pp. 199–209. Achenbaum, W. Andrew, "The Obsolescence of Old Age in America, 1865–1914," *Journal of Social History*, Vol. 8, Fall (1974), pp. 48–62.

Situational Factors Affecting Minority Aging

Joan W. Moore

It is part of the scientific credo that research should be motivated by the promise of knowledge that will contribute to the general understanding of phenomena. This credo is sometimes hard to follow in the study of aging. By and large the plight of the aging subjects is pathetic and the urgent desire to come up with an answer to some of their problems often prompts us to narrow research, often wildly over-generalized.

If this is true for aging in general, it is even more so for minority aging: as other papers in this section clearly show, this segment of the American population has an exponential share of the nation's problems. Nonetheless, a case can be made that whatever research we do on minority aging, no matter how narrow or problem-oriented, can begin to contribute substantially to the understanding of aging in general if we can agree on some research priorities.

The argument in this paper is simple. Whether we talk about individuals, group behavior, or the aged as a collectivity, most of our generalizations are based on the study of a limited sample—primarily middle-majority Anglos. We do not really know how much such sample limitations constrain these generalizations—for example, generalizations about "disengagement," about the "generation gap," and

From *The Gerontologist*, Vol. 11, No. 1:2, Spring 1971. Reprinted by permission of the Gerontological Society and the author.

about the aged as a "minority group." The life experiences and present situations of the minority aged can present such general theoretical issues in a fresh and often clearer light.

Let us look for a moment at a few things that go into the making of an American minority and see what can be learned from them about aging. This examination of necessity omits much of relevance to any particular minority or to the understanding of minorities *per se*. It is focused on what is inherent in the minority situation that is important to the study of aging rather than to minority status. All five of the characteristics to be mentioned have relevance for the aging of all Americans. With the minorities these characteristics are clearer.

First, each minority has a *special history*—a collective experience that has placed its members in their present position in the American social system. That special history differs from one minority to another; but in all cases it entails subordination. The particular process was different: conquest, prolonged conflict and expropriation in the case of American Indians and Mexicans; slavery and its aftermath for the blacks; migration into special economic slots for Puerto Ricans, Mexicans, and Asians, a transplanted European culture of racism in the case of all groups. Since the "generation gap" is in no small part a resultant of the reinterpretation of collective history, the position of the minorities in having a *special* history makes the study of this controversial issue a bit easier, as we shall enlarge upon below.

Second, in every case this special history has been accompanied by *discrimination*—and the development of strong and predominantly negative *stereotypes* about the minority. Although the content of the particular stereotype and the nature of the discrimination has varied from one group to another, in every case members of the minority populations have been viewed by the larger society as special and as requiring special treatment in all institutional areas. This characteristic has relevance for all Americans, in that we are increasingly concerned about the *age* category as a basis for minority status. The combination of two categorical bases for discrimination—minority status *and* old age—offers special interest for the gerontologist, as detailed below.

Third, in every case some *variant subculture* has been developed in the minority. In some cases, like many American Indian tribes, the subculture is strong and distinctive. In some cases, like the Jews and the blacks, the subculture has been much closer to that of the dominant culture. The subculture includes value sets of significance to aging, e.g., values about the importance of work or physical prowess to personal identity. It also may include specific definitions of the timing of statuses and norms relating to behavior in particular age statuses. In addition, these subcultures differ one from another. The combination of these features promises further insight into the generation gap—as discussed below.

Fourth, in almost all cases (whether in reservation, ghetto, or barrio) substructures have developed, and often been institutionalized, that could very loosely be termed *"coping structures."* The Negro church, the Mexican-American family structure, the Jewish voluntary association, the Chinese benevolent society—all of these have supported the minority individual in his difficulties in coping with economic uncertainty and a hostile and exclusionary larger society. "Coping" here is used to refer to many things, ranging from help with bare survival needs (as with the extension of the family network), to avenues for meaningful social participation, internal prestige and power (as with the Negro church), to a diffuse but still important opportunity for a sense of belonging to *some* collectivity (provided by all residential concentrations of minorities). These ingroup supports, with their variability, offer considerable promise of fruitful study in the general process of aging.

Finally, all of these things have been *changing rapidly* and with increasing obviousness. History is being re-thought, and actually being re-written. Discriminatory stereotypes and practices are being attacked head-on. The internal institutions and subcultures are being eroded, attacked, and displaced. At the same time, there are many continuities: exploitation, discrimination, and prejudice continue, as do many of the subcultural "old ways," while many of the lost "old ways" are being consciously resuscitated.

All of these features of the general minority situation have special relevance for the aged. All of them are exaggerations, amplifications, researchable deviations of what is happening for all Americans. The entire society is changing, although changes for minority persons are more easily seen and more accessible to study. One of the most critical issues in social gerontology is the problem of role continuity and discontinuity—how either one develops, how continuity or discontinuity in various roles are handled by people of widely varying social characteristics and background. The minority person offers the "natural laboratory" for at least the gross delineation of significant aspects of the aging process. Of course, the proper scientific controls are lacking: attempts to place the minorities on a precise continuum, where minority A and B share all but, say, dark skin, have met with perennial frustration. But all such attempts have led to a clarification of the processes involved, and this is greatly to be desired, given the present state of development of social gerontology.

Let us now turn to some specific illustrations of issues in social gerontology that might fruitfully be approached through the study of minority groups. One of the most conspicuous in terms of popular interest is the question of the importance of the "generation gap" to the aging individual. As an obvious consequence of rapid social change, the value differences between old and young in society have given rise to a variety of speculations about their effects. Most such speculations are concerned with integration of the society at large; very few have attempted to search out the implications of a severe generation gap for particular age groups. For gerontologists, it would seem that defining the generation gap and its significance for aging would be of prime importance. It is obviously quite different to grow old in a society in which your children and grandchildren agree with you totally about your life work compared with a society in which, at the very least, one may feel the need to "keep up" with the times, and at the worst, one feels alienated from the new values apparently espoused by the young. Research is, in fact, being conducted on such matters (Bengtson, 1969), but in the larger system, such research must of necessity be extremely broad.

Studying minorities would permit specification of *particular* values in the hypothesized generation gap, and particular kinds of continuities and discontinuities that might be related to "successful" aging.

For example, the special history of many minorities is now being redefined. This redefinition entails action by the young based on their re-evaluation of the collective past. This particular form of the "generation gap" has been hypothesized by one psychiatrist (Elam, 1970) as having some specific consequences for the successful accomplishment of age-specific psychological tasks—that is, ego integrity among the black aged. He argues that the black revolution provides more positive input for the old black than does the "normal aging" person's reflection on a past lifetime, since the past for many blacks has been one of frustration and failure. The young people's reinterpretation of collective problems helps the old black give a positive meaning to his failures. At least it removes the stigma of failure as a consequence of personal inadequacy. In this respect, the reinterpretation of the collective special history helps the black old person make positive sense out of his unique experiences and helps him to ego integrity rather than despair.[1] By contrast, a social worker has put forth some specific counter-hypotheses about the relevance of this reinterpretation of black history for the attainment of ego integrity, arguing that the young people's rejection of the past as the "only possible way" tends to produce despair in the old black (Solomon, 1970). Both arguments emphasize a specific change in values which is specifically relevant to a universal problem in aging—namely the frame of reference used by the old person in evaluating his life experiences.

There are alternatives for the blacks. For example, the old black may reaffirm that his own particular life *had* significance, that "Uncle Tomism" was the only possible—and an honorable—way. This may involve a rejection of the young person's reinterpretation—a particular form of the generation gap. Or, following Elam, he may take greater pride in the collective future—certainly a form of generational solidarity. Finally, following Solomon, he may be confused, resentful, or bewildered by the reinterpretations taking place around him.

Thus the existence of a special collective history, which provides the context within which the aging minority individual must interpret the meaning of his particular life, can permit the researcher to specify a significant dimension of the "generation gap." This task is more difficult in the larger society because of the greater diffuseness of the relationship between the aging individual's particular history and the collective experience on the one hand and the re-evaluation of that collective experience by the young on the other hand. Lifelong pacifists, for example, may find their lifelong "deviant" adaptations re-affirmed by the young people's collective reinterpretation of one American war as evil. But the reinterpretation of America's past and future is far from confined to particular issues such as war and peace. Reinterpretation is broader and more pervasive than one issue and thus far more difficult to pin down than in the case of minorities.

Because minority populations have developed subcultures, they permit another kind of specification of what might be meant by "generation gap" and its consequences for the elderly. American Indian tribes represent the best case. The traditional role of the elderly varies widely from tribe to tribe: in the Northwest Coast tribes, the young men assume the work and political responsibilities of the tribe, while in Southern Arizona and California, it is the older man. No matter what the norms, any changes (and recent changes have been drastic) mean a change in the role of the aged (Kelly, 1969). These changes, of course, are tightly interwoven with changes in the social structure of the tribal society, and in particular with the kinship structure. But it still seems valid to isolate them analytically. Thus studying the generation gap among minority groups permits the researcher to specify a set of traditional values regarding age itself as a principal value difference between old and young. By contrast, "the role of the aged" is far less clear-cut in the society as a whole, and the changes are far less specifiable as a consequence. Gerontological literature is full of speculations about the consequences for the elderly of "the changing role of the aged," but data usually fall into a morass of normative speculation. With a sample of Indian tribes as an illustration we could specify and vary *particular* changes.

Another example of the kind of issue that can be elevated from the plane of normative rhetoric is the blurred question of whether the aged in American society are themselves a minority group. This much overworked metaphor can be given some specificity in a population with a lifetime of discrimination. Active discrimination and pervasive stereotypes are the normal environment of most minority persons from early childhood. If, in fact, old age carries some of these social and psychological handicaps, does the life experience of discrimination and prejudice on the basis of minority characteristics prepare one for this new kind of discrimination? Is the elderly minority person more able to cope with yet another negative categorization? Or does the lifetime of discrimination wear him down so that he is especially vulnerable to this new form of discrimination?

In this formulation any such questions are, of course, fatuous. But their very fatuity casts light on one of the problems in the transformation of rhetoric to research. Discrimination which pervades the life experience of the minority person has been studied from many perspectives, ranging from the economic to the psychological. Individual and collective ways of "coping" are now in the process of being more intensively analyzed. In particular, the importance of reference groups is now being emphasized. The focus on minority aged and how they cope with this new form of prejudice and discrimination can help us clarify what is meant by "minority status" when applied to the old person. We can explore the relative significance of family members, age peers and juniors, members of the same ethnic group and members of other ethnic groups, potential employers (who are still salient for many minority aged), potential landlords, and the whole host of individuals with whom the minority person—poor or middle-class—must deal. We can explore the shifts in significance of these various groups with aging. We can explore the importance of class status. We can explore the variations in the content of stereotype—how they vary from, say, landlord to younger member of the same minority group—and how the old minority person responds to these issues. (We have already suggested the importance of the content of the intra-group stereotype above, when discussing the generation gap: now we are suggesting the utility of expanding this kind of perspective to include other people than just the young.) Most important, we can see if the discrimination entailed in being "put on the shelf" is similar to that entailed in the active rejection characterizing younger *and* older minority persons.

Thus far, we have illustrated the utility of studying minority old people, with their special situations, in order to clarify general research issues in gerontology. These are research issues which have been muddied by the stir of emotionalism and controversy that accompanies social change and the unexpectedly painful consequences to particular age groups. The much discussed generation gap and minority status of the Anglo aged are such issues. The special features of minority status—their distinctive collective histories and subcultures, common past experiences of prejudice and discrimination, might force the researcher into greater specification of the actual behavioral and attitudinal variables involved.

The existence of ghetto, reservation, or *barrio* institutions suggests another opportunity for gerontologists interested in age in general. By and large, Anglo old people in metropolitan areas do not live in tightly knit communities, unless there are some very special circumstances (Rosow, 1967). By contrast, poor minority old people may live in socially integrated communities. The strength of bonds in the minority kinship group and in the minority ghettos varies widely, from, say a high point in some Indian reservations to, perhaps, a low point in some of the more conflictful metropolitan ghettos. Potential community supports for the aging person have generally eroded in the society at large. The study of minority aged persons permits an exploration of the extent to which such community supports do in fact help the aging process.

In addition, potential kinship and community supports among the minorities are undergoing drastic change, providing yet another opportunity for generalizable research. For example, many observers have suggested that the old black woman is in some respects "better off" than the old white woman because the combination of poverty and a prolonged period of childbearing have tended to permit her to retain a meaningful functional role. A grandmother is often involved in active mothering both of her own children born late in life and of her children's children. This is true for other minorities as well and tends to be part of the norms attached to that status. Further, the role of the old person in a poor family may be significant because he may make a substantial contribution to the whole family's economic welfare. The small sums provided by Social Security or other pension or welfare plans may be a substantial portion of the household income. In addition, many elderly poor continue to work at unskilled and service jobs until very late in life, also providing income resources for all. The prevailing minority situation of poverty, in short, may have one minor side benefit for the aging individual in that a survival-oriented family system provides a potential contribution to his continued sense of personal worth.

This "benefit," however, is probably bought at the expense of increased fatigue and anxiety. Very few families will reject a higher standard of living in order to maintain the old person's functional role. Ironically, any improvement in the family's economic status may erode what little contribution the existing system might have made to the successful aging of the old poor minority person (Elam, 1970; Moore, 1971; Solomon, 1970). To return to the point of this lengthy excursion, exactly such changes are occurring. Economic or occupational mobility of young minority people is the point of much of the pressure for social change among minorities. The more successful it is, the more detrimental may be the effect on minority old people.

Another opportunity for study presents itself here, however. In some minority communities, new roles are being sought for old people. For example, community control of schools on one Indian reservation has meant that the old are finding a revived role as the repository of tribal tradition: something of the same is potentially present in all ethnic studies programs.[2] Thus change in some minority communities may be regarded as releasing the old people for new roles: self-conscious programs of cultural exploration have developed that may provide an opportunity for research on the invention of functional roles for the elderly. Change as drastic as that now occurring in minority communities, no matter what its direction, offers an opportunity for the researcher.

Kinship supports are one aspect of ingroup supports for the aging individual: many of the same generalizations can be applied to other ghetto institutional supports. As indicated, ghetto supports vary from place to place and minority to minority. They may range from total support to nothing much more than the comfort that comes from being with people who look like oneself and talk like oneself after a lifetime of prejudice and discrimination on "the outside." Under present conditions such ghetto supports are precarious at best. They also shrivel along with collective progress just as the emotional supports in the family may erode away with individual progress. For example, the Mexican areas of formerly lively settlements in middle-western cities have shrunk to a few restaurants and a few old people, while the economically mobile second and third generations follow the classic patterns of movement to "better" areas of the town. In addition such ghettos are frequently located in those parts of town most susceptible to redevelopment either by means of urban-renewal projects or private development and expansion efforts. Barrio or ghetto supports may thus be particularly susceptible to destruction. They are rarely replaced in whatever alternative housing may be provided for those relocated.

Adjustments of minority old people that depend on the minority community may be precarious. One story illustrates this point beautifully. South Texas is an area of high Mexican concentration, with considerable anti-Mexican feeling in the Anglo population. One old poor man, with no driver's license, and no English, finds his major pleasure in driving to church bingo games in a nearby town. He has been stopped several times in his slow, rickety car, but every time—so far—the policeman involved has also been Mexican, and not only has been able to communicate with the old man but also to tolerate, and even be amused by, his behavior. This man's life pattern is extremely vulnerable: all it would take to destroy his life is a tough policeman. He would have almost no meaningful alternative pleasures. Not to press the point too hard, adaptations made by poor minority people are often just this precarious. "Making out" in the face of a hostile system has often meant taking a minor advantage of a situation which can arbitrarily be changed completely. People at the bottom of any social hierarchy can rarely impose the conditions of their life: their adjustments are thus easily disrupted. Nowhere is this more probable than with the minority old person.

This is shown by the abject destitution of El Paso's Mexican-American elderly discussed in the US Senate hearing held in that city in 1969 (US Senate Committee on Aging, 1969). Here, where half the city is a poor and traditional barrio, where traditional family structure is strong, but where the external system is hostile and impersonal welfare supports are below minimum levels, old Mexicans literally starve if they have no family. If the ingroup supports fail, there is nothing but starvation. Quite obviously, if this is true for physical survival, it must be true for psychological well-being.

The same factors that militate against a minority person's well-being at earlier ages continue to operate without abatement: in many respects, things are worse. Though an able-bodied young man may suffer from job insecurity, an old man with a lifetime of job insecurity will also face a future without retirement benefits. For a very high proportion of minority elderly, this grim statement represents reality. Past collective problems are, if anything, increased with age. As the society as a whole becomes more bureaucratized, the badly educated person of any group becomes relatively worse off: minority elderly lag far behind the dominant group in such resources as education, linguistic fluency and so on, that might help them overcome problems as they arise (Moore, forthcoming). It is also plain that the gap between Anglo and minority elderly will increase in future decades.

The discussion of in-group support—kin and communal—and their changes and their variations provides obvious opportunities not only for research on existing situations but also for the development of programs. Such programs might build on the strengths of past situations, while avoiding the precariousness of minority adaptations in the past. If there is any validity to the hypothesis that collective and individual progress will erode kin and communal supports for the aged, it seems ridiculous for practitioners not to attempt some kind of ameliorative effort. In turn, such efforts may provide fruitful research opportunities. The "natural laboratory" provided by local variations in community strength need not be left untouched.

The discussion in this paper has illustrated ways in which five special characteristic situations of American minorities could help illuminate general issues in the study of aging. These general issues relate to three levels of analysis: the functioning of aging individuals, the functioning of aging individuals in groups, and the functioning of the aged as distinctive collectivities. Although American minorities found their modern shape in pain and in conflict and although there are many indications that both the pain and the conflict will continue, there is every reason to urge their further study. The study of minorities must always alert the social scientist to those aspects of society and its functions that he may as an individual prefer to ignore. Problems and conflict are part of every society and of the experiences of every individual in the society. The gerontologist all too often forgets this in his search for correlates of "successful aging." Minorities require that we enlarge our generalizations and deepen our conceptual framework.

References

Bengtson, V. Generational differences: Correlates and consequences, Unpublished ms., 1969.

Elam, L. C. Critical factors for mental health in aging black populations. Paper delivered at workshop on Ethnicity, Mental Health, and Aging, Los Angeles, Calif., April, 1970.

Kelly, W., & Levy, J. Indians. Paper delivered at NICHD Conference on Ethnic Differences in Retirement, Tucson, April, 1969.

Moore, J. Retirement and the Mexican American Aged, *Proceedings of the NICHD Conference on Ethnic Differences in Retirement*, 1971.

Rosow, I. *Social integration of the aged.* New York: Free Press, 1967.

Solomon, B. Ethnicity, mental health and the older black aged. In *Ethnicity, mental health and aging.* Los Angeles: University of Southern California, Gerontology Center, 1970.

US Senate Committee on Aging, 90th & 91st Congress. *Availability and usefulness of federal programs and services to elderly Mexican Americans*, Parts 1–4. Washington: US Government Printing Office, 1969.

[1] This argument was developed in the paper as actually presented by Dr. Elam, and does not appear in the condensed, published version.

[2] This pattern developed in San Francisco's Chinatown, with the local college's Asian studies program. Personal communication, Sam Yuen, 1970.

A Gerontological Look at Ethnicity, Human Capacities, and Individual Adjustment

Richard A. Kalish

Professional investigators, at least those of the behavioral sciences, seem to wear with pride the badge that permits them to claim membership in clubs whose exclusivity is based upon the small number of persons conducting studies in a given area. The testimony to one's innovative capacities is to begin the third paragraph of the introduction in the research article with the words "Research findings in this area are sparse," or "This matter appears to have been unexamined in previous literature." If prestige is, indeed, based upon probing into previously untouched areas, I should rise quickly to the pinnacle of the academic status ladder. I believe I have uncovered subject matter some of which has never been discussed by anyone. Whether such inattention should be decried as one more of the many shortcomings of shortsighted behavioral scientists or whether the lack of concern is well-deserved may be better evaluated upon reading the subsequent pages. I must admit to having begun the task of writing this piece with very little idea as to where it would take me at its completion.

The focus of this article, for which I have claimed such esoteric qualities, is ethnicity as a factor in the individual capacities and adjustment of the aging and the aged. Limitations have been set upon the boundaries of this paper, not because human behavior can be divided into neat packages, but because the inter-relatedness of all aspects of humanity, while a valid notion, makes communication virtually impossible. Thus, although *ethnicity* will be discussed in its broader meaning, as having applicability to all ethnic groups and, hopefully, to many non-ethnic divisions of the population (e.g., geographic regions, socio-economic, rural-suburban-urban, etc.), particular attention will be given those groups that are the source of major concern today. Similarly, although the following pages will hopefully have meaning for all kinds of research and speculation regarding subcultures in the United States, reference will be primarily to those aspects of human behavior that you may have confronted initially in your introductory psychology course: *(a)* human capacities, e.g., sensorimotor behavior, cognitive behavior, and *(b)* adjustment, e.g., motivation, emotion, personality, stress and coping with stress, and mental health and mental illness.

From *The Gerontologist*, Vol. 11, No. 1:2, Spring 1971. Reprinted by permission of the Gerontological Society and the author.

There exist, of course, innumerable articles and books dealing with ethnicity as a factor in personality, stress, mental illness, and mental health; a moderate literature is available on the capacities and adjustments of the elderly. But the interstices, the juxtapositioning, the points of overlap, the juncture, the whatever youmaycallit, has received scant attention—and, regarding some elements, none.

To some degree, this paper will undoubtedly intrude upon the others in this sequence, since individual adjustment is a function of social role and expectations, and cognitive functioning is related to social relationships. Redundancy is preferable to gaps, but we will attempt to avoid both.

Our charge for this section was not that of reviewing the literature, but rather that of outlining future research directions, based in part upon the discussions in the previous section and in part upon the vast store of non-ethnic research that may be brought to bear upon the topic. Ethnic group research serves two purposes: *(a)* gaining greater understanding of the group being studied, and *(b)* shedding light on human behavior in general through the use of ethnicity as an independent variable. This paper will consider both these elements, but will place relatively greater emphasis upon the former.

Ethnic Research and Gerontological Researchers

There was a time when good will, reasonable sensitivity, some insights, an advanced degree, and a few ethnic friends were sufficient to open the doors of ethnic communities to Anglo (to be defined in its broadest context) research investigators. Although some respondents were undoubtedly tailoring their comments and behavior either to upset or pacify the researcher, the study could proceed unhindered and most probably attain reasonably accurate results.

Today opposition to research from within the ethnic community is much greater. Anyone wishing to do research of any sort involving members of the more volatile ethnic communities (e.g., black Americans, Mexican-Americans, Puerto Ricans, Asian-Americans, American Indians) needs to take these feelings into consideration.

Perhaps the most frequent objections are that the research provides jobs for a token number of members of the ethnic community and a substantial number of Anglos, permits the Anglo research director to gain "brownie points" at his university and national acclaim as an expert on this ethnic group, and leaves the members of the ethnic community no better off than had the study never been done. These feelings are intensified by a history of researchers expressing their intent to use their results to improve life for the members of the ethnic community, then disappearing into the academic wilderness because of their unwillingness or inability to replace words with action. In addition, the gathering of knowledge for its own sake or for the building of a theory of human behavior is frequently seen as both inconsequential in the face of immediate problems and an academic putdown because of the obvious implication that the individual is not important in and of himself, but only as he might contribute to theory. These concerns affect many aspects of behavioral and social research today.

Exacerbating the situation is the role of the researcher. Rarely is he in a position to affect social policy directly. Frequently he does not even have access to the practitioners who would be most directly affected by his research. Research investigators, in some instances, do not report their results in sources readily available to practitioners and policy makers. On the other hand, I am certain that many behavioral scientists have shared with me the experience of asking a complaining practitioner what he had read recently and citing six or eight easily available books and journals, only to learn that he was unfamiliar with them and, besides, he was too busy with his "practical" work to have time to read much anyway.

Obviously, the potential recipient of the service is the victim of this breakdown in communication, and when such persons are members of an ethnic minority, they are liable to blame conscious racism rather than professional ineptness as the responsible agent. While seeking villains for this piece, I would like to nominate one more group that rarely receives blame: the social administrators and government decision-makers who control the funds and who are most likely to delete money for in-service training at the slightest threat of a cutback, although such training is often the major source of providing practitioners with the insights of research. The rundown on villains can eventually include everybody: researcher, practitioner, administrator, legislator, politician. And perhaps we have operationalized what the elderly member of an ethnic group means when he claims "the Establishment" is against him, that whenever *they* try to do something for him, the greater part of the pie is divided up among the powerful.

Sometimes the accusations are even more serious than mere exploitation: the research is perceived as degrading the ethnic group and playing into the hands of racists by showing that, according to the values of the Anglo community, the ethnic community has a greater incidence of an undesirable characteristic or fewer persons exhibiting a desirable behavior. Still more serious is the claim that the research is part of an attempt by the Anglo community to manipulate and, thus, control the ethnic community. That is, the investigator is seen as the counterpart of the CIA or Army, intent on gaining the kinds of knowledge and insight that will render the ethnic community helpless in the face of the powerful and aggressive Anglo overlords.

Social gerontologists have, in some instances, found among their geriatric subjects the kernel of similar views, but normally expressed without the intensity that ethnic militants proclaim. Since older members of ethnic groups have not received much attention, I would speculate that, at least initially, they will offer substantial cooperation. Eventually, however, the social gerontologist studying in this area can expect such attacks as "invasion of privacy" and "just give us the money instead of spending it studying us."[1]

The impact of values upon research does not affect only the more militant members of the ethnic communities. The researcher must, himself, be very much aware of the biases that his own values bring to the research. The bright and verbal militant in the ethnic community, in spite of limited formal education, frequently has unerring ability to pin the researcher to the wall with his own value biases. Even studies of sensorimotor and simple cognitive tests may not be exempt. We must be able to re-evaluate our own views and biases without, however, automatically assuming that in situations when they conflict, every value statement of an older person or a member of a minority group must take precedence over our own values.

Assume, for the moment, a bright and eager young (or not-so-young) behavioral scientist anxious to strike his blow for ethnic and age equality. He wishes to learn whether the present life style of elderly members of Ethnic Community is conducive to self-actualization. His measure of self-actualization has been validated (face, construct, concurrent, and predictive) through several studies in various Anglo communities. His scale is based in good part upon items that probe into the respondent's activities, giving plus scores to involvement in creative, social, and productive activities and negative scores to self-sacrificing homebound activities. "Taking grand-children to zoo" is good; "cleaning house so that my daughter-in-law can work" is bad.

Unfortunately for Eager Investigator, the values of this segment of Ethnic Community are that the ability to fulfill a reciprocal relationship with an offspring is very important, while expenditure of time and money on play is seen as unnecessary. Although the example may be transparent, its implications are frequently overlooked.

Thus what begins as a problem of values becomes a problem of methodology. The validity of an instrument is population-specific, i.e., any given measuring device varies in validity as a function of the population with which it is being used. As researchers we need to understand the meaning of our measuring instruments and our procedures both to older people and to the ethnic community.

Other methodological pitfalls are well known, yet even the most alert investigator falls into them. Jackson (1967) warns of two: first, we need constantly to remind ourselves and others that no ethnic community can be represented by any one group, unless that group is a well-selected sample of the entire community; we must focus not only upon means and modes, but upon ranges and standard deviations, upon groups within groups and upon individuals within groups. Second, we must avoid confounding ethnic differences with social class or other bases for differences that do not arise from the ethnic experience.

These two concerns are closely related. Kalish, Maloney and Arkoff (1966) studied marital role preferences of university students of Japanese-American and Caucasian backgrounds and compared their findings with results from students in Japan and Hawaii. Among women, students at one Japanese university showed the greatest desire for egalitarian marriages while those at another showed the least; both Japanese-American and Caucasian women from Los Angeles and Hawaii were intermediate. Had either of these Japanese universities been sampled with the assumption that it represented Japan, results would have been totally misleading. Yet we tend to generalize quickly from results of studies with Mexican-Americans in California to those in Texas, from urban ghetto low-income blacks to urban middle-class blacks, from Chinese-Americans in San Francisco to all Asian-Americans wherever they may be.

Jackson's second point is important, but does not go far enough. We are well aware that the social class and economic distributions of the various ethnic communities are not identical with each other or with the Anglo community. We obviously need to take precautions that all cross-ethnic research controls carefully for socio-economic differences. Another approach might be more useful: to determine those factors to which the variance of inter-ethnic-group differences can be attributed. It would be immensely useful to tease out of our data how much variance is actually the result of social class differences, how much arises from self-image, how much from regional differences in early socialization, and so forth.

Social and economic considerations are not the only variables that need to be considered when evaluating ethnic differences among the elderly. It is also important to be aware of the geographical origins of those being studied. The 65-year-old Nisei might well be different from the 65-year-old Issei; the Mexican-American octogenarian who moved to San Antonio in 1950 will differ from his age cohort counterpart who entered Texas in 1930 or their friend who was born in San Antonio. A comparable concern regarding the black American is related more to geography then generation, i.e., when (or if) he left the Southeastern section of the United States.

At the risk of belaboring the obvious, I wish to mention one more issue in doing gerontological research in ethnic communities. With a very few notable and known exceptions, members of the ethnic communities have shown no inclination to study their own elderly. Their priorities, as gerontologists are well aware, reside in the young. Therefore, those Anglos conducting the research are forced to rely more upon their own grasp of the situation and upon informants whose first interest in the elderly of their own communities may have occurred at the time they were approached to serve as informant. I would be hesitant to place much faith in the insights of most Anglo behavioral scientists into the meaning of aging in the Anglo community (or communities); there is little reason to be less skeptical about what I am told by members of other ethnic groups who are not tuned in to social gerontology.

Closely related to this concern is the anomalous role of the professional person who does offer to help with research. Recall the beginning of this discussion that ethnic research, especially that done by Anglos, is viewed with suspicion and hostility in the ethnic community. Members of the ethnic community may become belligerent in the face of naive interpretations of data; they may also respond with equal fervor to justifiable but unfavorable interpretations of data.

The behavioral scientist in the ethnic community may find himself caught between his dedication to his craft and his responsibility to the ethnic community. (Similar statements could be made regarding other kinds of groups.) Part of the difficulty evolves from the selection of research topic. For example, sex behavior in older persons has been reported in several papers: would there be a purpose in tabulating this in a cross-ethnic context? If we learn that elderly black males have a higher orgasm rate than older non-black males, have we learned anything of consequence? Assume that a medical sociologist learns that those elderly members of minority ethnicities who seek medical care from physicians of their own ethnic group receive superior treatment: should this be reported? After all, it implies that non-minority physicians who treat minority group members provide them with less adequate care. A "normal" liberal would declare withholding this information to be unethical and, most likely, racist. However, what should the researcher do if his data establish the opposite, i.e., that minority group members get inferior care from physicians of their own groups? Consider the headlines and the hollering. Or, with the present climate regarding welfare, how would you report the results of a study showing that a substantial proportion of elderly welfare clients of various ethnic groups were not reporting some of their income?

What we write and report on is open for public inspection. I previously mentioned the desirability of reaching practitioners and policy-makers—are there occasions when we need to demand that our results not be available for those outside our select group? Can we expect the media, attuned to behavioral science papers and meetings only after many years of having been proselytized, to ignore stories because the principal investigator is unhappy about the potential policy changes produced by his data?

Each person must make his own decision in terms of his own value system. However, many readers will demand that physicists and biologists need to reconsider their moral responsibilities, particularly in regard to war-related activities and environmental issues. Behavioral scientists can no longer sit smugly on the statement "Scientists and science must remain amoral—any ill effects evolve from the decisions of those who use our information incorrectly."

There, Here, and How They Made the Journey

Having grappled with writing this paper for many frustrating hours, I feel that I have little in the way of facts or data to impart. The most valuable contribution that I can make is to organize my thoughts in such a fashion that some coherence emerges for me—and hope that this organization will serve to structure or to stimulate you.

To study ethnicity as a factor in the individual capacities and adjustment of the aging and the aged, we need three kinds of information: where these people came from, where they are, and how they got from there to here. Naturally we also wish to learn where they are going, but that will emerge from the other considerations.

Where They Began

Psychology has been referred to as the science of the behavior of rats and sophomores. After doing the research for this paper, I would surmise that a disproportionate number of the latter and virtually all of the former have been white. It would be interesting to learn what percentage of subjects in studies of vision, thirst, need for achievement, pursuit rotor manipulation, operant learning, mirror drawing, or schizophrenia has been Anglo. Excluding those studies in which ethnicity was an independent variable, I would guess 99% to be a safe estimate.

When we want to investigate ethnic differences in the elderly of 1970, we lack the baseline data of knowing what differences existed among these people in 1910. Is enough known about reaction time or hand dynamometer grip or depth perception of black children or Indian adolescents or Mexican-American young adults to make comparisons among the elderly? Thus, if we find differences existing in either over-all performance or rate of change of capacities as a function of ethnicity, we are likely to be ignorant as to whether these are continuations of differences that occur at prior age levels or whether they emerged in later life as the result of factors impinging at that point. The same considerations hold for those variables categorized for this paper as adjustment variables (motivation, emotion, personality, and so forth).

In some instances, there is little reason to believe that ethnicity would have a meaningful impact upon behavior. Many studies of depth perception, critical flicker fusion, thirst, or card-sorting could probably ignore ethnicity as a variable. Perhaps nutritional differences or differential susceptibility to disease or even some genetically transmitted condition might lead to the importance of ethnicity, but the nature of the studies make this unlikely.

For other kinds of research, we know very well that ethnic differences exist. The larger the role played by learning and environmental factors, the greater the likelihood that ethnicity is a meaningful variable. A study of psychomotor performance following 24 hours of food deprivation might show little or no difference among ethnic groups, assuming social class is controlled. However, if the famous study of long-term food deprivation conducted during World War II with conscientious objectors (Keys, Brozek, Henschel, Mickelsen, & Taylor, 1950) were replicated with black Americans or Puerto Ricans, we might speculate on different results, at least to some extent. Most certainly the need for achievement, feelings regarding self-actualization, reactions to threats to security, and so forth will differ greatly as a function of ethnicity at all ages.

Some of these variables have been studied in relationship to ethnicity. Others have received little or no attention. Although I personally concur with the implicit opinion that ethnicity will not be a meaningful variable in studies of pursuit rotor, reaction time, and conditionability (although I am not familiar enough with this literature to know whether such studies have, in all cases, been conducted), it would seem to be worth a little effort to give experimental support to what is now assumed. There are, anthropologists inform me, some longitudinal reports of this nature interwoven in the writings on preliterate cultures. Ferreting such out, however, appears to be difficult, and experimental conditions were rarely if ever controlled in a fashion that would satisfy even a tender-minded psychologist.

The practical problems of obtaining baseline data for today's 70-year-olds are insurmountable. Until the imagination of H. G. Wells becomes reality, we have no way of retracing steps in time. We cannot conduct longitudinal research retroactively. We can do three other things, however. First, we can obtain baseline data on today's young, so that future researchers can do what we cannot, even though our experiences tell us that whatever we attempt now may have only limited use to our successors. Second, we can conduct good cross-sectional research using cohorts widely separated by age. Third, we can carry out longitudinal research covering brief time spans or apply the research paradigms proposed by Schaie and others (e.g., Schaie, 1965; Schaie & Strother, 1968) to determine that variance produced by cohort, that produced by time, and the interaction effect.

A few paragraphs ago, I stated that 99% of subjects in most studies in which ethnicity is not an independent variable have probably been Anglo. The accuracy of the statement would, of course, be difficult to determine. Fortunately, there have been some studies comparing ethnic groups on human capacities, especially cognitive capacities, and innumerable studies involving individual adjustment.

Two excellent articles summarize the psychological literature through 1965 (Dreger & Miller, 1960; 1968), with bibliographies of approximately 300 and 350 items, respectively. These deal entirely with differences between blacks and whites (or, at least, non-blacks). It is doubtful whether a comparable article on other non-Anglo groups would reach a fraction of this number.

As would be assumed, many statistically significant differences occurred in studies of cognitive capacities, personality, attitudes and values, mental illness, and related concerns. Even for psychomotor tasks and sensory and perceptual responses, however, some differences were obtained, although most reported (and, I would assume, many unreported) studies showed no differences. Thus blacks displayed greater needle deflections for galvanic skin responses than did whites, both among 7-year-olds and among 23-year-olds; blacks appear to have better vision, at least when measured among military inductees; they also have lower thresholds for pain. Those who wish fuller discussion should turn to the Dreger and Miller articles. Suffice it to say that the majority of the studies discussed had been conducted in public schools or colleges, with most of the remainder being done with military personnel, through the Veterans Administration, or in mental hospitals.

Not one reference was made to a study in which subjects were in their later years, except for those that were primarily demographic in scope. That Jackson's 1967 literature review on older blacks did refer to several such studies brings up the question as to why Dreger and Mason did not report these sources. One explanation is that very few of Jackson's studies would suggest an ethnic concern by their titles, and their focus was sometimes not particularly involved with ethnicity. In addition, Jackson's article must have appeared after the completion of the later Dreger and Miller article, and many of Jackson's references were dissertations, conference papers, and other sources specifically avoided by Dreger and Miller.

In summary, base data do exist for some aspects of human capacities and individual adjustment against which present studies of aging could be conducted. It would, of course, be most helpful to utilize the same respondents, but this is usually out of the question for many reasons. Some of the studies were conducted long enough ago that a present-day follow-up could compare 1970 capabilities of an elderly cohort against 1936 capabilities of that age cohort in early years. However, since the original respondents will not usually be available, such research would need to pay careful heed to Jackson's (1967) warning to avoid assuming comparability among members of an ethnic group merely because they share ethnic membership. Thus if someone wished to follow up a 1935 study of rural Georgia blacks and whites, would he be able to justify returning to Georgia to conduct the study? What proportion of those blacks have migrated from Georgia, how do they compare with those who stayed, and how does the difference between black migrant and black "remainee" compare to the difference between those whites who left and those who stayed home?

Other methodological problems are well-known and may be reviewed in the three articles referred to above. It might well be more fruitful to conduct cross-sectional research today, hoping that the experimental controls possible will outweigh the disadvantages of known age cohort non-comparability between young, middle-aged, and old at any given time.

Where They Are

Although the reverse switch on our time machine is yet not operative, we can still study older persons today, and we have certainly made a reasonable start. Botwinick's recent book (1967), for example, surveys a substantial portion of the gerontological literature on cognitive processes.

Psychologists and others have traced the age-related changes and age cohort differences in a great variety of motor and sensory areas. We have good evidence that older persons display less capacity for many visual and auditory tasks, less capacity to taste and to smell, longer reaction times to respond to stimuli, less strength, and so forth. Although some of the research results may be questioned because of physical health differences between the populations or other factors not directly involving age-related changes, the overwhelming weight of opinion is that, in varying degrees for different persons, these decrements emerge as part of the aging process.

The importance of sensorimotor changes with age is not restricted to performance decrement (or lack of decrement), but extends to the meaning such decrement may have to various ethnic groups. Assuming, for example, that the research showing a slowing in reaction time with age is valid, we might ask whether reaction time is of equal importance among ethnic groups. Is age-related loss more threatening to certain ethnic groups because of its implications for work effectiveness? Is masculine self-image dependent upon reaction time? Is the entire process of aging, for which increased reaction time serves as portent, more disturbing for some ethnic groups than others? If reaction time appears to be unimportant in this regard, substitute "physical strength and endurance" or "depth perception," or "response to complex stimuli."

Another consideration is the coping strategies used by people to deal with loss (or perceived loss) of sensorimotor functioning. In what ways are the losses compensated for? When and how does denial occur? Is withdrawal a frequent outcome? As reduced mastery and reduced independence take place, what sorts of social interactions come into play?

So far I have been discussing the kinds of sensorimotor losses that do not incapacitate people. When we become concerned with extensive decrement in visual or auditory functioning, in depth perception, in reaction time, in physical strength, a new constellation of factors emerges. To begin with, we need to have reasonably accurate epidemiological data concerning sensory and motor disabilities. Such data are very difficult to obtain, since most present statistics are based upon agency figures, and these are most often limited to agency contacts plus an indeterminate estimate regarding the prevalence of those not seen. However, we are well aware that ethnic groups do not appear on agency rolls in exact proportion to their percentage in the population. We may be far under-estimating the number of elderly persons of certain ethnic groups who have significant loss of visual, auditory, or other capacities.

In addition to epidemiological data, we need to become aware of the meaning of the disability to the individual, as influenced by his ethnicity. In traditional Japan, the blind person became a masseur and the deaf, a barber; what meanings exist today and are they, in any way influenced by these traditions? How does the individual person perceive himself as the result of his disability? Does he seem worthless in his own eyes? Does he view himself as being reduced to begging? Obviously his self-perception is greatly influenced by his role in the nuclear family, the extended family, and the community. Does the community have a network of interrelationships that will provide emotional, physical, and financial support for the disabled when needed? Is the nuclear or extended family obligated to come to his aid? Is disability seen as the result of chance, a bad karma, divine retribution?

And, finally, what sorts of interventions are seen as ameliorating the loss? Does the individual feel that he must intensify his efforts? Turn to prayer? Seek medical help? Enter psychotherapy? What sort of care is provided? In an institution? In the home? Strictly custodial? Primarily rehabilitative?

Like motor and sensory behavior, cognitive processes show decline beginning in the middle adult years and accelerating in the late 60s and beyond. Individual differences are substantial, and recent research has indicated that not all processes diminish at the same rate. Some cognitive capacities appear to hold up well with age, perhaps even improving slightly through the late middle years; if we could operationalize *wisdom* and find reasonable acceptance of its measurement, we might find that this capacity continues to rise throughout life.

Certain forms of illness, such as those relating to the cardiovascular system, produce cognitive decrement, in some instances to the point that the reduced cognitive effectiveness is sometimes assumed to be prognostic of impending death prior to normal medical testing. Thus, ethnic groups whose members are more susceptible to illnesses that produce cognitive decrement would probably show steeper rates of decline with age in various measures of learning and intelligence.

At the same time, it is well known that the median scores on intelligence tests differ among ethnic groups at all ages beyond infancy. Investigators differ as to the reasons for this, some placing more emphasis upon genetic variables while others focus upon the environmental factors, including early medical care, nutritional background, and early opportunities for learning and stimulation. Although evidence is very good, I feel, for the claims that genetic transmission influences differences in cognitive capacities among individuals, a comparable argument for differences among ethnic groups is dubious. The recent controversy concerning Jensen's position is cogent in this regard (Jensen, 1969; Kagan, 1969).

As with sensorimotor behavior, it may be more important to understand the meaning of cognitive change to the individual, as reflecting his ethnic identification, than to plot the actual changes. We might hypothesize that such decline is less tolerated by groups who place a high value on verbal competence and intellectual endeavors. (Here again we need to remind ourselves to avoid the danger of confounding ethnicity with social class.) Does the self-image of a person whose ethnic reference group emphasizes learning skills and intelligence (as traditionally defined) suffer more when memory for recent events declines? How do his ethnic compatriots treat him when he becomes forgetful and a little confused? Is he rushed into a maelstrom of agencies, social workers, and—eventually—institutions? Or does he receive the tolerance and support of kinship and community support networks, permitting him to remain in familiar (and less confusing) surroundings? Numerous members of non-Anglo communities have contrasted their willingness to tolerate a wide range of behavior of the elderly, including sensorimotor and cognitive losses, to what they perceive as the Anglo's uptight demands for immediate placement in convalescent care facilities at the first sign of distress.

Is it true that the general Anglo community is less tolerant of the old person with sensorimotor or cognitive failings? If so, does this affect the self-concepts of their members? Are there different patterns of coping strategies that result from the different roles they are called upon to perform? And what are the patterns of community and family intervention?

For the sake of illustration, let me assume that the elderly black and the elderly Anglo display the same patterns of cognitive decline, but that the former's change is seen by his community as an unfortunate but natural outgrowth of age, while the latter is called to the attention of a physician or social worker. The subsequent events thus set into motion may well produce entirely different roles, behavior, expectations, health and illness patterns, self-concepts, and so forth.

Although it seems doubtful that the biological needs for food, water, sleep, air, or elimination vary much in intensity from one ethnic group to another, the ways in which these needs are satisfied very obviously differ. Food preferences not only vary according to ethnicity, but older persons differ in their eating habits from younger persons of the same ethnic group. To select an obvious example, the much-discussed soul food of the Southern black may be enjoyed by the 70-year-old because of his early memories and by the 20-year-old because of its in-group associations, but be disliked by the 45-year-old because it reminds him of an environment he is trying to forget. Food preferences, then, may be age-related as the direct result of the era and region of early socialization.

It is not only the foods that have ethnic saliency, but the ways in which they are consumed. The entire social milieu of eating, e.g., with whom one eats, silverware and utensils, at home or in a restaurant, all these factors may affect the satisfaction of a biological need and may differ according to ethnic background.

When we consider the more socially oriented motives, we find substantial ethnic differences. The need for companionship, for displaying aggressivity, for power, for knowledge, all these can be seen to differ along ethnic lines. However, we know little or nothing about how these needs change over the decades. Longitudinal research is almost non-existent, and even cross-sectional research is sparse. One obvious avenue for research would be the use of questionnaires such as the Edwards Personal Preference Scale Schedule. This has been widely administered both in the United States and abroad. It measures the relative strength of 15 social needs, including need for exhibitionism, etc. The potential usefulness of longitudinal data is apparent, but even good cross-sectional studies in which both Anglo and non-Anglo groups of comparable background would receive this questionnaire would be helpful. We could better determine whether the differences existing between college students of different ethnic backgrounds are comparable to differences between older generations. Do intergenerational disputes involve the same concerns among all ethnic groups?

To my knowledge, there is no evidence that decrements for any of these kinds of performance are related to ethnicity or what might be called "the ethnic experience," assuming social class is kept constant. If such differences were to be found, it could shed considerable light on both the aging process and the meaning of ethnic experience.

Almost nothing has been written about ways in which ethnic communities may make the aging process and the life of the older person easier or more difficult. Being elderly in an ethnic community that supports young militants may be especially troublesome today, since the changes being demanded reduce the status and power of the elderly. But this may be compensated for if the import of some of the American core values that discriminate systematically against the aged is reduced. Moreover, if the community accepts its members without regard for their sensory, motor, or cognitive losses, the older person can be a participating member of that community for a longer time period and with much less anxiety; his feelings of self-worth will diminish minimally. Similarly, if the ethnic community places pressure upon the family to keep the older person as a functioning family member, even after losses occur, the older person receives another support network.

Thus, when the militant black or brown, who has just finished attacking the elderly of his community as Uncle Toms or Taco Toms, insists that these same persons are welcome members of his community, it may be more than rhetoric. He may be claiming, with justification, that the losses suffered by these persons in the aging process do not place them outside the pale of community membership. These community and family reactions, in turn, may influence the rates and the nature of performance and personality changes in the elderly.

A handful of publications on ethnicity and aging do exist, most of them discussed earlier in this sequence of articles and most of them tangential to the parameters of the present article. Jackson's work at Duke University has been referred to previously; Donald Kent and others at Pennsylvania State University are concentrating on older blacks; Margaret Clark at the University of California, San Francisco Medical Center campus has done excellent work (e.g. Clark & Anderson, 1967); and at UCLA, the author and anthropologist David

Reynolds are studying ethnic differences in the meaning of death and bereavement, a research program that will have implications for social gerontology.

The Clark and Anderson book does discuss the meaning of independence and dependence for ethnic groups and how this reflects upon the elderly and upon others as they approach aging. Other individual adjustment problems are also covered, including the conflict produced by acculturation, in which the first generation in the United States (now primarily elderly) adhere to traditional values that affect the role of the elderly and perceptions of aging and the aged, while younger persons tend to be socialized to the value schemes of the cultural core values of their own generation. Their book is a necessary starting point for anyone engaged in this topic.

Making the Journey

We are concerned not only with baseline data on the young and behavioral and functional data on the elderly, but on what occurs in between, i.e., we are concerned with adult development, the process as well as the end result. What transpired, as the result of ethnic association, that led to the differences that we find among the elderly? Do the curves upon which we can plot change in performance look alike, regardless of ethnicity? Do changes in measured personality occur in the same or different ways among ethnic groups? What are the age-related changes in life style according to ethnicity? Would we find essentially the same pattern of cognitive decrement for each of the ethnic groups? If not, are we able to explain the basis for the variance? Good longitudinal studies of change involving the middle and later years are rare, and none to my knowledge have used non-Anglo subjects.

Inevitably, not all those who began the journey will live to complete it. In what ways do ethnic death rates and death causes differ from each other? Are there factors, other than those tied to social class and income, that differentiate life-span and cause of mortality of ethnic groups?

Priorities

When I began to write this paper, I had planned to focus upon the psychology of aging and aged, with specific reference to ethnic group differences. As the paper unfolded, it turned into a discussion of the difficulties of doing good research on ethnicity. My final statements reflect the latter concerns.

The first priority, and probably the simplest, would be to conduct research into ethnic differences in performance on simple sensory, motor, and cognitive tasks. Although I *believe* that differences among ethnic groups, when controlled for social class, would be nil, I feel that this testable hypothesis needs testing. If this can be done—and it might make good fodder for a few master's theses—then we can at least lay some claim to building our science and our theories upon all men, not just Anglos. Since comparable information is not often available for other age groups, I would suggest that these studies be conducted on three age groups. These studies could best be conducted by psychologists.

For the second priority (and I do not consider these priorities competing—they should all receive equivalent consideration in terms of timing), I will shift to the more complex cognitive tasks, plus individual adjustment. A small beginning has been made in the evaluation of differences among the elderly of ethnic groups regarding personality, adjustment, values, roles, and so forth. This requires great expansion. All behavioral scientists can participate in this phase.

For the third priority, I suggest focusing upon the meaning of age-related changes to the various ethnic groups (and the sub-groups within the ethnic group). How does the loss of certain capabilities affect the elderly person's standing in his ethnic group? What is the meaning of role changes? Again, all behavioral scientists can combine forces for this aspect. In studying these concerns, we can also learn something about the impact of the dominant Anglo culture vis-à-vis the strength of association with the ethnic reference group in regard to shaping the attitudes that impinge upon the older person and the changes he is undergoing.

Fourth, and related to the third, we need to understand how each ethnic group (or sub-group within the group) defines good adjustment. We need to know what the group, from within its frame of reference, wishes to attain in later years before we can understand their adjustment and, before we suggest certain appropriate interventions. The tools of the anthropologist impress me as most effective in this regard.

And fifth, we need to learn about the kinds of people who will be the concern of social gerontologists in one, two, three, or more decades. We need to learn about people in their 50s and 60s, how they differ from the 65-plus populations of today and how their aging process may make them different 75-year-olds than today's 75-year-olds.

Throughout the entire research program, we must remain aware that the individual personality functions in an environment that is affected by economic conditions, climate, international relations, pollution, health services, and so forth.

Although I feel that these five priorities should proceed simultaneously in terms of timing, I doubt whether the first priority described will require a substantial effort. It is important to verify our implicit assumptions, and this should be done quickly, but—unless some unexpected results occur—this phase will not be extensive. The second priority is presently receiving some attention; it demands a great deal more. The next two priorities will not be satisfied with a crash program (as the second might), but with concentrated effort from a handful of knowledgeable investigators, including some who are members of the minority groups themselves. The last priority must begin immediately, since we now know that successive age cohorts are different and that plans for the future should not be imitations of the successes of today.

Throughout the entire effort, all investigators should take great care to remain attuned to differences not only between ethnic groups, but within ethnic groups. We must learn a great deal more about the kinds of individual differences obtained and how these differences are related to other factors.

References

Botwinick, J. *Cognitive processes in maturity and old age.* New York: Springer, 1967.

Clark, M., & Anderson, B. G. *Culture and aging: An anthropological study of older Americans.* Springfield, Ill.: Charles C Thomas, 1967.

Dreger, R. M., & Miller, K. S. Comparative psychological studies of Negroes and whites in the United States. *Psychological Bulletin*, 1960, *57*, 361–402.

Dreger, R. M., & Miller, K. S. Comparative psychological studies of Negroes and whites in the United States: 1959–1965. *Psychological Bulletin*, 1968, *70*, Monogr. Suppl. Pt. 2, 1–58.

Jackson, J. J. Social gerontology and the Negro: A review. *Journal of Gerontology*, 1967, *22*, 168–178.

Jensen, A. R. How much can we boost IQ and scholastic achievement? *Harvard Educational Review*, 1969, *39*, 2–123.

Kagan, J. S. Inadequate evidence and illogical conclusions? *Harvard Educational Review*, 1969, *39*, 274–277.

Kalish, R. A., Maloney, M., & Arkoff, A. Cross-cultural comparisons of marital role expectations. *Journal of Social Psychology*, 1966, *68*, 41–47.

Keys, A., Brozek, J., Henschel, A., Mickelsen, O., & Taylor, H. L. *The biology of human starvation.* Minneapolis: University of Minnesota Press, 1950.

Schaie, K. W. A general model for the study of developmental problems. *Psychological Bulletin*, 1965, *64*, 92–107.

Schaie, K. W., & Strother, C. R. A cross-sequential study of age changes in cognitive behavior. *Psychological Bulletin*, 1968, *70*, 671–680.

[1]It is platitudinous to exhort the academic and research establishment to communicate more effectively; it is ineffectual to attempt to persuade the practitioner and the
policymaker to read and contemplate more; it is too late to expect the minority
community members to "trust us" and to "have faith." And I personally resent such
comments as "Of course there are some bad apples, but . . ." or "It is only that 5% who
make trouble for the rest of us." The point is that we have something to offer as behavioral and social gerontologists; that we are human beings with individual competencies
and individual inadequacies; and hand-wringing and soul-searching are not substitutes for the development of policies, programs, and approaches to thinking to produce
a more accurate recognition of the significance of research and its potential utility.
(This issue is discussed in a different context in the article in this issue by Kalish &
Yuen.)

Growing Old Black

Donald L. Davis

"If programs are set up it's going to be hard to convince elderly Negroes they
should get involved. Many of them are basically distrustful of the outside world because
they don't understand it, and they don't understand it because of ignorance. This ignorance pervades their entire life-style, and—unless they are encouraged from without by
people they trust—they won't move in any direction other than the accustomed ones."
Thomas Pettigrew, *Toward a National Urban Policy.*

The People

Many aged black people live on tenaciously, in urban ghettos and the
recesses of rural areas all over America. They learned years ago to live
within prescribed arenas—physical, social, economic—that limited
their full participation in the American social scene. This paper describes these barriers and how they relate to the anguish and the
frailties that are, many times, inseparable from the pain of aging in a
youth oriented society.

The National Urban League has recently completed a study, *Double Jeopardy,* which states that: "Today's Negro is different from today's aged white because he is Negro . . . and this alone should be
enough basis for differential treatment."

Consequently, while many persons and agencies involved in the
field of aging recognize the responsibility of a complete network of
services to meet the individualized needs of our aged, we often fail to
realize that we may have very few relevant programs for the black
segment of the aged population. For, as W. E. B. DuBois cited in his
classic 1899 study of *The Philadelphia Negro:*

From *The Multiple Hazards of Age and Race: The Situation of Blacks in the United
States.* Washington, US Senate Special Committee on Aging, 1971.

The existence of certain social problems affecting Negro people is plainly manifest. Here is a large group of people . . . who do not form an integral part of the larger social group. This in itself is not altogether unusual; there are other unassimilated groups . . . And yet in the case of the Negro, the segregation is more conspicuous, more patent to the eye and so intertwined with a long historic evolution, with particularly pressing social problems in poverty, ignorance, crime and labor that the Negro problem far surpasses in scientific interest and social gravity most of the other race or class questions.

Black Americans, for the most part, are people who have spent their prime working years contributing to the growth of large central cities where they now live. Of this group, three out of every 10 persons, 65 years or over, live in four of the most populous States—New York, California, Pennsylvania and Illinois—each of which has more than 1 million such persons.

These people, for the most part, are now confined to some of the most decaying areas of the inner cities in these States. Current inflation, coupled with the inability to find work, continues to increase the despair of these aged citizens.

It has been stated by Kent and Hirsch,[1] in their recently completed study, that our current lack of knowledge in the field of gerontology applies primarily to noninstitutionalized, low-income, elderly white and black persons. Despite the high percentage of these groups living in our central cities and who comprise a large percentage of the client populations of health and welfare agencies, neither racial group had undergone an extensive study prior to the Kent and Hirsch study.

The Pathway of Black People to the Cities   In most decades since 1860, the black population has increased less rapidly than that of whites. However, in the last 40 years, the black population has reversed its earlier trend and has shown more growth than the white population. Since 1860, blacks have formed the following percentages of the U.S. population.

1860	14.1		1920	9.9
1870	13.5		1930	9.7
1880	13.1		1940	9.8
1890	11.9		1950	10.0
1900	11.6		1960	10.6
1910	10.7		1969	11.0

Source: U.S. Department of Commerce, Bureau of the Census.

These statistics reveal that the black population decreased from 14.1 percent in 1860 to 9.7 percent in 1930. But in 1969 the black population significantly increased to 11.9, and totaled a little above 22 million people. The recent rapid increase in the proportion of blacks within our population is largely due to an increase in life expectancy among blacks. Although the birth rate has long been higher among blacks than whites, a higher death rate decreased or held constant the proportion of blacks in the population. For instance, the life expectancy of blacks in this century has increased at a faster rate than that of whites: 38.4 years for nonwhite as compared with 20.7 for white men, and 32.7 years for nonwhite as compared with 25.2 for white women. Although life expectancies for nonwhites have increased at significant rates in recent years, their life expectancy continues to be lower than that for whites.

The black population appears proportionately greater nationwide than it really is, largely because massive migration of blacks into the central cities of large metropolitan areas has been accentuated by out-migration of whites from the cities to the suburbs. The percentage of blacks within the total population has shown minimal change in this century. However, the black population has instead been characterized by rapid migration from the South and farms into central cities of metropolitan areas where 55 percent of all blacks lived in 1969.

The black migration from South to North and from country to city has probably been one of the most massive population changes in the history of our country. Sixty years ago, in 1910, approximately eight of 10 blacks lived in one of the 11 states of the "Old Confederacy." As Silberman stated:

Over 90 percent of these Negroes, moreover, lived in rural areas. Negroes began moving to the North during World War I and continued to move during the 1920's, when restrictive legislation slowed down the flow of immigrants from southern and eastern Europe. By 1940, the Negro population in the Old Confederacy had increased by only 12 percent, whereas in the same period the Negro population elsewhere in the U.S. had more than doubled, from 1.9 to 4 million.[2]

In the half century ending in 1960, the black population of the United States had increased 92 percent, but less than 3 percent of this increase occurred in the five Southern States which had the greatest black population in 1910. In contrast, almost half of the increase took place in the States of New York, Illinois, California, Pennsylvania and Ohio. Among these States, in 1960, for instance, were located the first three cities with greatest concentration of black population. In 1969, the six cities with largest black population were as follows:

New York, 1,087,931; Chicago, 812,637; Philadelphia, 529,240; Detroit, 482,223; Washington, 411,737; and Los Angeles, 334,916.

Growing Old Black

As a result of the significant population growth shown in the above table, it would appear that the aging black population will expand at a very rapid rate in these States and, therefore, should receive close attention from State, local and Federal agencies. The extent of migration and urbanization is best illustrated in observing the population composition of those 10 northern and western cities with the greatest black concentration. We found that nearly one-half of the black residents were not born in the city of residence, since most of this group was born in the South.

Why did such a rapid migration occur among the black population during the 50-year period from 1910 to 1960? Primarily to find better opportunities for employment in the North. After World War I reduced immigration from Europe, northern employers were forced to meet some of their needs for unskilled and semiskilled workers among the black population. Closely related to these circumstances is the fact that the wages paid for unskilled and semiskilled work—the type of employment for most blacks at that time—were and remain higher in the North than in the South. In addition, living conditions were not as oppressive in the North. Although the North was characterized by extreme prejudice, discrimination, and de facto segregation, cities outside the South were not committed to the pervasive and rigid system of legal segregation which limited job opportunities for blacks.

It has been mentioned that the increased life expectancy for blacks has resulted in a larger overall black population group with a similar significant increase of aged blacks in the total population. In 1969, for instance, "Negro and other" composed 12.3 percent of the total population; 9.6 percent of the 45–64 age group, and 7.9 percent of the age 65-and-above group. By 1969, Brotman[3] reported that 60.7 percent of the black population aged 65-and-above lived in metropolitan areas compared to 61.2 percent of the white population aged 65-and-above living in the same area. Of the black total, a significant 47.5 percent resided within the central city compared to only 33.4 percent whites who lived in the central city. Further, the Committee for Economic Development has estimated that the nonwhite elderly population (65-and-over) living within our central cities will more than double during the period 1960–1985, rising by a total of 600,000 (108.7 percent) or 24,000 per year. In contrast, the estimated growth of the white population age 65-and-above in the central cities will rise only 3 percent in this same period (155,000 or 6,200 per year). Future growth of the aged white population, it appears, will occur primarily in suburban areas.

If this estimated growth in the elderly nonwhite central city population does occur, they will comprise a much greater proportion of all

Aging and Social Stratification

elderly poor in those cities, perhaps one-fourth rather than one-sixth as in 1968. Further, the increased growth of the nonwhite elderly population could be much more significant because the Committee for Economic Development based its estimated population expansion upon census data which contained a reported undercount of at least 10 percent in some black inner city areas. Based upon these criteria, we can probably expect the nonwhite elderly population in our central cities to expand as fast as our nonwhite age group under age 15 living in the same area. This rapid expansion of these age groups will pose grave problems for the future, since the same age groups now comprise a large percentage of the poor people in our central cities. Both of these age groups now and for the foreseeable future represent essentially a drain on the economic resources of the community unless and until appropriate planning and actions occur.

Family Living Patterns We are told in *Double Jeopardy*, which studied approximately 2.5 million old age recipients, that a higher percentage of elderly blacks than whites were heads of households, but that most of the blacks lived under deprived conditions. For example, nearly the same percentage, 30 percent, white and black household heads lived alone, but 20 percent of the blacks and only 12.5 percent of the whites had other persons besides husband or wife living with them.

Although overcrowding seldom appears to be an obstacle among the general aging population, a 1963 study by the U.S. Housing and Home Finance Agency found that among elderly nonwhite renters, 9 percent did live under extremely overcrowded conditions with more than 1½ persons per room while 5 percent of home owners were living in similar conditions. In contrast, among the total population, only 3 percent of the aged renters and 1 percent of the owners lived in these same conditions. Older blacks are more apt to live in large family groups than the aging population in general. Again, *Double Jeopardy* identified a larger proportion of black Old Age Assistance recipients than whites living in someone else's household—28 percent as compared with 23 percent. This same study also cited that approximately 5 percent of all elderly blacks resided with nonrelatives, as compared with a 2 percent average of all elderly persons.

As a result of this tendency of older blacks to live in someone else's household:

It means . . . . they must carry on the energy-consuming household work for large families and care (for) younger children at an age when the older person's health is poorest, energies lowest and the need for less stress is greatest.

A larger proportion of older blacks than whites are not living with their spouses. In testimony before the Special Committee on Aging, Miss Jeweldean Jones of the National Urban League commented that the higher percentage of older black males and women who are single can be attributed to greater broken marriages, shorter life expectancies of black males, and family patterns. According to Miss Jones' testimony, the present public welfare laws encourage the male to leave the family which results in family separations while blacks are in early adulthood. Consequently, the chances of blacks becoming old and single are much greater than their white counterparts. This same welfare system helps to perpetuate feelings of helplessness and dependency which the poor black youth carries with him throughout his life and into old age.

Although living alone without a spouse is accepted as a common experience of older persons regardless of race and economic characteristics, Kent and Hirsch found that over half of their low income inner city respondents living alone had been without their spouses for 15 years or more. As we know, the problem of adjusting to aging is apparently magnified by the loss of spouse. If this assessment is characteristic of most urban inner city elderly populations, the Negro aged fares less well than the white, since at all levels in both sex groups, more blacks than whites have been without a spouse for 15 years.

Since the aged black in our inner cities does not have as long a residency in these areas as the aged white, we can expect that among blacks, the proportion without living kin will increase with age. Among whites, on the other hand, fewer can be expected to be without living kin at an advanced age. We learn from the Kent and Hirsch study that 11 out of every 100 blacks had no living kin, in contrast with 6 out of every 100 whites who had no living kin.

It is unlikely that there will be dramatic changes in the family patterns of the black aged population rapidly enough to modify the trend of a large proportion of black aged households composed either of persons living alone or many persons living together.

Social and Economic Conditions   The Senate Committee on Aging heard much about the inadequate financial resources available to elderly, poor black people. Miss Jeweldean Jones testified at these hearings that it was "bad enough to be black in our society . . . also bad to be old in a youth-oriented culture. But to be old and black is indeed to be in double jeopardy." In this testimony, Miss Jones commented:

The pitifully low incomes of elderly people, especially elderly Negroes, is reflected in terms of daily bread and medical care. The $3,010 minimum annual income set by the Bureau of Labor Statistics as a modest but adequate budget for an elderly couple provides not quite an egg a day per person, about a half pound of meat and no provision for special diet or the expensive kinds of medical care all too often associated with the terminal illness that strike one in 10 aged couples every year.

Seven out of every 10 elderly Negro couples have less than $3,000 a year; one in two couples, less than $2,000; and one couple in 10 must live on less than $1,000 a year.

The older Negro man or woman who lives alone faces a daily existence even more bleak than that of married couples. $1,800 is the figure set by the BLS for a minimum sustenance budget for the lone elderly person, a budget which does not cover such basic items as medical care, car fare to the clinic, replacement of worn out clothing.

Yet, 76.6 percent of the older men and 96.5 percent of the women have less than $2,000 a year; 45.7 percent of these men and 68.5 percent of lone older Negro women must try to get along on less than $1,000 a year.

Retirement for the aged black is primarily a logical sequence of the deprivation which faced him prior to retirement. Accordingly, the black in retirement usually suffers because of his unstable employment and low wage background which result in smaller Social Security benefits. In 1962, for instance, black retired couples averaged about two-thirds of white retirement income and fully half of them had less than $1,960 for the year. Further, as Jackson and Velten cited, for the year 1966, in those families headed by individuals 65-and-over, 47 percent of the nonwhite families were poor as compared with 20 percent of the white families.

Work and Black Men Although we have observed an improvement in the employment status of blacks during the last decade, black men of all ages are still less likely than white men to find full-time employment. In 1964, little more than half of all nonwhite males who worked had full time, year-round jobs, compared with two-thirds of all white males. Moreover, long-term unemployment is quite prevalent among older nonwhite men as they tend to have relatively less education and training than whites of the same age group, and are likely to be employed in heavy manual labor, and in occupations particularly subject to seasonality or high turnover. During the period 1948–1964, labor force participation rates in the 55–64 age group dropped more among nonwhite males than white males. In 1948, for example, nearly 89 percent of all black males aged 55–64 were in the labor force, but by 1964, their labor force participation had dropped to almost 79 percent. In contrast, the labor force participation during this same period for white males in the same age group dropped from nearly 90 percent to only 87 percent.

In 1969, among those over 65, both white and black males had relatively sharp declines in employment as both groups together average only about 26.5 percent labor force participation rates—25 percent for blacks and 27 percent for whites. With reference to the proportion of older black males who do not participate, Beattie pointed out that:

> The aged and aging Negro faces a difficult, if not impossible situation in trying to remain in or re-enter the labor market . . . the Urban League has been able to place only one Negro male applicant who was beyond 45 years of age, in a St. Louis industry . . . the Negro is still the last hired and the first fired.[4]

Work and Black Women   Aged black women work outside their homes more often and longer than white women. In 1965, only 9.7 percent of white women aged 65 and over were in the labor force whereas 12.9 percent of black women were still working. As we have pointed out previously, the black aged male is forced into early retirement; in contrast, his spouse may continue in the labor force, but her employment is usually confined to domestic work. These differences in labor force participation are highly significant because they imply that the black aged male is not the breadwinner and thus enters old age without a defined social function since the black aged female's continued participation in the labor force means that she will be head of the household. Kent and Hirsch, in their study, for instance, found that after age 65, black women and white men were most likely to be employed. Although these roles are not radically different from those family patterns that existed for today's aged black families in their early adulthood years, they still mean that the aged black male's problems in adjusting to retirement are much different from those of the white aged male.

Occupational Diversity of Black Workers   Although the proportion of nonwhite workers has increased in fields from which they have previously tended to be excluded such as professional and technical jobs, approximately two-fifths of these workers were still engaged in service, laborer, or farm occupations in 1969 which was more than twice the proportion of whites in these same occupations. Regardless of improvement in the overall occupational situation for blacks, most older blacks are likely to be engaged in labor or service work which is unskilled and subject to low pay or unstable seasonal employment. Of all employed blacks in 1969, only 6 percent were employed in professional or technical occupations whereas more than half were employed as farm laborers, domestics, and service workers. Furthermore, in 1969, 20 percent of all employed black females were private household or domestic workers compared to only 3 percent white females involved in similar work. A large percentage of the domestic female workers are middle aged and elderly blacks, and according to the President's 1970 Manpower Report, half of all families headed by domestic workers were considered as poor.

Today's aged black population has entered old age with a wide gap between their retirement income and that of whites. In 1968, the median income of black families for those age 65-and-above was only 65 percent of that for white families in the same age group. In its 1969 report on *Developments in Aging*, the U.S. Senate Special Committee on Aging cited that although about one of every four persons age 65-and-above is poor, the percentage among black aged is practically twice as great since almost one of every two—47.7 percent—blacks 65-and-older can be considered poor. Furthermore, the efforts of the aged black to escape from poverty are frequently multiplied by prejudices in our society which, according to Dr. Inabel B. Lindsay, means that the family head cannot look forward to increased earning potential through better education, job training and decreases in employment discrimination.

As Berkowitz and Burkhauser stated,[5] for the older worker who is also a black man, or poorly educated, or not highly skilled, the chances of becoming unemployed are more likely than that of the white older worker who is also unskilled and poorly educated. These same authors commented that if the older black worker has skills that have become technologically inefficient or if he is caught in a stagnant industry, his unemployment probability is further compounded.

Work and Educational Attainment

If present economic policies of this country continue, we can expect the aging black population in our inner cities to comprise a large "under-class" depending on government assistance for daily existence. Even if every racial barrier were immediately eliminated for the aged black worker, the mass of aged blacks would still face a disastrous economic future. Their limited educational attainment in part was the starting point of a vicious cycle which failed to prepare them for skilled jobs or for upgrading opportunities. Although we have observed a higher educational attainment of young adult blacks in recent years, the educational levels of middle aged and elderly blacks are very low.

The Manpower Report to the President, 1970, indicated that approximately 3 of every 5 blacks, age 25 to 29, have completed high school—which is almost twice the proportion among those blacks age 45-to-54 and four times that for the 55-to-64 black group. When educational achievements are compared between black and white middle aged and older persons, the results reveal significant gaps in the two age groups. In the 45-to-54 group, for instance, 59 percent whites had completed high school whereas only 29 percent blacks completed similar educational levels. Further, in the age groups 55-to-64, only 15 percent blacks had completed high school compared to 45 percent whites who had done likewise. In 1969, the percent distribution by median years of school completed for persons aged 20 years and above was as follows:

	Median years of school completed	
Age	Black	White
20 and 21 years	12.2	12.8
21 to 24 years old	12.2	12.7
25 to 29 years old	12.1	12.6
30 to 34 years old	12.0	12.5
35 to 44 years old	10.6	12.4
45 to 54 years old	9.1	12.2
55 to 64 years old	7.6	10.9
65 to 74 years old	6.1	8.9
75 years and over	5.2	8.5

As we can readily observe from the above statistics, the aged black's inferior educational attainment has probably contributed to his few job opportunities, less steady work, a high rate of unemployment and low pay scales which make inevitable the insecurity and poverty of aging Negroes. There appears to be a close relationship between the aged black's meager education and his poor socioeconomic conditions. Lumber observed the same relationship and commented that "poverty feeds inferior education; inferior education feeds poverty."

Social Security Benefits

The result of the aged black person's employment in most low level occupations is a marked differential in the incomes of black and white Social Security beneficiaries, even though liberal amendments have been added to the Social Security Act since 1955. Dr. Lindsay submitted a statement to the U.S. Senate Committee on Aging which stated that the benefits gained for women and children through these liberalizations were of considerably greater significance than those for retirees. Of this latter group only 8 percent were nonwhites at the end of 1967, as compared with a mere 6 percent in 1955—the average benefit for nonwhites than whites age 65-and-over (on the basis of the number of recipients per 1,000 population of this age). For instance, public assistance in 1962 accounted for 70 percent of the income re-

Aging and Social Stratification

ceived by nonwhite married women who seldom owned any income-producing assets such as private individual annuities, and so forth. In contrast, among the white aged, two-thirds of the couples and about half of the nonmarried reported such income. Although the necessity for public assistance may be a new experience for most whites, many elderly blacks merely retire from general public assistance to Old Age Assistance at the age of 65. For instance, the Kent and Hirsch Pennsylvania study found some highly significant differences between their low income black and white sample with reference to public assistance:

Over 20 percent of the black respondents received Old Age Assistance benefits whereas only 10 percent of the white respondents received this type of aid.

Although many factors contributed to the difference in recipients of Old Age Assistance, the basic underlying factor appeared to result from the average Social Security benefit being smaller for the blacks than for whites thus permitting more blacks to be eligible for supplementary assistance.

In addition to having more frequent dependence on Old Age Assistance, in the two lowest age groups (65–74 and 75–84), more blacks than whites also implied they were once welfare recipients.

Among those respondents either receiving welfare assistance or who applied for welfare since age 65, 20 percent of the respondents reported that they felt they needed welfare assistance since reaching age 65. The difference between races was highly significant as almost one-fourth of the black respondents implied a felt need whereas only slightly more than one-tenth of the whites in each age group indicated such need.

When asked why they did not apply for Old Age Assistance benefits, the group who responded specified that they failed to apply because of reasons including the following:
   1.   Felt an imposition on personal life and children;
   2.   Fear of losing their owned home; and also,
   3.   Aspects of delivery of service which indicate that the aged have difficulty coping with both travel to the district welfare office and the "red tape" of intake procedures.
   4.   Aspects of delivery of service which implies that there is a lack of accurate information concerning eligibility among the potentially eligible aged groups.

We can conclude from this Pennsylvania study that large numbers of aged blacks are forced to retire to being an Old Age Assistance recipient, to climax a lifetime of social and economic indignities.

Health Conditions

Although we have observed that the elderly black is often handicapped economically and educationally, his health needs also pose serious problems in adjusting to old age. Despite the fact that there has been a significant increase in life expectancies for blacks, their death rate continues to be disproportionately high, and the morbidity rates for blacks exceed that of whites in comparable age groups.

In 1967, at birth, whites could expect a life expectancy of 71.3 years compared to only 64.6 years of life expectancy among blacks. In this same year, the white male at birth could expect to reach his 68th birthday whereas the black male could only expect to live 61 years. However, Beattie reported that after age 75 nonwhite mortality is lower than white. Thus, although fewer nonwhites survive to reach 75, those who do may, on the average, expect a remaining lifetime of about 2.5 years longer than the whites.

According to *Double Jeopardy*, the incidence of death from the leading killers—heart disease, cancer, brain hemorrhage, and accidents—is proportionately greater for older blacks than older white people. It has been cited also that deaths of nonwhites age 65-and-over from tuberculosis account for 15 percent of all deaths; those from influenza and pneumonia, 8 percent of all deaths—16 percent of all patients in tuberculosis hospitals are nonwhites.

Although the reasons why men are not in the labor force are similar for both nonwhites and whites, a much larger proportion of nonwhite males than white males are not working because they are ill and disabled. In 1969, in the age group 55-to-64, the number of nonwhite males who were unable to work was 38 percent compared to only 28 percent of white males. Among the age group 65-and-over, the ratio was quite similar as the number of nonwhite males unable to work was 19 percent compared to 9 percent in the white male group.

During the period of 1961–1963, nonwhite persons after age 25 reported a higher rate of restricted activity, bed disability, and a greater number of days lost from work than white persons. In spite of their greater need for medical attention, blacks of all ages visit physicians less often than white persons and got to the dentist about one-third as often.

Institutional Care and Medicare   In Miss Jones' testimony about the plight of our black aged, she cited the lack of skilled nursing home care as a national disaster for the country and an intolerable situation for blacks since few nursing homes have been willing to admit aged black patients. Chronically ill Negroes in many States have been condemned to live out their lives in custodial-care mental hospitals because there is literally no place for them to go.

Most Negroes cannot afford. . . . costs of medical care and must either do without or settle for that which the community provides at nominal or no cost—care which, more often than not, is offered with indifference, at best, and frequently in a way calculated to humiliate.

These problems reflect both the inadequacy and unavailability of preventive and remedial health services for our increasing aged black population. The cost of food and drugs in inner city ghetto areas is much higher than it is in the rest of the metropolitan areas. The income of the aged black buys relatively fewer of the items needed to sustain normal health. Health and housing are closely related and substandard housing adversely affects those who must live in these dwellings. Of all the housing occupied by nonwhites in the United States in 1968, 24 percent of these occupied by blacks were substandard, as compared to 6 percent for whites. In both races, it can be assumed that a disproportionate share of such housing is occupied by the aged. As we have earlier mentioned, aged blacks—to a much greater extent than whites—are forced to share housing with relatives or friends.

Social Services   In addition to the shortage of health practitioners who are working in inner city black areas, there is also a lack of related social services. The social or welfare worker for many aged black persons is his only contact and source of information regarding public health services. We all are aware of the scarcity of such workers who too seldom are able to actively serve this segment of the population.

Conclusion

Given the history and the reality of the lives of elderly black Americans, imperative action is clear. Their future, like the future of the Mexican American and the American Indian, is inextricably linked to efforts of this society to discharge its responsibility to all of its members. The dysfunction in the society endemic to the life space of elderly black Americans increasingly demands attention and contributes to the deepening crisis of the aged in our country. Facts and statistics notwithstanding, growing old black is a peculiar and perilous experience.

Their history usually reflects low paid employment, a disproportionate amount of unemployment and underemployment, inadequate health care with resulting high death rates, greater necessity to depend on public assistance and, for most aged blacks, family situations which offer little aid.

The deprived socioeconomic conditions of the elderly black population are rather complex and also require that we understand the need of special reaching out in order to motivate older blacks to participate in and utilize existing aging programs and services.

Since so many older blacks live in poverty and need additional income, but cannot gain entry to the labor force, we suggest the creation of an employment program based on human service jobs. We believe such a program would be helpful to both the elderly black population and the community, because it would permit the older blacks to realize their potential, maintain themselves economically, and bring meaning to their lives while enriching the services of the community. It would seem especially advantageous to involve elderly blacks in cases where, conditioned by a heritage of segregation to resist free interchange with whites, they might participate more freely with other blacks to help provide some of the substantial service needs that exist within the black community, as well as in other communities.

[1]Kent, Donald P., and Carl Hirsch. *Social, Economic and Health Conditions of Negro and White Aged and Their Utilization of Community Resources.* Final report submitted to the Administration on Aging. Grant AA-4-68-028-01. 1971.

[2]Silberman, Charles E., "The City and the Negro," *Fortune*, March 1962.

[3]Brotman, Herman, "The Older Population: Some Facts We Should Know" (draft), *Administration on Aging*, HEW, April 1970.

[4]Beattie, W. M., Jr., "The Aging Negro: Some implications for Social Welfare Services," *Phylon*, 21:131–135, 1960.

[5]Berkowitz, Monroe, and Richard Burkhauser, "Unemployment and the Middle-Aged Worker," *Industrial Gerontology*, 3 (October 1969).

Attitudes toward Aging and the Aged among Black Americans: Some Historical Perspectives

Floyd M. Wylie

There is a dearth of substantial data on attitudes toward aging and the aged among black Americans of the present day. Most of the information is impressionistic. It is clear, however, that even on a subjective and impressionistic basis, the behavior of black Americans toward their older folk and the attitudes of the older folk toward themselves and their senior citizenship is strikingly different from those of the majority white culture in many ways.

It is generally accepted that black Americans are more inclined than whites to include the elderly in the family structure and to regard the elderly with respect, if not veneration. Studies of American blacks by sociologists and anthropologists have indicated blacks' wider

From the *Journal of Aging and Human Development*, Vol. 2, No. 1, 1971. Copyright Baywood Publishing Company, Inc., 1971. Reprinted by permission of the publisher.

acceptance of the extended family, including persons of older generations. Moreover, it is generally agreed that, traditionally, blacks accept old age and look forward to the rewards of advanced years. Messer (1968) indicates that older blacks are more likely to show high morale than older whites. According to his study, blacks perceive old age as a reward in itself, and they are less likely to deny their advanced age.

Blacks' respect for the elderly and their greater acceptance of their own aging are seldom studied. This paper will attempt to provide some perspective on these phenomena.

There is increasingly abundant and detailed historical evidence concerning the highly complicated cultures which existed and continue to exist in Africa. Much of the material referred to in this paper is related to notions of death and dying and, correlatively, to ideas and practices of ancestor worship.

Old Age in Africa

Herskovitz (1941) and Davidson (1961) provide lengthy explanations of the complex familial relationships and patterns which existed in Africa prior to its "discovery" by Europeans. There are many commonalities among the various African cultures, one of the most frequent of which is ancestor worship. This practice is still very widespread in West Africa, the area from which most African slaves were taken. The particular forms of ancestor worship bear some striking, if superficial, similarities to certain oriental religious teachings, notably to those of early Christianity and Islam. Parrinder (1967), writing about Nigeria, details the African belief in survival after death and notes also that the idea of total death is unacceptable to the African mind. Both Parrinder and Lewzinger (1960) indicate that Africans view all creatures, including the departed, as linked closely together by the fact that they share in the same "eternal power." Fagg and Plass (1964) report that African art expresses life as a continuum; art, particularly sculpture, in many instances displays the togetherness of the clan. Age, rather than being represented as ravages on skin and flesh, is shown as a kind of fourth dimension, referring to life as a whole rather than to a specific phase of it.

Among Africans, in addition to the sense of continuity of life and death, is the regard for old age as a sign of dignity, something to be respected. Moreover, the African oral-historical tradition continues to this day both in Africa and in the United States, and apparently in all areas where Africans or descendants of Africans are found. One consequence of this tradition is the reinforcing of the importance of the elders, particularly those trained to remember in minutest detail the history of the family or group of families. In addition, African religious art and practices continue to be supervised by priests chosen by councils of elders.

The writer's own recent (1969) experiences in parts of West Africa confirm the continuing high regard for family structure, and particularly for older family members. One outstanding incident took place in a small, bustling Hausa village in Nigeria. New visitors to this village were conducted to the "Grandfathers' Place," where a group of older men sat on rugs in an awning-shaded area near the center of commercial activity. These men were accorded great respect and referred to by all simply as "the grandfathers." This panel of elders served as a kind of advisory group, presumably on all matters concerning the village, but apparently most frequently on matters of business, since the village was the center of the kola nut industry in that area.

It was interesting also to note that older members of the group touring West Africa with this writer were often referred to as "mother," or "father," or "grandfather" by otherwise officious customs officers, and accorded respect and deference to a degree seldom seen in this country.

One of the problems of older people in the United States has to do with surviving family members, particularly widows. Bohannan (1964) discusses the ways in which African societies cope with widows, getting them back into families quickly and simply. Loneliness is not indigenous to Europe and the United States; but our societies cope less well with older widows who are, especially in the United States, something of an anomaly.

The continuity of life and support of the clan and extended family continues strong in various areas of Africa. Bohannan reports that African children grow up in an intense situation of kinship and family. They continue throughout their lives to learn their family obligations and family histories. As a result, the abrupt break, such as Westerners know, between children's culture and adult's culture, is not to be found in Africa.

Parenthood is an important event everywhere. However, in African societies, only on the birth of a grandchild is a man or woman in a position to be truly sure that his name and spirit will live in the history and genealogy of his people. Grandparenthood allows a perfect and rewarding position for summing up the meaning of a life cycle. Grandparenthood is enviable and elderhood is the finest estate.

Current African cultural values have been discussed recently by Arth (1968) and Shelton (1968). The aged in the Ibo culture are much respected, maintaining high status and continuing relevance in that society. According to Arth, senior men of lineage have numerous ritual functions to perform, and elders, who are regarded as closest to the ancestors, are the most revered persons in the typical Ibo village.

Shelton reports a low level of senility among the Igbo people of eastern Nigeria. He attributes this low incidence to the older persons' involvement in the most prestigious affairs of the community and to a reduction in the level of stress of living. Living members of the lineage are regarded as "reincarnations of the ancestors." Shelton notes that the average American is conditioned to what he terms several "contradictory myths." The myths are those of personal independence and the extremely high value of youthfulness. Among the Africans, on the other hand, dependency on the group is fostered throughout the life cycle, so that when a person becomes old, he is not suddenly thrust into a dependent state. The Igbo elder is no more productive than his American counterpart, but he can demand care in his old age as his publicly acknowledged right, without any sense of guilt, ego damage, or loss of face. Whoever fails in giving such care is culpable and subject to scorn and ridicule, and runs the risk of being cut off from the ancestors.

Effect of Slavery

The strength of the cultural traditions of the extended family and clan, the regard for life, the reverence for old age and ancestors were not, contrary to some opinions, dissolved or broken by slavery. A case could be made for the dropping away of the cultural traditions, were it not for the fact that young Africans from their earliest days were inculcated with these values. Naturally, slave-traders did not seek out or obtain very young children; rather, they took healthy "specimens" largely in the age range from pre-teen to young adulthood. These Africans would have had, of course, a number of years of conditioning to the values of the village, the clan, and the extended family. Little additional documentation or proof is required to indicate that "Africanisms," in a variety of forms, continue to the present time among people of African heritage.

According to Lincoln (1967), the African family was virtually destroyed by the peculiar form that slavery took in North America. However, it is clear that many vestiges remained. For example, black slave mothers retained the West African tradition of naming their children for the time of their birth: a month, a day, or even a time of day. Frazier (1957), in his celebrated book, *Black Bourgeoisie,* took a short-sighted position, maintaining that the African family system was destroyed when the slaves were separated from family and friends, and because the majority of young slaves taken were males.

However, despite this systematic family breakup, it would have been impossible to divest older children or young adults of cultural patterns learned from very early life within the family or larger group. The "seasoning process," or slave-breaking processes which took place in South America and the Caribbean, clearly served the purpose of the slave-traders and buyers, but it did not, contrary to Frazier's opinion, strip away all African values, including, no doubt, values and perceptions about life, death, and familial relationships such as those between the young and the old. On the contrary, one could take the position that the family breakups and sales of various family members led, instead, to new group relationships. An even more extended inclusiveness of people became the rule. Botkin (1954) indicates that when blood kin were often destroyed or sold, never to be regained, non-blood kin came to be included in family and larger social groups. The sharing of bondage surely provided some glue for familial and other social relationships. In many cases, according to Frazier (1939), the affectional ties between mother and child somehow survived the ordeals of the slave-markets and even the Middle passage. It would be logical to assume, then, that affectional ties, regard for kin and others, were strengthened rather than weakened by common suffering.

Powdermaker (1968) refers to the slave family as "elastic." This very elasticity so necessary for psychological survival naturally extended into the post-slavery times and, in modified forms, to the present day.

Post-slavery times found elderly women in their seventies and their middle-aged daughters forming one household with the older woman at the head. Personnel of these matriarchal families was reportedly higher variable, and even casual. Stepchildren, "illegitimate" children, and adopted children mingled with the children of the house. No matter how crowded the home, there was always room for an orphaned child, an elderly grandmother, an indigent aunt or homeless friend.

Frazier (1939) notes that in post-slavery times, age added dignity to the grandmother's position and to her regime, which sometimes extended to three generations. With the grandmother or the grandfather were the accumulated lore, history, and superstition of the slaves. The older person here became, as in Africa, the repository of folk wisdom and medicine. Younger adult men and women, not directly related, referred—and still refer—to the grandmother as a second mother, sometimes showing the same deference and respect for her that they would accord their own mothers. This writer's own experience with people of his grandfather's generation (persons born in the 1880s and 1890s) indicates not only a respect for older generations, but a kind of hierarchy of respect in which older brothers and sisters were referred to as Brother William or Sister Mary, while younger siblings were referred to by name only.

Conclusion

Although there is a paucity of sound data on the phenomena of respect for the elderly and greater acceptance of their own aging by blacks, the cultural heritage of West African values and attitudes toward aging and the aged is an important factor in any consideration of these phenomena.

Fortunately, many of the cultural values and attitudes regarding the elderly have apparently changed little over the several centuries since Africans were snatched from their home continent. Studies of the Ibo and Igbo people, and observations of the Hausa, probably reflect in most important respects the West African view toward continuity of life, the importance of ancestors, and especially the inculcation of these values into the lives of younger people.

The period of the slave trade and slavery did not, contrary to the opinions of some writers, divest Africans and their descendants of many basically African cultural values. It is clear that among the more important of these values that continue to the present time are a certain respect and even veneration of age, and frequently strikingly different attitudes about the aging process and the role and place of the older person within the culture. Issues of "belongingness" rather than of productivity appear to be dominant in these regards.

This brief historical perspective will hopefully provide a different understanding, appreciation, and recognition of the essentially humanitarian view that black Americans take of their older folk.

References

Arth, M. Ideals and behavior: A comment on Ibo respect patterns. *Gerontologist*, 1968, *8* (4), 242–244.

Bohannon, P. *Africa and Africans.* New York: The Natural History Press, 1964.

Botkin, B. A. (Ed.). *Lay my burden down.* Chicago: University of Chicago Press, 1945.

Buckmaster, H. *Freedom bound.* New York: Macmillan, 1967.

Davidson, B. *The African slave trade: Precolonial history, 1450–1850.* Boston: Atlantic-Little, Brown. 1961.

Fagg, W., & Plass, M. *African sculpture: An anthology of studies.* London: Vista, 1964.

Frazier, E. F. *Black bourgeoisie.* New York: Macmillan, 1957.

Frazier, E. F. *The negro family in the United States.* Chicago: University of Chicago Press, 1939.

Herskovits, Melville J. *The Myth of the Negro Past*. Boston: Beacon Press, 1941.

Lewzinger, E. *Africa—The art of the negro people*. Baden-Baden, Holle Verlag GMBH, 1960.

Lincoln, C. E. *The negro pilgrimage in America*. New York: Bantam Books, 1967.

Messer, M. Race differences in selected attitudinal dimensions of the elderly. 17250 *Gerontologist*. 1968, *8*, (4), 245–249.

Parrinder, G. *African mythology*. Middless, England: Hamlyn, 1967.

Powdermaker, H. *After freedom*. Kingsport, Tenn.: Atheneum, 1967.

Shelton, A. J. Igbo child-raising, eldership and dependence: further notes for gerontologists and others. *Gerontologist*, 1968, *8* (4), 236–241.

Selected Social and Psychological Sex Differences in Later Life

Robert C. Atchley

In recent years there has been a great deal of speculation concerning how the social and psychological characteristics of older men and women differ. Riley and Foner (1968) reviewed sex comparisons on more than eighty topics. However, because these comparisons failed to control the effects of sizable sex differences in average age, marital status, education, and income, they are of limited value. It is widely known that compared to older men, older women are older, more likely to be widowed, more likely to be less well-educated, and more likely to have inadequate incomes. Studies which have included sex comparisons usually lump all respondents into a single age category, usually age 65 and over. Even those studies that do include more detailed age breakdowns almost never control for the large sex differences in marital status, education, or income. Yet this lack of controlled description of sex differences in later life has not stopped theorists from developing hypotheses about them. Unfortunately, the controlled research necessary to discipline these hypotheses has lagged behind.

This paper reports male-female comparisons that have been controlled for age, marital status, education, and income adequacy. The comparisons cover attitudes toward work and retirement, self concept, psychological well-being, self-reported health, perceived income adequacy, and perceived social participation. The implications of these findings for previous hypotheses about sex differences are also

From *Research Studies in Social Gerontology*, 1975, Scripps Foundation Gerontology Center, Oxford, Ohio.

discussed, and some new theoretical assumptions are developed about sex differences in later life.

Data were gathered via questionnaires mailed to a random sample of retired teachers in a large midwestern state and to the entire population of people retired from a midwestern telephone company. A total of 3630 questionnaires were returned. 922 respondents were still in the labor force. The response rate varied from 50 percent for retired males to 70 percent for female former phone company employees and 81 percent for female retired teachers. These response rates compare favorably with those from interview studies of older people.

The variables were measured either through self assignment (voluntary retirement, attitude toward retirement, time required to become accustomed to retirement, labor force status, marital status, education, age, age identification, loneliness, work as a self value, health, income adequacy, and social participation) or through preexisting scales (anomie, anxiety, self esteem, self stability, sensitivity to criticism, and depression). For a more detailed discussion of the measures used, see Atchley (1976).

In this study, test factor standardization (Rosenberg, 1962; Atchley, 1968) was used to control the effects of age, marital status, education, and perceived income adequacy in order to get a better measure of sex differences. Test factor standardization is a technique which weights the distribution of cases in a two-variable, cross-break table using as weights the percentage of distribution for the same sample on a third variable called a test factor. This technique allows the logic of partial correlation to be applied to data that is at a categorical level of measurement rather than ordinal or interval. More than one test factor can be used if there are enough cases in the sample to yield no more than one zero per column in the n- dimensional cross-break table. In this study, the number of cases was sufficient to allow the use of four test factors.

Table 1 illustrates the importance of test factor standardization. The uncontrolled, zero-order findings indicate that females are significantly more likely to perceive themselves as having retired voluntarily, but only among retired phone company workers. However, age and marital status have a particularly strong effect on perceived voluntary retirement. Never married women in older cohorts are much less likely to see themselves as having retired voluntarily, and the sample contained a large number of women in this category. The standardized findings reveal that there is indeed a significant sex difference among retired teachers in the prevalence of perceived voluntary retirement. In fact, the controlled difference is greater among retired teachers than among retired telephone employees. Thus, test

Table 1 Zero-Order and Standardized Percent Distribution of Voluntary Retirement, by Sex and Industry

| | Percent Voluntary Retirement | | | | | |
| | Male | | | Female | | |
	Total	Phone	Teacher	Total	Phone	Teacher
Zero-order	37.4	34.3	42.8	46.9	50.2	45.3
Standardized*	35.3	35.4	35.3	54.1	47.6	57.1
N = 3630	1364	862	502	2266	710	1556

*Standardized on Age, Marital Status, Education, and Income Adequacy.

factor standardization unmasked an effect of sex on voluntary retirement that was substantially different from the uncontrolled relationships.

The results are broken down not only by sex but by industry as well because there were significant differences between the industry groups. The women teachers were overwhelmingly classroom teachers when they retired (96 percent), while the men contained a sizable proportion (31 percent) who had been administrators at the time of their retirement. Among telephone company retirees, 92 percent of the women were operators, operator supervisors, or clerks at the time of retirement while 87 percent of the men were linemen, installers or maintenance personnel. Thus, the sample has within it two distinct occupational categories for both sexes; therefore, for analytical purposes, it is often invalid to lump the categories together as the data in Table 2 show. Table 2 summarizes the findings, subdivided by sex and industry group. Keep in mind that the results are controlled for age, marital status, education, and income adequacy.

Work and Retirement

Being considered good at their work was important for the majority of respondents; more so for former teachers than for former telephone employees. However, there were no significant sex differences in the importance of work.

Former men teachers are significantly more likely to still be in the labor force than are former women teachers. There is no sex difference among former phone employees. Former men teachers are more likely to have had administrative experience which is more transferable to other jobs than are the skills of classroom teachers or telephone employees. Thus, the larger percentage of former men teachers in the labor force is probably at least partly due to differences in employment opportunities.

The findings in Table 1 concerning voluntary retirement show

Table 2 Sex Differences among Retired People by Industry for Selected Variables Standardized by Age, Marital Status, Education, and Income Adequacy (In Percent)

	Male			Female		
	Total	Phone	Teacher	Total	Phone	Teacher
Work important	60.9	53.0	73.2	65.5	57.1	71.1
In labor force	27.4	22.3	36.4*	24.2	25.2	23.7
Like retirement	85.7	89.1*	79.4	81.8	84.1	80.7
Quickly used to retirement	54.9*	58.2*	46.7*	44.2	53.5	38.6
Often lonely	21.1	20.9	21.4*	28.9	22.5	31.5
High anomie	22.1*	22.1*	22.2*	17.3	17.3	17.3
High anxiety	31.3*	31.6*	31.0*	43.8	48.4	41.8
Identifies as old	85.6*	84.3*	87.9*	70.9	59.6	76.2
Low self esteem	16.5	15.2	19.0*	25.4	18.9	28.5
Low stability of self concept	8.4*	9.6*	6.7*	23.6	17.9	26.4
High sensitivity to criticism	27.1*	24.6*	31.5*	50.7	40.5	55.4
High depression	20.1*	17.0*	25.9*	29.6	25.4	31.7
Poor health	11.7	10.6	13.9	12.6	9.4	14.6
Inadequate income†	17.1*	13.9*	23.0*	28.1	26.8	28.7
Less contact with friends	26.7	31.5*	18.3	19.7	23.1	18.1
More contact with friends	35.6	31.4	42.7*	34.5	29.5	36.8
Less participation in organizations	21.6	23.0*	19.5*	25.0	27.4	23.9
More participation in organizations	29.6	30.1	28.7	30.0	27.0	31.4
N (3630)	1,364	862	502	2,266	710	1,556

*Sex differences significant at the .05 level or below. Unless both phone and teacher categories show significant sex differences, the total is not shown as significant, even though the percentage difference may be technically significant.

†Income adequacy controlled only on age, marital status, and education.

that older women are more likely to report their retirement as voluntary. However, there is a serious problem concerning definitions of *voluntary* that makes this finding less than clear-cut. Both sexes tended to see the issue in relation to the mandatory retirement date. Those who retired before the mandatory date defined their retirement as "voluntary," while those who waited until the mandatory date to retire defined their retirement as "involuntary." However, many of the women in this study were married at the time they retired, and their husbands tended to be older than they were. In order for the couple to retire at the same time, the man often worked until the mandatory age and the woman retired early. Many of these men eagerly awaited the mandatory retirement age. Streib and Schneider (1971) found a similar pattern. Accordingly, it does not seem prudent to make a great deal of the sex difference in responses to the voluntary retirement question.

More than four-fifths of the respondents like retirement. But among retired phone company workers, men were significantly more apt to like retirement than the women were. Older men in general are more likely than older women to become accustomed to retirement in three months or less.

These findings show in sum that both sexes seriously embrace job success as a life goal and that women are less likely than men to make a quick adjustment to giving up their jobs.

Psychological Characteristics

Loneliness is significantly more prevalent among older women than among older men, and the gap is greater among former telephone workers. High anomie is not very prevalent among the respondents, but older men were significantly more likely to have high anomie as compared to older women. Older women displayed high anxiety as compared to older men, and again the gap was greatest among former phone company workers. When actual age is controlled, a higher proportion of older men see themselves as old (rather than middle aged or just past middle age) compared to older women, and the gap is greater among former telephone workers.

Low self esteem is more likely among former women teachers than among former men teachers, but there is no significant sex difference among former phone company employees. However, both industry groups of older women have a significantly higher prevalence of uncertain self concepts. On the other hand, the overwhelming majority of respondents of both sexes report high self esteem and stable self concepts.

Older women are much more likely than older men to be highly sensitive to criticism, and the gap is greater among former teachers. More than half of the former women teachers are highly sensitive to criticism. Older women are also more likely than older men to be highly depressed.

Thus, older women show a greater prevalence of "negative" psychological characteristics compared to older men. Older women are more often lonely, anxious, unstable in self concept, highly sensitive to criticism and highly depressed. There are also some important variations among older women. Former women phone workers have a significantly larger proportion who are highly anxious, while former teachers show significantly larger proportions with low self esteem and stability of self concept, high sensitivity to criticism, and high depression.

Health

Very few of the respondents reported themselves to be in poor health, and there were no significant sex differences in this respect.

Income

Older women are significantly more likely than older men to report their incomes as inadequate, particularly among former telephone company workers. Note that over a quarter of the older women, even in this relatively advantaged sample, reported inadequate incomes.

Social Interaction

Among former telephone employees, compared to women, older men more often see themselves as having less contact with friends and less participation in voluntary associations now than in the past. Among former teachers, the pattern is practically the opposite. Contrasted with earlier in their lives, the men more often see themselves as having *more* contact with friends and less often see themselves as having less participation in voluntary associations as compared to women.

Discussion

The findings concerning sex differences in attitudes toward work and retirement raise some interesting questions. The absence of sex differences in the importance of work matches results obtained by Streib and Schneider (1971) and Clark and Anderson (1967) who used different measures of the importance of work. These empirical results do not match the oft-voiced assumption in the literature to the effect that work is not a primary role for women who work. Cumming and Henry (1961:144) state that: "Retirement is not an important problem for women because . . . working seems to make little difference to them." Based on a review of then-current literature, Donahue, Orbach, and Pollak (1960:398) state that: "The working role for women still does not have a social value equivalent to homemaker or user of leisure. It is, therefore, not unlikely that to leave a second- or third-class role presents an individual with less of a dilemma than to leave one which is recognized as a prime function of the individual." The fact of the matter is, however, that women do indeed think that work is important. In addition, the women in this sample more often reported difficulty in getting used to retirement than did the men. And among the former phone employees, women were less likely to like retirement than were the men. The implication is obvious. Past assumptions about male-female differences in attitudes toward work and retirement have not borne the empirical test. In their place should go theoretical assumptions that women can be highly committed toward work, and that retirement can present problems for women, perhaps even more so than for men. Future research should also take into account the idea that the overwhelming majority of both women and men like retirement; and nearly half get used to retirement in a very short time.

The findings concerning psychological characteristics are also relevant to theory in gerontology. Rosow (1974:11) develops a theoretical statement which holds that the ambiguity associated with the role of older person affects the older person's psychological stability and leads to depression, anxiety, anomie, and refusal to view the self as old. Rosow's argument is primarily social-structural in that the problems cited above are said to be due to role loss and lack of clear-cut norms. Using Rosow's argument, we might expect widespread incidence of psychological problems among older people. And we would expect this to show up particularly among men since they are often held to be traditionally more connected with the external social structure.

The findings of this research do not support Rosow's view. Despite the fact that two-thirds of the sample is retired and a fifth is widowed, the prevalence of loneliness, anomie, anxiety, low self esteem, or depression is not very high in this sample. In addition, where sex differences exist, it is more often older women rather than older men who show the high incidence of these psychological problems.

One problem with this interpretation is that the research reported here is cross-sectional. We can only say that *in later life* these are the incidences of various symptoms and sex differences. Whether the magnitude of the sex differences has increased or decreased with age is still an unanswered question. Thus, it is possible that the prevalence of negative psychological characteristics has increased among men as they have grown older, but the generally low incidence of these characteristics among men reduces the plausibility of this argument.

It could also be argued that these sex differences result from a tendency for women to be more willing and to find it more appropriate to *admit* to problems. (Phillips and Segal, 1969; Coopersmith, 1971). However, Clancy and Gove (1974) examined the effect of various forms of response bias on sex differences in scores on the Langner (1962) scale of psychiatric symptoms and found that controlling for response bias *increased* the magnitude of sex differences rather than reducing them.

Thus, it would seem plausible to hypothesize that the impact of aging on symptoms such as anxiety, depression, low self esteem, sensitivity to criticism, or uncertainty of self concept is greater among women than among men. On the other hand, men seem to be more susceptible than women to anomie and to identification of self as old. More will be said about the significance of this later.

The findings on health and income adequacy were unsurprising.

The findings on social participation show that more than half of the total sample feel that their levels of contacts with friends and participation in organizations have changed since earlier in their lives. Among those who perceive change, those who see an increase in participation outnumber those who see a decrease. Earlier studies reported no sex differences in friendship behavior (Shanas, 1962; Powers, Keith, and Goudy, 1975; Hunter and Maurice, 1953). However, the question in this research was sex differences in *perceived change* in friendship behavior. Here there are sex differences, with men seeing more change than women do.

Based on the findings of this research, it is possible to sketch a broad theoretical picture of some of the ways that older men differ from older women, apart from differences due to factors such as average age, marital status, education, or income adequacy. Men often respond to aging in terms of how it affects their relation to the social system. Among working-class men (the former telephone employees) aging seems to bring desirable disengagement. Compared to middle-class men, they less often remain in the labor force, they more often see themselves as less involved with friends and organizations as compared with the past, yet they are more likely to like retirement. It is important to note, however, that this sample of older working-class men has reasonably good health and adequate incomes. In a less advantaged working-class sample, disengagement may not be so well-received. (Rosenberg, 1970).

The older men who were teachers are more often men of action. They are more often still in the labor force, and they more often see themselves as more involved with friends and organizations as compared to older women.

Compared to older men, older women are less likely to respond to aging in active terms such as staying in the labor force or increasing social participation. They less often see ambiguity in norms and they more often deny that they are old. Yet older women *are* more likely to be lonely, anxious, and depressed. They also are more likely to have low self esteem and to be highly sensitive to criticism. Thus, men tend to perceive aging in structural terms and to respond to it by accepting a new position in the social structure happily and/or by realigning their energies and commitments toward the social structure through either disengagement or reengagement. Men are not very likely to respond to aging by becoming "psychologically stressed." On the other hand, women neither accept social aging nor try to fend it off by continued engagement. Instead, women respond to aging with high levels of psychological stress.

Obviously this theoretical portrait extends far beyond the data of this study. It is intended as a brief speculative picture of what longitudinal research of the future may find, if it will only look.

Of course, the sex differentials in psychological symptoms may also be hold-overs from earlier periods in the life cycle. It is also possible that the differences observed here will not be the same for the upcoming cohorts of "new old people." (Cain, 1967) All of these are alternative hypotheses which deserve serious consideration. The picture of sex differences painted in this paper offers researchers and practitioners a different set of theoretical assumptions than those that often have been used in the past.

References

Atchley, R. C. A qualification of test factor standardization. *Social Forces,* 1968, *47,* 84–85.

Atchley, R. C., and George, L. K. Symptomatic measurement of age. *The Gerontologist,* 1973, *13,* 332–336.

Cain, L. D. Age status and generational phenomena: the new old people in contemporary America. *The Gerontologist,* 1967, *7,* 83–92.

Clancy, K., and Gove, W. Sex differences in mental illness: an analysis of response bias in self-reports. *American Journal of Sociology,* 1974, *80,* 205–216.

Clark, M., and Anderson, B. *Culture and Aging.* Charles C. Thomas, Springfield, Ill., 1967.

Cooperstock, R. Sex differences in the use of mood modifying drugs: an explanatory model. *Journal of Health and Social Behavior,* 1971, *12,* 238–244.

Cottrell, W. F., and Atchley, R. C. *Women in retirement: a preliminary report.* Scripps Foundation, Oxford, O., 1969.

Cumming, M., and Henry, W. E. *Growing old: the process of disengagement.* Basic Books, N.Y., 1961.

Donahue, W., Orbach, H., and Pollak, O. Retirement: the emerging social pattern. In C. Tibbitts (ed.), *Handbook of social gerontology,* University of Chicago Press, Chicago, 1960.

Hunter, W., and Maurice, H. *Older people tell their story.* Institute of Human Adjustment, Ann Arbor, Mich., 1953.

Maas, S., and Kuypers, J. A. *From thirty to seventy.* Jossey-Bass, San Francisco, 1974.

Phillips, D., and Segal, B. Sexual status and psychiatric symptoms. *American Sociological Review,* 1969, *34,* 58–72.

Powers, E. A., Keith, P., and Goudy, W. J. Family relations and friendships. In R. C. Atchley (ed.), *Environments and the rural aged.* The Gerontological Society, Washington, D.C., 1975.

Riley, M. W., and Foner, A. *Aging and Society. Volume one. An inventory of research findings.* Russell Sage Foundation, New York, 1968.

Rosenberg, M. Test factor standardization as a method of interpretation. *Social Forces,* 1962, *41,* 53–61.

———. *Society and the adolescent self image.* Princeton University Press, Princeton, N.J., 1964.

Aging and Social Stratification

Rosow, I. *Socialization to old age.* University of California Press, Berkeley, Calif., 1974.

Shanas, E. *The health of older people.* Harvard University Press, Cambridge, Mass., 1962.

Streib, G. F., and Schneider, C. J. *Retirement in American society.* Cornell University Press, Ithaca, N.Y., 1971.

F
M